Women and the Family:
Two Decades of Change

The *Marriage & Family Review* series:

- *Family Medicine: A New Approach to Health Care,* edited by Betty E. Cogswell and Marvin B. Sussman

- *Cults and the Family,* edited by Florence Kaslow and Marvin B. Sussman

- *Alternatives to Traditional Family Living,* edited by Harriet Gross and Marvin B. Sussman

- *Intermarriage in the United States,* edited by Gary A. Crester and Joseph J. Leon

- *Family Systems and Inheritance Patterns,* edited by Judith N. Cates and Marvin B. Sussman

- *The Ties that Bind: Men's and Women's Social Networks,* edited by Laura Lein and Marvin B. Sussman

- *Social Stress and the Family: Advances and Developments in Family Stress Theory and Research,* edited by Hamilton I. Mc-Cubbin, Marvin B. Sussman, and Joan M. Patterson

- *Human Sexuality and the Family,* edited by James W. Maddock, Gerhard Neubeck, and Marvin B. Sussman

- *Obesity and the Family,* edited by David J. Kallen and Marvin B. Sussman

- *Women and the Family: Two Decades of Change,* edited by Beth B. Hess and Marvin B. Sussman

Women and the Family:
Two Decades of Change

Beth B. Hess and Marvin B. Sussman
Editors

The Haworth Press
New York • London

Women and the Family: Two Decades of Change has also been published as *Marriage & Family Review*, Volume 7, Numbers 3/4, Fall/Winter 1984.

The Haworth Press, Inc., 12 West 32 Street, New York, New York 10001
EUROSPAN/Haworth, 3 Henrietta Street, London WC2E 8LU England

Library of Congress Cataloging in Publication Data
Main entry under title:

Women and the family.

"Has also been published as Marriage & family review, volume 7, numbers 3/4, fall/winter, 1984" — T.p. verso.
Includes bibliographical references.
1. Feminism — United States — Addresses, essays, lectures. 2. Women — United States — Social Conditions — Addresses, essays, lectures. 3. Family — United States — Addresses, essays, lectures. 4. United States — Social conditions — 1960- — Addresses, essays, lectures. I. Hess, Beth B., 1928- . II. Sussman, Marvin B.
HQ 1426.W636   1984   305.4'2'0973   84-12967
ISBN 0-86656-291-5
ISBN 0-86656-292-3 (pbk.)

Women and the Family:
Two Decades of Change

Marriage & Family Review
Volume 7, Numbers 3/4

CONTENTS

Women and the Family:
Two Decades of Change

Chapter 1

Women's Roles in Mythic Tradition and a Planetary Culture

Marvin B. Sussman

The epic myth of Eros and Psyche is a tale of trials, tribulations, and triumphs. Aphrodite, alias Venus, subjects Psyche to a series of impossible tasks. The reason for this godless action is that Venus is jealous of Psyche's beauty as a mortal. Fearful of the competition, she sends her son, Eros, alias Cupid, to destroy Psyche. Instead, Cupid falls in love with Psyche and Psyche becomes with child. Angry, fretful, alienated, and a bit fearful, Venus sends her agents to bring Psyche to her. She treats her abominably and subjects her to a series of trials, intended to guarantee defeat, depression, and succombing behaviors with the only recourses being death at the hands of the angry goddess or suicide.

The first trial involved the sorting of mixed grains. Venus called for large quantities of wheat, barley, millet, beans, lentils, poppy seeds and similar grains and mixes them together in a pile. The task is for Psyche to sort and stack the grains in separate heaps and to do this before nightfall. The test was for Psyche to demonstrate her industriousness, and to warrant having Eros as a lover and husband would require her to demonstrate hard work.

Psyche completely frustrated, overwhelmed, and in a deep depression made no attempt to set about this stupendous task. A small ant had witnessed what had occurred, had heard the wild curses of the cruel mother-in-law who was trying to destroy Psyche, the wife of the god of love, Eros. As quick as his six legs could carry him he went about the countryside rounding up all the ants telling them what has occurred and they came in waves working furiously sorting out the piles of grain and putting them in the appropriate piles.

1

Venus returned at the setting of the sun, somewhat tipsy from an afternoon garden party, and to her surprise and great disbelief found the grains all sorted. She accuses Psyche of not doing the task but having the ability to beguile and bewitch some wretched soul or many of them to help her with the sorting test.

In this myth of trials, tribulations, and triumphs, animals and human beings, gods and goddesses, nature and the environs rise to the occasion and save the poor and stricken Psyche in ingenious and creative ways. Another illustration is the task of the second trial. Psyche is asked to fill a crystal cup with pure water from a stream on top of the mountain. To scale this mountain involves passage through the deeper realms which are inhabited by wild creatures, demons, quick sand, illusions, extremes in temperature, dragons, ghosts and witches. One has to cross the river Styx. The water must be delivered to Aphrodite before the sun sets in the west.

Psyche is in despair and decides to commit suicide. But a voice on high believed to be that of Jupiter angrily admonished her for giving up. His utterings take the form of an impassioned lecture and with concern and compassion knowing in his heart that he wants to bring Psyche to a godly status without diminishing the ego of Aphrodite, dispatches one of his faithful carriers, the royal eagle, who with the speed of Mercury, comes out of the heavens and seizes the crystal cup and on strong wings soars and takes it high over the grasping limbs of the demons of the deep. The eagle, exhausted from the mission, convinces the stream, which is reluctant to give up its pure waters, that it is Venus' desire, and fills the crystal cup. It is brought to Psyche who subsequently delivers it to a shaken and angered Venus.

Voices on high, emanating from above, metaphorically represent the great controllers of culture, of our lives. It is the metaphor of the tower. It is from the oracles or from the mounts, or from the burning bush on the hill to which we have lifted our eyes and hearts, for the important message, to determine the tower in our life, our calling. Is it a profession, family, friendship, network, or spirituality?

From a close examination of the eclectic writings of experienced authors on the women's movement and families whose work is represented in this volume, there are many voices or towers which purport to clarify and enlighten the primary mission of the women's movement, one which is achievable and in keeping in the long cultural, social, biological and genetic history of humankind and womenhood. The many voices juxtapose the rights of the individual for self fulfillment, particularly women, and the primacy of the family as a unit with the consequential commitments to its endurance, providing a safe haven for the nurturance and development of its young. Other voices call for the transformation of long ingrained and almost instinctual ideologies which emphasize generosity and the giving of one's self, especially the giving nature of women. The Tower in the Eros and Psyche myth tells her to curb her generosity, to avoid giving away critical parts of herself automatically and spontaneously before integration and wholeness of self occurs. The issues today of women's jobs or careers and families and the very survival of the planet remain unresolved. The reeds in waters are multivoiced and are playing a score not inconsonant with the tunnel visioned perspective of a male dominated corporate world.

Another emergent theme from this collection of articles on the women's movement and families is that the movement and its advocates and scholars are using paradigms and endemic behaviors suited to current institutional patterns. This explains why the success rate in the drive towards equity in gender relationships is less than robust. The movement would prosper if those in it supported a paradigmatic revolution suggested by T.S. Kuhn. Such a revolution would transform current states of consciousness attuned to cultural practices and societal constraints and the symbolic imagery of current institutions, their demands and functions. Only with the unfettering of the symbolic universe of current institutional patterns can the linkages between gender equity, human needs and planetary resources be established.

As Kuhn indicates, a paradigmatic transformation of consciousness and institutions cannot be achieved using current educational, managerial, media, scientific and technical processes. The desired outcomes of the gender revolution can be realized by adoption of beliefs and values alternative to existing ones. These beliefs and values provide new perceptions and uses of administrative, educational, and technical processes in the quest of gender equity (Gutting, 1980).

A change in paradigms for our planetary culture of high complexity and integration is necessary to obtain a complementarity of men and women's roles. We cannot use existing paradigms whose behaviors are inhibited by cultural constraints, habitual patterns, and symbolic universes which provide the realities for current institutional forms and practices. Ours is a social order built around corporate and bureaucratic structures and ideologies with paradigms supporting acquisitive, competitive, hierarchical, inegalitarian, and self oriented tendencies and practices. A dramatically different paradigm, and requisite for the success of the gender movement, professes egalitarian and cooperative practices and horizontal over vertical structures with relationships based on trust, negotiation, and cooperation. Internalized in the consciousness of society's members and imbedded in its institutional forms are the values and norms of equity and shared decision making. The consequences are harmony with nature, the thoughtful use of natural resources and humaneness in interpersonal relationships. There is a high identification with the belief systems of the social order; social institutions and structures are people oriented, which work for the benefit of individuals and groups. A sense of harmony, belonging, and security prevails.

To transcend the prevailing paradigm with its foci on acquisition, competition, control, and me-ness requires beliefs, techniques, and strategies that are not derived from current corporate structures, or its symbolic universe and consciousness. A new paradigm which incorporates concerns for human emotions and reason demands a transformation strategy which can promulgate democratic, cooperative practices, and equitable relationships.

A transformation strategy should aim to correct the fallacious perceptions of interest which are now dominant in people's consciousness, according to which security, need satisfaction and survival can be attained within prevailing institutional arrangements. People everywhere, but especially in the privileged, powerful, and supposedly developed countries, have to be challenged to discover that in spite of their statistical wealth and their military power, the quality of their lives is now deeply unsatisfactory and continues to deteriorate; their basic needs go often unmet; their social and psychological needs for meaningful human relations, meaningful work, self-direction and self-actualization are generally unfulfilled. They are afflicted with a pervasive sense of insecurity; and their own future and that of their children seems threatened (Houston, 1982).

This change in paradigms, essentially a humanistic revolution provides possibilities for strategies and tactics toward decentralized yet co-ordinated, cooperative, egalitarian social orders, in which people can become self-directing, self-reliant, self-actualizing, and above all rational in the conduct of their public affairs. It should be stressed that the social orders implied here do not require a return to "primitive," tribal ways of human existence. Rather, these should be social orders in which people will make optimum use of science and of a humanized technology and industry. People will be subjects and masters of these processes rather than their objects and slaves. They will use and control scientific and productive resources and processes for their shared well-being.

Implicit in the strategy and goals suggested is a notion of self-interest which is fundamentally different from both selfishness and altruism. It is a notion of self-interest that affirms the self-interest of one's ego along with the self-interest of the "generalized other." It incorporates the realization that the liberty, security and needs of the self will be assured only when everyone's needs, security and liberty are assured. As such a redefinition of self-interest takes hold in the consciousness of growing numbers of people, values and motivations will emerge which will be supportive of an institutional order geared to everyone's free and full development, need satisfaction and self-actualization.

Women roles will change grudgingly and slowly as part of the evolutionary process, as current corporate paradigms modify to accommodate change induced by "have nots" in the system. The equity or fairness in the role behaviors and status of men and women will not be achieved in a millennium or until the messages from the reeds in the waters or towers on high are listened to and accepted. A cosmic unity evolves on what men and women should want for each other and from one another and their families, and the complementarity of independent and autonomous self with well being of the family and other primary groups.

Concomitant with this illumination is the acceptance and implementation of behaviors endemic with new paradigms, those which lead to a transformed culture and society, those which lead to horizontal connectedness with multiple prospects for rooting deeply, fostering a balanced, systematic and sensible relationship between needs and resources, rather than vertical, hierarchial structures rooted in power and control. There is a Don Quixotic tone to this posture, at first blush. Yet my perception of reality is that, to the contrary, the current struggles for gender equity are truly Quixotic, thrusting at the windmills of encrusted paradigms and attendant behaviors is action without fulfillment.

You, the reader, experienced in the ways of life and living in the not so brave new world of 1984, will after reading these juicy, penetrating and convoluted papers, accept or reject my thesis. I had to take this position, it was my "calling." I chose to be a lion for a day rather than a mouse for a life time. So it goes.

REFERENCES

Houston, J. Lecture, Possible Human in A Possible Society Seminar, 1982.

Gutting, G. *Appraisals and Applications of Thomas Kuhn's Philosophy of Science.* Notre Dame: University of Notre Dame Press, 1980.

Chapter 2

The Women's Movement and the Family: A Socio-Historical Analysis of Constraints on Social Change

Maren Lockwood Carden

INTRODUCTION

In this paper I discuss why the nineteenth and the twentieth century women's movements have been shown to have relatively little impact on patterns of family life (Bird, 1979; Hoffert and Moore, 1979; Hunt and Hunt, 1982; Oakley, 1981; Vanek, 1980; Weinman-Schram, 1983). Chapters in this issue of *Marriage & Family Review* provide additional evidence that even today's supposedly enlightened middle-class families are not equalitarian, and that, in all social classes, the responsibilities of motherhood still make it exceedingly difficult for women to take full advantage of the world outside the home.

HISTORICAL PERSPECTIVE ON THE MOVEMENTS

Although agitation began earlier, the nineteenth-century women's movement was formally inaugurated in 1848, the date of the first women's rights convention, organized by Elizabeth Cady Stanton and Lucretia Mott and held in Seneca Falls, New York. These

Maren Lockwood Carden is Associate Professor, Department of Sociology, Long Island University, Brooklyn Center, Brooklyn, NY.
I should like to thank Betty Lyerle, Eileen Moran, and Barbara Katz Rothman for their very useful, constructive comments on earlier versions of this paper.

women became involved in feminist issues while working for abolition, while others were brought directly into the women's movement through the organizing skills of such talented women as Susan B. Anthony. During this early period, feminist leaders explored a range of ideas. While by today's standards, their agenda for change was modest, by nineteenth century standards, such ideas were radical. Women, it was argued, should be educated, admitted to the professions, have increased opportunities for employment outside the home, and receive higher wages. They should attain an independent legal status and not be dependent on their husbands. In dress, social, and recreational activities they should not be restricted by the excessive sensibilities of the nineteenth-century view of women. In all these areas, feminists fought for change. They achieved it in only a few.

By 1870, these broader objectives had been abandoned and feminists limited their actions, if not always their discussions, to the issue of suffrage. In fact, the first major organizations devoted exclusively to women's rights were the suffrage groups: the American Woman Suffrage Association and the National Women Suffrage Association. Fifty years later, in 1920, women gained the vote.

In discussing the work of the nineteenth century feminists, I shall concentrate on the period before suffrage became the dominant concern; that is, on the years between 1848 and 1869 when women sought the greater range of changes. I shall refer to the feminist movement of this period as "the mid-nineteenth century movement."

Once suffrage was achieved in the twentieth century, the organized feminist movement virtually died. It revived suddenly in the 1960s. At first, the then conservative National Organization for Women (NOW) and the radical "women's liberation" consciousness-raising groups were its sole proponents. But soon the movement diversified into hundreds of small and a few very large groups (such as NOW, the Women's Equity Action League, and the National Women's Political Caucus) working for change at local and national levels. Later, these independent groups were joined by feminist constituencies working within such established organizations as the YWCA, or the National Federation of Business and Professional Women's Clubs, the major political parties, and academic disciplines.

The contemporary feminists' objectives have been even more

varied than their forms of organization. Although the extreme radicals of the late 60s and early 70s are less visible today, feminists still hold a wide range of views about such matters as the extent of inherent differences between men and women, the degree to which male and female roles should become androgynous, and about the relative importance of working for change in areas like the rights of minorities, working class and poor women, employment opportunity, party politics, lesbians' rights, older women's rights, and child care.

Neither the contemporary movement nor the mid-nineteenth century movement is or was composed, therefore, of a single organization pursuing a single set of objectives. Each is a loosely coordinated collection of groups, different in size, degree of formality, styles of action, and objectives. It is the objectives and the achievements of these composite groups in the areas of marriage and family which are the focus of this paper. I shall suggest three main reasons why the members of these groups have said, done, and achieved so little in transforming these institutions of marriage and, particularly, the family.

THE COMPLEXITY OF THE RELATIONSHIP BETWEEN THE FAMILY, SOCIETY, AND WOMEN'S STATUS

Almost all the mid-nineteenth century feminists and many contemporary feminists have failed to realize the complexity of the relationship between the family, other social structures, and women's liberation. Consequently, their suggestions for change in the family are inadequate. In addition, those theorists who have addressed the issue with the perspicuity it deserves, have for the most part been unable to come up with analyses that suggest either significant or immediate change in the family.

Mid-Nineteenth Century Feminist Movement

The liberalism that formed the underpinnings of American society provided the rationale for mid-nineteenth century feminism: women, like other citizens, had the right to such civil liberties as education and admission to the professions; and they should retain legal rights after marriage.[1] Insofar as they went, these ideas were in women's interests, but they did little to promote changes in male/female role relationships and nothing for changes in family patterns.

A few women went beyond the usual interpretation of nineteenth-century liberalism in explaining women's inferior position but they were hesitant to express themselves publicly. Elizabeth Cady Stanton, in her private correspondence, saw marriage as a source of inequality. Anticipating in 1856 John Stuart Mill's celebrated analogy (1869) she argued that marriage "makes man master, woman slave": whenever the interests of husband and wife conflict, as they must, those of the husband are gratified and those of the wife sacrificed because the husband has the legal and economic power over the wife.[2] Some others, like Lucy Stone, Paulina Wright Davis, and Susan B. Anthony, reached similar conclusions. Even fewer feminists, notably Susan B. Anthony, recognized that the economic exploitation of women workers was another reason for women's subordinate status in society (Flexner, 1966, p. 85).[3] While they touched upon the issues of patriarchy and class conflict, none of these feminists went beyond an initial exploration of the topics. For the most part, even these women subscribed to the prevailing view that equality outside the home and legal equality inside the home would resolve women's problems.

The Contemporary Feminist Movement

Contemporary feminists have access to many recent probing analyses of women's status. Early in the contemporary movement, some theoreticians took a Marxist/Engels or a neo-Marxist position: they saw class oppression as the underlying cause of women's inequality, and revolution (followed by the creation of the socialist state) as the solution to that inequality (Benston, 1969; Reed, 1969). Others have asserted that childbearing and childrearing are the basic cause of oppression: responsibility for children has confined women to the home in all or almost all societies while men acquired the power that comes from control over the political and economic spheres (Lamphere, 1977; Rubin, 1975). The more radical of these theorists place special emphasis on the patriarchal nature of society, and advocate the creation of women-centered and women-controlled forms of social organization as the means to liberation (Bunch, 1975; Daly, 1978).

Larger than either of the two previous groups of theorists are those who contend that *both* childrearing and class are the roots of women's oppression: they look forward to a transformation of the structure of both society and family (Eisenstein, 1981; Mitchell, 1966, 1971; Rowbotham, 1974; Zaretsky, 1976).[4]

Today's radical theorists, therefore, disagree over the causes of women's oppression and, it follows, over its solutions. For their part, activist feminists find these theorists' work difficult to understand and even more difficult to apply. In contrast, liberal feminism with its emphasis on equal rights is easy to understand and to apply, particularly in areas outside the family. Although no liberal analysis compares in explanatory power with the radical analyses, feminist liberalism makes up in practical applicability for what it lacks in intellectual depth.

PRACTICAL PROBLEMS OF ACHIEVING EQUALITY IN THE FAMILY AS OPPOSED TO ACHIEVING EQUALITY IN THE LARGER SOCIETY

In both periods under consideration, liberal feminism has suggested many changes that would improve women's condition. Some of these changes have been sought, and some achieved; but most of the successes have been made within the larger society, not within marriage and the family.

Mid-Nineteenth Century Feminist Movement

Insofar as marriage and the family were concerned, the mid-nineteenth century feminists sought equality under the law in areas relating to the control of property and wages, and the guardianship of children. Very few women tried to extend the notion of equality to the relationship between husband and wife. Nonetheless, the marriage agreements and subsequent careers of such pioneers as Lucy Stone and Antoinette Brown Blackwell showed that some feminists believed in and achieved a broader definition of equality than was generally accepted.

While a few people could envision equalitarian marriage, no one could envision equalitarian parenthood. Motherhood then was an even more demanding job than it is today. For the middle class woman, servants helped, but they were not enough to change her situation significantly. The nineteenth-century feminist could not anticipate the availability and acceptance of birth control, the labor-saving devices, the mass-produced food and clothing, or the medical advances in the control of childhood diseases that enabled twentieth-century women to spend more time outside the home in paid or unpaid activities. Furthermore, she could not imagine the enormous growth in job opportunities, albeit ill-paid and routine, that in recent decades have made it possible to find employment.

Even working class women of the nineteenth century were unlikely to be employed because few jobs were available.[5] Those who were employed labored long hours in the home as well as in the factory. Rheta Dorr described the mill town of Fall River, Massachusetts, "Eleven o'clock at night seemed the conventional hour for clothesline pulleys to begin creaking all over town" (Scott, 1971, p. 20).

In the nineteenth century, therefore, no one could foresee a time when technological changes inside and outside the home would make it possible to combine motherhood with a career. The only married women who worked did so out of sheer economic necessity.

The Contemporary Feminist Movement

In recent years, feminist ideas have encouraged couples to believe that equalitarian marriages are possible. Indeed, much of the movement's early protests were directed at sex-role stereotyping and its implications for male-female relationships inside and outside the home. From a practical point of view, therefore, it is reasonable today to seek equality in marriage.

In contrast, equality seems an impractical ideal once a couple has children. The technological advances of the past hundred years have enabled mothers to move out into the world beyond the home but they have by no means eliminated the responsibilities of parenthood (Bird, 1979; Hoffert and Moore, 1979; Hunt and Hunt, 1982; Oakley, 1981; Vanek, 1980, Weinman-Schram, 1983).

At least three suggestions for coping with parenting have emerged from the contemporary women's movement: child care, household help, and shared parenting. None of these is practical in more than a small minority of cases. Quality child care is prohibitively expensive for individual families and for most organizations. Household help can be afforded only by the prosperous.[6] Most women's attempts to share family responsibilities with their husbands have failed. Indeed, the movement has made no more than a nominal attack upon the problem of male indifference to parenting: its members know that no privileged group gives up its prerogatives simply out of a sense of justice. Since contemporary fathers can experience most of the joys of parenting without assuming its liabilities, they have no incentive to change.

MOTHERHOOD

In addition to the complexity of feminist theory of the family and the practical and psychological difficulties of introducing changes in either male or female roles within a household where there are children, a third formidable obstacle to change is the high value we place on motherhood. For many people this value extends beyond motherhood to marriage and the traditional family. The following argument focuses upon motherhood because it is the central part of the familial role whose importance is universally accepted.

The respect in which motherhood is held occurs at two intertwined but intellectually distinct levels. First, this respect is based upon human considerations. It is hard to imagine a mother, feminist or non-feminist, from the nineteenth or twentieth century, who does not agree that the rearing of children is an enormously important, difficult, and rewarding process.

The second level at which motherhood is valued is societal: no one can violate this value with impunity, whether the person be a presidential candidate or a mother who leaves her children. This value obviously reflects the human condition described above: it is found in all societies and at all times; but its relative importance changes with time, place, and gender.

American women are and were supposed to make parenthood their primary value. Men are and were not. Yet, if parenthood had a uniformly recognized high social value, mothers would receive greater rewards for their efforts, suggestions regarding payment for housewives would not have been ridiculed, no one would say apologetically "I'm just a housewife," and men would be competing for the job.

As a result of these two different bases to our veneration of motherhood, working mothers face two sets of conflicts. First, they cannot, as Myrdal and Klein (1956) point out, perform their "two roles: home and work" adequately; combined, the roles are simply too demanding. Second, women who attempt the task face social disapproval because they are upsetting the traditional notions of what is a woman's—and a man's—place.

The Mid-Nineteenth Century Feminist Movement

Nineteenth-century society extolled the virtues of marriage and motherhood. Woman had no other role: she needed none. Motherhood in particular was her God-given purpose. By extension, woman was guardian of the children's and her husband's morals and, by some alchemy, she performed these mentally and physically demanding responsibilities while remaining the embodiment of feminine delicacy and frailty.

In this enervating climate of opinion, even hardy feminists had difficulty conceiving of the idea that motherhood might be contributing to their sense of dissatisfaction and even to the psychosomatic ailments through which so many women escaped their prescribed role (while incidentally affirming the belief in their frailty). Even so outspoken a feminist as Elizabeth Cady Stanton accepted motherhood as woman's primary role in life. In proposing change, she, like others, couched her demands in terms of their contribution to the family well-being. Education would make women better mothers because they would impart more knowledge to their children. Exercise would make women healthier and better able to withstand the demands of motherhood. Shorter dresses and simpler clothes would enhance the performance of household duties.

Although mid-nineteenth century feminists decried the lack of legal protection available to married women, only the more radical of them argued that such protection was a woman's inherent right. The others put their argument in terms of the children: women whose husbands failed to provide for and protect their children should be awarded control of their own property or guardianship of their children. While women should welcome dependence on a good husband, they must be freed from dependence on a bad husband.

Other demands, such as entry into the professions, would inevitably take women out of the home. Those who followed this road, however, were seen as belonging to a tiny minority who were exceptions to the general rule of familial involvement. Entrance to the professions was an alternative to marriage for a few high-status women: it was not seen as an appropriate goal for most women, and certainly not for mothers.

The Contemporary Feminist Movement

By the time the new feminist movement had emerged in the 1960s, women's roles had changed greatly. Large proportions of married as well as single women were at work; some women, both single and married, had succeeded in business and the professions; and many middle class women attended college. College graduates were no longer expected to follow the rule of the 1920s and 30s and choose between marriage or a career. However, those who elected to pursue both objectives learned quickly that a woman's life was like a sandwich; career, the bread, was placed around the real meat of life, the family. Thus women were no longer closeted in the home, but to be a wife and mother was still a woman's primary goal and most rewarded status.

Like their nineteenth-century predecessors, contemporary feminists accept the motherhood role, but unlike their predecessors they expect their lives to include more than marriage and motherhood. The world outside the home should be as available to them as it is to men. Their vigorous efforts to achieve equality, particularly in the work force, have been accepted with relative equanimity because employment does not, on the face of it, prevent them from being successful mothers. They themselves believe that the 60s and 70s have brought new opportunities to combine the two roles. Although recent literature belies that optimism, women of all classes continue to have babies and to remain primary parent to these babies, even as their labor force participation rates continue to rise.

The vast majority of contemporary feminists who demanded greater opportunity in the world of work assumed that they and other working women would continue to be mothers. They affirmed their belief in motherhood. In other areas, particularly that of fair treatment for poor women, they addressed mothers' needs directly. Feminist groups, for example, carefully monitor federal policy changes that would affect welfare or other forms of assistance to poor mothers (with or without husbands) and, when these policies would increase the burdens on such women, feminists have lobbied strenuously. At local levels, feminists, for example, have fought effectively against high school rules that once required expulsion of pregnant girls, thus depriving them for life of both a diploma and any but a menial job through which to support their children.

A more controversial change—the idea of voluntary single parenthood—was first suggested by feminists. While a few men have chosen to become such single parents, the vast majority are women. Some women have adopted children; others are biological parents. This trend, however small the number involved, is another affirmation of motherhood. Single women are willingly assuming the responsibilities and the joys of being a mother and they have assumed the economic and emotional responsibility that, traditionally, was held by two parents.

THE WOMEN'S MOVEMENT
AND THE FAMILY OF THE FUTURE

I have suggested three reasons why the nineteenth and twentieth century feminist movements have not brought about significant change in family patterns: (1) the theoretically complex nature of the relationship between the family, social structure, and women's status; (2) the practical problems of establishing equalitarian relationships in the home, even if wives achieve equality in the world of work; (3) the high value placed on motherhood by society and, to a greater extent, by individual women whether feminist or not.

In the contemporary movement's early years, a few radicals predicted that the family, including motherhood, would disappear. Others, perhaps a slightly larger number, envisioned the ascendence of androgyny for the betterment of everyone. Neither of these visions has been realized: motherhood remains central to feminists as well as non-feminists lives; and androgyny remains largely a hope.

Today the movement has demonstrated both its commitment to motherhood and to women having access to the world outside the home. Most feminists want women to fulfill both of these commitments—to strike a balance between motherhood and work, or, in more traditional terms, between family and work. Some would call this a balance between individualism and familism (Degler, 1980), but that distinction is not entirely accurate because work contains elements of contributing to the group while family activity can often be self-interested individualism. Nonetheless, work, on the whole, requires more individualism, and the family (or motherhood) less. What hope is there that a balance between the more and the less individualistic demands of the two spheres can be achieved?

I believe that we give "the feminist movement" an impossible task when we expect it to "solve" this problem. It is one aspect of a far larger problem inherent to the human condition: the conflict between the individual and society. The fact that the problem is part of a larger human dilemma helps explain the feminists' difficulties in creating an adequate feminist theory of the family, in introducing change, and in dealing with the sacred nature of the family.

Another aspect of the rise of individualism has been the often-deplored decline in community and the accompanying rationalization of society. Discussion of the individualism/familism issue therefore also requires discussion of broad historical trends affecting all modern societies.

The radical right attempts to resolve the problems of community and the family by a retreat to the past. Even if one could do the impossible and retrace the steps of history, forgotten conflicts would emerge, as if we had removed the rose-tinted spectacles of age. Retreat cannot work: we can only go on, seeking the best solutions in our own generation to the human dilemma of individual freedom and the social good. Feminists have their responsibilities here: so do all the thinkers of our time.

NOTES

1. Interestingly, mid-nineteenth century feminists rarely referred to the work of the early liberal feminist Mary Wollstonecraft (1792, 1967).

2. Letter to Lucy Stone, November 24, 1856. Quoted in O'Neil (1969), p. 21.

3. Charlotte Perkins Gilman was the only nineteenth-century theorist to make a systematic analysis of the relationship between domesticity and inequality. She did not publish her first book, however, until 1898 by which point the movement was devoted to suffrage. While Gilman became famous and her books sold well, the movement could not at that time be deflected from its singleminded purpose.

4. The classification used in the two preceding paragraphs is adapted from Andersen (1983) and Jagger and Struhl (1978).

5. Statistics broken down by class are not available, but since as late as 1890 only 4.6% of *all* American married women were in the labor force (U.S. Bureau of Census, 1975, 133), the proportion of employed working class wives must have been relatively small.

6. In both these cases it is still women who care for the children.

BIBLIOGRAPHY

Andersen, M. L. *Thinking About Women: Sociological and Feminist Perspectives.* New York: Macmillan, 1983.

Benston, M. The political economy of women's liberation. *Monthly Review,* September, 1969, pp. 13-25.

Bird, C. *The Two-Paycheck Marriage.* Rawson, Wade, 1979.

Bunch, C. Lesbians in revolt. In N. Myron and C. Bunch (Eds.), *Lesbianism and the Women's Movement.* Oakland, Calif.: Diana Press, 1975.

Daly, M. *Gyn/Ecology.* Boston: Beacon Press, 1978.

Degler, C. N. *At Odds: Women and Family in America from the Revolution to the Present.* New York: Oxford, 1980.

Eisenstein, Z. R. *The Radical Future of Liberal Feminism.* New York: Longman, 1981.

Flexner, E. *Century of Struggle: The Woman's Rights Movement in the United States.* Cambridge: Harvard, 1966.

Gilman, C. P. *Women and Economics: A Study of the Economic Relation Between Men and Women as a Factor in Social Evolution.* Edited by Carl N. Degler. New York: Harper and Row, 1966. First published 1898.

Hoffert, S. L. and K. A. Moore. Women's employment and marriage. In R. E. Smith (Ed.), *The Subtle Revolution.* Washington, D.C.: The Urban Institute, 1979, pp. 99-125.

Hunt, J. G. and L. L. Hunt. The dualities of careers and families: new integrations or new polarizations. *Social Problems,* 1982, 29(5), 499-510.

Jaggar, A. M. and P. R. Struhl. *Feminist Framework: Alternative Theoretical Accounts of the Relations between Men and Women.* New York: McGraw-Hill, 1978.

Lampere, L. Anthropology. *Signs,* 1977, 2(3), 612-627.

Mill, J. S. *The Subjection of Women.* Cambridge, MIT Press, 1970. First published 1869.

Mitchell, J. *Woman's Estate.* New York: Pantheon, 1971.

Mitchell, J. The longest revolution. *The New Left Review,* November-December, 1966, pp. 11-37.

Myrdal, A. and V. Klein. *Women's Two Roles: Home and Work.* London: Routledge & Kegan Paul, 1956.

Oakley, A. *Subject Women.* New York: Pantheon Books, 1981.

O'Neill, W. L. *Everyone Was Brave: The Rise and Fall of Feminism in America.* Chicago: Quadrangle, 1969.

Reed, E. *Problems of Women's Liberation: A Marxist Approach.* New York: Merit, 1969.

Rowbotham, S. *Women, Resistance and Revolution: A History of Women and Revolution in the Modern World.* New York: Vintage, 1974.

Rubin, G. The traffic in women. In R. Reiter, (Ed.), *Toward an Anthropology of Women.* New York: Monthly Review Press, 1975, pp. 157-211.

Scott, A. F. (Ed.) *The American Woman: Who Was She?* Englewood Cliffs, N.J.: Prentice-Hall, 1971.

U.S. Bureau of the Census. *Historical Statistics of the United States.* Washington, D.C.: Government Printing Office, 1975.

Vanek, J. J. Household work, wage work, and sexual equality. In S. F. Berk (Ed.), *Women and Household Labor.* Beverly Hills: Sage, 1980, pp. 275-291.

Weinman-Schram, R. *Late childbearers: An analysis of their experiences with and attitudes toward marriage, parenting, and work.* Ph.D. Dissertation, Rutgers University, 1983.

Wollstonecraft, M. *A Vindication of the Rights of Women.* New York: Norton, 1967. First published, 1792.

Zaretsky, E. *Capitalism, the Family, and Personal Life.* New York: Harper and Row, 1976.

Chapter 3

In Defense of Traditional Values: The Anti-Feminist Movement

Ruth Murray Brown

That there have been changes in the American family and in the roles of women in the last two decades is unquestioned. There have been dramatic increases in the number and percentage of women in the labor force (Levitan and Belous, 1981, p. 88) in the number and percentage of households headed by women (Levitan, 1981, p. 110), in the number and percentage of divorces (Levitan and Belous, 1981, p. 28), and in the number and rate of pregnancies among unmarried women, and especially among unmarried teenagers (Spain and Bianchi, 1983; Levitan and Belous, 1981, p. 65). There has been a significant decline in the size of households (Kobrin, 1983, p. 103) and the ideal family, as reported to survey researchers, is two children or less, for a larger percentage of Americans than at any previous time in our history (*Gallup Opinion Index,* 1977, p. 25).

Less well-documented, and less dramatic, but nonetheless real, is the increase in the number of men (primarily young men, to be sure) who are taking an active role in the care of their children, and of divorced men who are seeking custody of their children (Pleck, 1982). Concomitant with these changes in the situation at home are the changes in women's roles in other institutions of society: more women seeking baccalaureate degrees, more women attending professional schools of medicine, law, and business, more women entering the professions and other traditionally male occupations,

---

Ruth Murray Brown is a member of the Division of Social Sciences, Rose State College, Midwest City, OK.

19

more women seeking and attaining elective and appointive office in the political system. The rebirth of feminism is both cause and effect of these other changes (Ferree and Hess, 1984).

These changes, demographic, attitudinal, economic, educational, and political, however, are viewed differently by different segments of the population. While younger women and professional women are likely to applaud most of them, older women and those who remain homemakers by choice are less likely to do so. Some see the rising divorce rate as a healthy corrective to women's traditional passivity and willingness to tolerate a bad marriage, while others see it as a tragedy for men, women, children, and society. It is members of these latter groups who have given impetus to the anti-feminist movement.

American society has changed in other ways in the last two decades: a dramatic rise in crime rates, increased incidence of drug use and teenage suicide, and a decline in Scholastic Aptitude Test scores. Hardly anyone is pleased with these changes; anti-feminists who deplore the shift in women's roles suspect that if mothers had only stayed home rather than going out to work, some of these undesirable trends could have been prevented. Feminists and others, more sanguine about women's new roles, attribute the other problems to other causes, such as increasing urbanization, to the changing age structure of the population, to the TV generation, or dismiss them as an artifact of an improvement in reporting procedures. With so many changes occurring almost in tandem, the relationships among them are difficult to sort out—and almost any causal relationship can be made to seem plausible.

These contrasting preferences and competing explanations form the rationale for the feminist movement, which was at least partially responsible for some of the changes, and for the anti-feminist movement, which deplores most of them. A social movement, of which these are examples, is here defined as a collectivity organized to promote or to resist social change. In this case, the anti-feminist movement came into being to oppose the feminist movement, as well as to oppose the changes that the feminists favored.

America's political system is conducive to the growth of social movements. Because our electoral system discourages the proliferation of parties, a set of preferences which in a Western European nation might be embodied in a new political party is here more likely to result in a social movement. The "structural conduciveness" of our political system has been noted by many observers, from de

Tocqueville on. It is also the first of the theoretical components in Neil Smelser's (1962) "value-added" scheme for analyzing the development of a social movement. Knowing that a system is conducive to the growth of a social movement tells nothing about the type of movements which might occur, but each succeeding component of Smelser's scheme adds to the specificity of the conditions and restricts the range within which the next component can vary.

Smelser's second component is "structural strain." The structural strain in American society in the early 1970s is revealed in public opinion polls of that period. A significant number of Americans were saying that they were dissatisfied with American society and would welcome a return to the "old values" and a slowdown in the rate of change, which had been so rapid during the 1960s (Gallup, 1972, p. 123; 1973, p. 3). The social movements of the 1960s had promoted change, but they had also created strains which prepared the way for social movements resisting change. But what form would the resistance take, and what would be its focus? There were, in fact, incipient social movements protesting integration, busing, and other trends in the public schools. There were also a number of social movements opposing pornography, but none of these proved to be as durable or as visible as the highly-organized social movement focused initially on the defeat of Equal Rights Amendment, and drawing ecumenical support from religious conservatives of the Catholic, Protestant, and Jewish faiths.

No one in the early 1970s predicted that the backlash would take this form. Neither the potential opposition to the ERA, nor the potential political power of religious conservatives was recognized in advance. With hindsight, we may be able to understand their role in the development of the anti-feminist movement by a further look at Smelser's "value-added" components.

The third component is a system of "generalized beliefs" which serves to tie the strains and discontents in society to a possible method of dealing with them, thus motivating participants to social action. The various causal explanations for the social problems of the 1970s were available for use in this way, but even more important were the religious beliefs which gave these causal explanations the sanction of God's truth. Not only were the changes in moral standards responsible for the problems, according to the anti-feminists, they were part of God's judgment because the U.S. had strayed from His commandments—and further disasters would surely follow, unless things were "turned around."

Smelser's fourth component is a "precipitating factor." When and where it occurs is largely a matter of chance, but it provides the spark that ignites the social movement. The Equal Rights Amendment precipitated the birth of the anti-feminist movement, which later called itself the pro-family movement, and it was by chance that the ERA served this function. Phyllis Schlafly, whose brilliant leadership was crucial to the success of the anti-feminist movement, had no interest in ERA until December of 1971, when a friend persuaded her to participate in a debate on the subject. All of her previous efforts had been directed toward the issues of national defense, military policy, and anti-Communism. She was quickly joined in her campaign against the ERA by rightist organizations such as the John Birch Society and Billy James Hargis' Christian Crusade. Later the organizations formed under the aegis of Richard Viguerie, Howard Phillips, and Paul Weyrich, which Viguerie himself categorizes as the New Right, joined Schlafly in establishing the Pro-Family Coalition. But neither the Old Right nor the New Right had shown any interest in women's issues before 1972.

The first four components of Smelser's value-added scheme may be present in situations which do not lead to the development of a social movement. Nor do they occur as the result of human volition, in most cases. Their contribution to the development of a social movement can best be discovered after the fact; it is difficult to decide in advance which of the various "strains," "beliefs," or even "precipitating factors" will be the significant ones. His fifth component, however, introduces the important variable of purposive human action. For that reason, the fifth component, *mobilization of participants for action,* has been expanded and made the major emphasis in recent work in the field of social movements. The resource mobilization, or resource management approach, as it is called, analyzes mobilization of all kinds of resources: commitment, personnel, finances, media attention, and beliefs or ideologies.

The key figure in the mobilization and management of the resources of the pro-family movement is Phyllis Schlafly herself. She brought important resources of her own to the task. First, there was a network of active rightist Republican women all over the country who admired her, and with whom she communicated monthly in the Phyllis Schlafly Report. Her skill in writing this four-page monthly policy analysis was another resource. Her style—bright, concise and forceful—is admirably suited to her purpose. She uses strong adjectives, powerful verbs, and frightening implications. She has learned to be very careful in what she actually says, but to write in such a way that readers are likely to draw some other, more extreme conclusion.

Her third personal resource was her lifelong association with anti-Communist groups and other rightist causes. When she turned her efforts against the ERA, the communication networks and financial resources of these other organizations were available to her.

The fourth resource, which Schlafly recognized before anyone else on the political right, was the commitment and dedication of the members of the conservative churches. It is these members, and the beliefs that motivate them to be politically active in the pro-family movement, that I want to describe in some detail in the rest of this chapter. They were a natural constituency; issue entrepreneurs like Carl McIntire, Billy James Hargis, and Fred Schwarz had for many years combined a religious appeal with anti-Communism and other issues of the political right. But for the most part, the conservative religious groups had been content to stay out of the political arena. Their entry into politics dramatically changed the terms of the ERA campaign.

The primary source of data for this discussion is my research on the anti-feminist movement in Oklahoma. The data were collected in six years of participant-observation which included more than one hundred brief interviews, fifty-six lengthy interviews with a random sample of those involved in the pro-family movement, eleven interviews with feminist leaders, and fifteen interviews with persons interested in pro-family issues, but not involved with either social movement. There is also the data from 168 Campaign Questionnaires, a 40% return from mailings to random samples of both pro-ERA and anti-ERA organizations, just after the final defeat of ERA in Oklahoma. While 40% is not a high rate of return, it is higher than that of any other study of anti-feminist groups. The Oklahoma material is supplemented by data from the published work of researchers in other states in the South, Southeast, and Northeast, and by my own participant observation and a series of brief interviews with those attending a pro-family rally for the Western states, held in Idaho in 1979.

National polls on the ERA have consistently shown that support is higher among men than among women (although this was no longer true after 1981), among blacks than whites, among those with college education than those with less education, and among those in the East than the South. Those who support the ERA are also more likely than those who oppose it to be under 50 years of age, to be in professional occupations, and to live in cities rather than in rural areas or small towns (*Gallup Opinion Index,* 1975, 1980, 1982). Consistent with these poll results are the results of small studies in Texas (Brady and Tedin, 1976), North Carolina (Arrington and Kyle, 1978), and Massachusetts (Mueller and Dimieri, Note 1). Each of these studies chose its sample in a different way. Some were limited to leaders or to those who took part in some public activity about the ERA, while others were taken from membership lists. Each study collected information in a slightly different form, and not all studies had information on all the variables, but where comparable information was available, it was consistent in all states. In every case, the Antis were older than the Pros, had less formal education, were less likely to be in professional occupations, were more likely to be of rural origin and to live in rural areas or small towns at the time of the survey, and were more likely to be married and to have more children.

These demographic facts are by now so well established that they do not need elaboration. But when combined with other facts about the political and religious affiliations and activities of the Antis, they suggest that the Antis belong to a particular culture tradition which plays an important role in their motivation to oppose the feminist movement.

Another consistent finding of all the studies of the anti-feminists is that religion is very important in their lives. In Oklahoma, only 53% of the Pros said that religion was very important in their lives, as compared to 96% of the Antis. In the Southern states where Protestantism is the dominant faith, 95% to 98% of the Antis are members of fundamentalist Protestant groups. In the Northeast, significant numbers are Catholic and some are Orthodox Jews; in the West, most are Mormons.

There is a striking difference in the degree of commitment that the Antis and Pros gave to the ERA campaign, as reported on the Campaign Questionnaire. Of the Antis, 72% had given a high or highest priority to the campaign during the previous six months, compared to only 28% of the Pros. Other questions, about the amount of time spent on the campaign, and the kinds of activities, revealed similar disparities between the two groups. The mailing list for the Antis was only about one-third as long as the Pros' list, but the numerical advantage was not enough to overcome the lack of commitment among the Pros. Why were the Antis so committed?

One of the continuing controversies is whether social movements arise because of the strong convictions or passionate concerns of the participants—the "hearts and minds" approach—or because the leaders and other elites in the society are skilled at mobilizing resources which make a social movement possible—the "resource management approach." This controversy is echoed among lay persons who hold differing views about the rightness of the social movement's cause. If they agree with it, they tend to assume that the participants are indeed motivated by sincere beliefs, but if they disagree with it, they suggest that sinister manipulation by outside forces is responsible for the movement's growth.

The anti-feminist movement is subject to the same kind of controversy. Feminists point to the right-wing connections, the insurance companies and other corporate interests that benefit from discrimination against women, and the male-dominated churches which have played an important part in the movement. All of these factors are important. The skillful leadership of right-wing leaders like Phyllis Schlafly and those in the various networks that she had available to her were an indispensable ingredient in the success of the pro-family movement. While there has been no direct evidence of insurance company involvement, it is clear that individual insurance agents contributed to the movement. And the male leadership of the conservative churches was also visible in all anti-feminist lobbying activities.

But the Antis themselves attribute their activity to their belief that they are helping to save America from God's wrath. The level of enthusiasm, dedication, and commitment which they brought to the campaign would have been hard to produce by outside manipulation alone. It springs from their religious convictions. On the one hand, their commitment is based on a combination of Biblical interpretation, taught by their pastors and religious leaders, and legal interpretation, taught by Phyllis Schlafly. On the other hand, this particular interpretation falls on deaf ears unless one is steeped in a particular religious tradition and believes it to be eternal truth.

American Protestantism includes two fairly distinct religious groups—the "mainline" or "liberal" churches, and the fundamentalist or evangelical churches. Because the term "mainline" implies a denigration of the churches in the other category, I use the term "liberal" which originally referred to a theological doctrine. Fundamentalists, on the other hand, take their name from *The Fundamentals,* a set of pamphlets published in 1910 in opposition to theological liberalism. Fundamentalists originally distinguished themselves from the liberals by believing in a literal interpretation of the Bible, a belief they now call "Biblical inerrancy." If they believed that the Bible was inerrant, or literally true, they also believed that the historic doctrines about Jesus' life contained in the Bible were literally true, i.e., that He was born of a Virgin, that He rose from the dead, and that the miracles which are described in the Bible happened in exactly that way.

By the latter half of the twentieth century, the ways in which liberals and fundamentalists interpreted the Bible had become the basis for two different broad cultural patterns which extended to many areas of life. As one after another of the older denominations moved into the liberal camp, fundamentalists have established their own seminaries for training ministers, and parochial school systems for the education of their young people. They have refused to participate in the National Council of Churches, which is dominated by the liberal denominations. Fundamentalists are more likely than liberals to hold to traditional values of sexual morality (*Connecticut Mutual Report,* 1981, p. 88), to disapprove of the use of all drugs, including alcohol and tobacco, and to be politically conservative.

Although the anti-feminist movement includes Catholics and Orthodox Jews as well as fundamentalist Protestants and Mormons, all but one of my respondents in Oklahoma were from the latter two groups. The values and religious beliefs of all these religious groups are very similar; in the broadest sense of the word, they are all fundamentalists. But the specific beliefs and historical antecedents described here are those of fundamentalist Protestants and Mormons.

Members of the pro-family movement, and of the New Right, which shares many of the goals of the pro-family movement, sometimes call themselves "traditionalists." This is an appropriate term for a subculture which upholds the traditional doctrines and values.

All Protestants were fundamentalists one hundred years ago, and until recently, upheld the traditional views of sexual morality. Their culture, which was the dominant one in those days, is now a subculture found in the South; in rural areas that have resisted the inroads of liberalism; among older people, who were reared and educated when those values were the dominant ones; and among women, who have traditionally been more religious and more conservative than men. It is not limited to older Southern women, however, although the majority of anti-feminists in Oklahoma are women over 45. The culture's values are aggressively taught by the fundamentalist churches; the men and the young people of these churches also absorb its values. The likelihood that anti-feminists are less well-educated and in lower-status occupations than feminists is partly an artifact of their being older and more rural. The men and the young people in the movement are often well-educated urban professionals, but they are more likely to have been educated in colleges which espouse the older values, often connected with traditionalist churches.

Among respondents to the ERA Campaign Questionnaire in Oklahoma, there is almost no overlap in the churches to which the Antis and Pros belonged. Almost half of the Antis belong to the fundamentalist Church of Christ, and another one-fourth were Baptists and Mormons. Over half of the Pros, on the other hand, were Methodist, Presbyterian, Episcopal, or Disciples of Christ, all liberal groups. Another twelve per cent were Unitarians, the most liberal denomination of all. The Church of Christ was also the largest group among Anti respondents in Texas (Brady and Tedin, 1976) and the second largest group in North Carolina (Arrington and Kyle, 1978).

Biblical inerrancy is not merely an obscure theological doctrine. As it is understood by the fundamentalists, it is the key to decision-making about relationships in the home, about church governance and the conduct of church services, and about every other aspect of daily life. The Bible can be interpreted so as to give guidance on all these matters, and Biblical prescriptions have the force of law handed down directly by God. In fact, the fundamentalists understand that the Bible, which cannot be in error, is inerrant precisely because the writers of the texts were inspired by God as they wrote.

Liberals, of course, do not reach the same conclusions from their study of the Bible, nor do they think it should be used as a literal guide to daily conduct in a society that is different from that in which the Bible writers lived. Disbelieving the doctrine of Biblical inerrancy, they fail to understand its power over the lives of the fundamentalists. The enthusiasm and dedication with which the anti-feminists have fought the ERA because they believe it to be anti-Biblical should be evidence enough of the intensity of that belief.

In response to the Campaign Questionnaire, 56% of the Antis gave as their first reason for opposing the ERA, that it was "against God's plan"; of those reporting that they had given the ERA campaign the highest priority in the last few months before the deadline,

100% chose "against God's plan" as the reason for their activity. Respondents were asked to list their first, second, third, and fourth choices of reasons from among a list of eight which had been mentioned in earlier interviews. After weighting the choices (a weight of 4 for a first choice, a weight of 3 for a second choice, etc.) the total scores were 398 for "against God's plan." The second reason, with 220, was that "it would weaken families." The third most popular reason, that it would "encourage an un-Biblical relationship between men and women" received a score of 200. In the minds of the anti-feminists, the Biblical and the family reasons were linked, as this statement by an interview respondent illustrates: ". . .(the ERA) is against God's will for the family, as set out in Ephesians. The husband is head of the house. The women's movement tries to uproot this God-ordained subjection of the wife to the husband's authority and control" (wife of Church of Christ minister). The passage to which she referred is Ephesians 5:21: "Wives, submit yourselves unto your husbands, as unto the Lord."

The anti-feminist belief that God's law calls for the husband to have the final authority in the family is easily misunderstood. My respondents insisted that it did not mean being a "doormat." This is reiterated in the books about marriage relationships sold in Christian bookstores. One such book (Hancock, 1975) lists three things submission does not mean. It does not mean denying selfhood, or personhood. It is not unquestioning acquiescence: women must "evaluate their husband's views, weigh them, and discuss them with him" (p. 32). Finally, submission is not an acceptance of inferiority. It does mean, however, submission in spiritual matters, submission in major decisions: "Once there has been full and free discussion, thoroughly assessing the situation, once reasonable alternatives. . . have been properly considered. . .then, ultimately, even if the wife remains in basic disagreement with her husband—pleasant acquiescence is her route" (Hancock, 1975, p. 33). And it means submission in the sexual relationship.

Marabel Morgan, whose book *Total Woman* was a best-seller in the early 1970s, calls it "adaptation" and explains it in roughly the same way: the woman must adapt to her husband, if no means of compromise can be found. The underlying reason for this doctrine is the fundamentalist understanding of the meaning of the Bible. According to one interpretation, the real meaning of the story of the Fall in the Garden of Eden is that wives must not usurp their husband's decision-making authority. Adam was created first, and it was Adam "who received God's word of prohibition regarding the fruit of the tree of the knowledge of good and evil. . .Satan's temptation to Eve was to make a spiritual decision on her own, against the command of God expressed to her by her husband" (Hancock, 1975, 25-27).

On the other hand, "submission is not refusing to take responsibility or make decisions when necessary. . .If her husband is not around and cannot be consulted, the wife then has the authority to make the decision" (Beardsley and Spry, 1975, p. 13).

In addition to the Biblical foundation for the principle of womanly submission, the fundamentalists argue that every human relationship must have a hierarchy. It is not practical for a human relationship to operate any other way. "It's the only way that you can live and have a good relationship in life. Even in a job, someone has to be the boss, and someone has to submit. That's the only way to have a relationship, is to have someone in charge" (wife of schoolteacher, Nazarene church member).

An especially articulate man among my respondents phrased it this way:

> I'm not talking about lording it over the family, understand, but in any organization, you need someone who is the dominant authority figure, and that's the responsibility of the father. That is a Biblically-given position. I also believe that it is the responsibility of the father to perform most of the sociological functions. . .I have nothing against men working at home. I know a lot that have. We have a lady working here whose husband stays home and takes care of the kids. I have no problem with that, but I don't think that relieves the husband of his God-given responsibility to the family. Every man has that responsibility. (owner of small business, Lutheran)

In addition to the Biblical and organizational reasons for submission, it has practical advantages. It provides a ready formula for settling disagreements. And most important of all, it is better than nagging. As Marabel Morgan says: "If Henpecked Harry is happy at home, then keep it up. But if he's not, then what? If all else has failed, what about love as a last resort?" (Morgan, 1976, p. 188).

And finally, Mrs. Morgan, whose program is summarized by the Four As—Admire, Accept, Adapt, and Appreciate—also suggests that it will bring a rain of gifts from a grateful husband. Beardsley and Spry's book, which is very similar to Morgan's, reports that one wife, "after following the project (suggested in their seminars) and cooking his favorite dinner, was rewarded with a new microwave oven from her husband" (p. xii). This particular aspect of the program offends many readers of these books, including some of my respondents: "The general idea that you have to work at marriage, I agree with that, but you don't have to go as far as she does" (wife of college professor, Mormon). "My husband even called the bookstore to complain and asked them to take it off the shelves, because he said it made the wife like a prostitute" (wife of lawyer, Baptist). Another respondent sums it up: "Part of it is goofy. But the idea that you give of yourself and you get a lot back is good. If we could quit being concerned about me, me, and put the other person first, we'd all come out ahead" (wife of insurance man, Church of Christ).

The view that men and women have different functions, ordained by God, explains why women are taught to submit, or adapt to their husbands. It also has ramifications for other areas of life. Fundamentalists believe that women should not speak in church, and that women should not be ordained, because of Paul's passage in the letter to the Corinthians: "Let your women be silent in church" (I Corinthians, 14:34). This teaching provides another reason to oppose ERA: "Now the church that I go to teaches that women are subject to their husbands, and that men have a say in church, and I like it that way. So I have to go up there and fight the ERA because I don't want anybody telling me that they have to have women deacons, and women preachers—and I resent that" (wife of farmer, Church of Christ).

The Church of Christ also believes that women should not teach groups which include men. Just as the man is the spiritual leader at home, he should be the spiritual leader in church activities. Some of my Church of Christ respondents were disturbed by the lack of men in leadership positions in the pro-family movement. "I really think it would be better if the men would take the leadership in this too, but they are so busy that the women have to do it" (wife of oil executive, Church of Christ).

But most important, men and women have different functions in the family because they are made differently and because they have God-given differences in the way they think and in what they are capable of doing best.

My basic understanding of woman's place is not that she's inferior or superior, but each of us has our own basic needs and they're different. Men are better suited for things like physical labor, and women are better suited for things like bearing children. I'm proud to be a woman. I'm proud that the Lord saw fit that I should be one to bear children. And if you're proud to be a woman, I don't know why you should want the same things that a man has. I don't want the responsibility that he's got, for one thing. I don't want to have to answer for everything. (wife of farmer, Mormon)

This quotation includes all three elements of the fundamentalist doctrine of women's roles: Women and men are equal in worth, competence, and in the sight of God. Women and men have different temperaments and different competencies. And women have the better part. Anti-feminist women are satisfied with what they believe is God's plan for families, with men and women fulfilling different functions. And they believe that ERA would undermine that family structure. Therefore, the second most popular reason for opposing ERA is that it would weaken families.

ERA would weaken the home, and weaken the place of women. I really think our prime purpose here is to be mothers and to raise children, and have that policy in force, and I think we'd lose that gentle influence of mother. It's more of a harsh—the more you push them out in society, and the more you put them up against men and create different roles—let's see, how can I verbalize this? I see a harshness, a difference in women now, than, say even five years ago—women's general attitudes. Feminism has affected women in general. In fact, now with young people, I don't think marriage and family is even a goal. And the law would bring more of this kind of thing. (wife of college professor, Mormon)

A man who had recently had to adjust to women working on his railroad crew expressed the same idea from the male viewpoint.

Most of the guys could do pretty well (at a particular task on the job), but I don't know if the women could handle that or not. I don't disapprove, but I just think it would probably cause a little bit less respect for the opposite sex, for my wife and daughters to receive. If you work with women all the time you just think of them as being another person, and you don't give her the same respect that I think they deserve. I think that women are special, because God created man first, then said, "I can do better," and created woman. That's the way I think of my mother, and that's the way I think of my wife and my daughters. I know if you work with a woman, day in and day out, and she does the same job that you do, and she gets the same pay you do, you're not going to have that reverence toward women." (railroad worker, Church of Christ)

Women think differently, our psychological and emotional make-up is different. We are more romantic, softer in our relationships. A mother has different feelings toward a child from the moment that the child is put in her arms. The father may love the child, but he can't love it in the same way that a mother does. This is ingrained in the nature of people, it's not from bringing up. Men are more competent in some areas, where emotions do not play a part, such as in mechanical things. My husband understands business and can make that kind of decisions better than I can. . .but women are better in human relations. They sense children's problems better. This is an inborn psychological trait. These are not going to change, because they are God-ordained. (wife of farmer, Church of Christ)

The anti-feminists have no objection to women being employed in jobs for which they are qualified, and all of them endorse the goal of equal pay for equal work, but they often add that the women may not be doing equal work: "I firmly believe in equal pay and equal opportunity. If they find a woman that can compete with men, that's well and good, but they raise a lot of stink over discrimination when the woman really isn't qualified. I've seen it happen here in the oil fields" (wife of oil-field supply worker, Church of Christ).

"You say equal work, equal pay. I really believe that women can't do equal work. I grew up on a farm, I lived on a farm, and I've worked hard, but I was never able to keep up with the men, and I don't think we are really physically fit for that" (wife of farmer, Assembly of God).

Seventy-nine per cent of the interviewees, however, believed that women should not be employed outside the home while their children are small, except in cases of dire financial necessity—and some add that even in a case like that, the church should provide help for her so that she does not have to be employed. The Mormon Church has a policy of helping its members in this way. "Women should not work out, at least when children are in the formative years. This is when they develop communication. A lot of my acquiantances do work because of the economy. I know of one family that broke up because of it" (wife of blue-collar worker, Church of Christ).

"I believe people can get by on a lot less, they just spend more than they need to spend, get in over their heads, and then they're dependent on that second income, and then they're strapped" (Baptist minister).

One woman told of going to work so that they could buy a car when her children were young, but she was so unhappy being away from the children that they decided to sell the car back and get along without one, so that she could stay with the children.

Fundamentalists believe that the ERA would take away the choice of women to stay home and be supported by their husbands.

> If my husband is the father of my children, even if we are no longer living together, he should be responsible for supporting them, and I think under the ERA, he could fight that. I think if the ERA is passed, the way that it is now, we are going to find ourselves saying "well, we'll change this a little, and that a little" Women are going to find themselves in a situation that they don't want to live with. (wife of lawyer, Mormon)

Then the next step would be that children would no longer be cared for at home by their mothers: "The thing that I've read is that the women should work and they'll put them in these government day care centers and take care of these children. I don't want the government taking care of my children" (wife of blue-collar worker, Church of Christ).

"You know, it's too much like the Russians, where the mothers work and the kids go to government day care centers" (wife of small businessman, Church of Christ).

The fear of enforced government day care was repeated over and over, by respondents in every part of the state. It was implied in Phyllis Schlafly's first Report against the ERA, although a careful reading shows that she did not actually say that ERA would bring that result. In fact, the Soviet experiment with forced day care was short-lived, because the government never did appropriate the necessary funds to provide the day care centers. Hedrick Smith, who was a New York Times correspondent in the Soviet Union, reports (1976, p. 193) that most Soviet pre-schoolers are raised at home, and that one of the most common complaints of Soviet women is that there are not enough day care centers.

Aside from the fear of government-run day care centers which might be "like Russia" anti-feminists respondents objected to day care centers of any kind on other grounds:

"Children tend to be noisier, and to share less when their mother is not with them" (wife of farmer, Mormon).

"I worked in a nursery once, and I was sick so much from the children's illnesses, that I wonder if it was a good idea for the children. If a person takes on the responsibility of being a mother, she should be there with the children" (wife of blue-collar worker, Church of Christ).

"I was appalled when I went to pick up a child for a friend, at the chaos and mayhem that was going on. I thought that particular child, who already had problems, was certainly not being helped by that day care center" (wife of businessman, Church of Christ).

If working is an absolute necessity, then "I would prefer an individual who would have the same values as the mother to care for the children."

"I hate day care centers. It's best to leave them with grandma, but that's a terrible thing to do to grandma. Aside from that, maybe a neighbor who takes care of only that child. And then down the line from that, a Christian day care center. The last resort would be a public day care center" (wife of doctor, Lutheran).

The fundamentalists' commitment to anti-feminism is based on a particular view of the ideal family and maternal roles which in turn is based on their view of Biblical prescriptions for the family. Without these deeply-held beliefs, they would not have been able to sustain such a high level of political activity during the long ERA campaign. On the other hand, most of them were inexperienced in politics. Without the skillful guidance of Phyllis Schlafly and her fellow-activists in the states, their commitment could not have been translated into effective political action.

Now that they have had a taste of political activity, many of them find it challenging and exciting. Will this first step out of the home-bound role tempt them to take other steps? Will it have an effect on their daughters as they observe their mothers going out to campaign day after day? Or will the fundamentalists retreat to their homes now that the main event is over?

The ERA campaign has transformed American politics, as women of both the left and the right have learned that they will have to work in politics if they expect to have laws that embody their preferences. The future of feminist issues depends on which side is more successful in both maintaining the "hearts and minds" commitment of its adherents, and in managing its resources effectively.

REFERENCE NOTE

1. Mueller, C., and Dimieri, T. "Oppositional Consciousness and ERA activism in Three States." Paper Presented at American Sociological Association Annual Meetings, San Francisco, California, 1982. Available from senior author at Center for Research on Women, Wellesley College.

REFERENCES

Arrington, T. S., and Kyle, P. A. Equal Rights Activists in North Carolina. *Signs,* 3 Spring, 1978, 666-680.

Beardsley, L., and Spry, T. *The Fulfilled Woman.* New York: Bantam Books, 1975

Brady, D. W., and Tedin, K. L. Ladies in Pink: Religion and Political Ideology in the Anti-ERA Movement. *Social Science Quarterly,* 56, March, 1976, 564-575.

Connecticut Mutual Life Insurance Co. *The Connecticut Mutual Life Report on American Values in the 80s.* Hartford, Connecticut, 1981.

Ferree, M. M., and Hess, B. *Controversy and Coalition: The New Feminist Movement.* Boston: Twayne, 1984.

Gallup Opinion Index. No. 185, May, 1972.

Gallup Opinion Index. No. 101, November, 1973.

Gallup Opinion Index. No. 118. April, 1975.

Gallup Opinion Index. No. 142. May, 1977.

Gallup Opinion Index. No. 178. June, 1980.

Gallup Opinion Index. No. 203. August, 1982.

Hancock, M. *Love, Honor and Be Free.* Chicago: Moody Bible Institute, 1975.

Kobrin, F. E. The Fall in Household Size and the Rise of the Primary Individual in the United States. In Gordon, Michael, ed. *The American Family in Social-Historical Perspective,* 3rd edition. New York: St. Martin's Press, 1983.

Levitan, S., and Belous, R. S. *What's Happening to the American Family?* Baltimore: Johns Hopkins University Press, 1981.

Morgan, M. *Total Joy.* Old Tappan, New Jersey: Fleming H. Revell Co., 1976.

Pleck, J. *Men's Family Work: Three Perspectives and Some New Data.* Paper presented at the New Jersey Council on Family Relations, October, 1982.

Smelser, N. *Theory of Collective Behavior.* New York: Free Press, 1962.

Smith, H. *The Russians.* New York: Ballantine, 1976.

Spain, D., and Bianchi, S. M. How Women Have Changed. *American Demographics,* Vol. 5: 18-25, 1983.

Chapter 4

Women's Work in the Home: Seems Like Old Times

Catherine White Berheide

This chapter examines the nature of household work: time budgets, the division of labor, working conditions, and women's feelings about their labor in the home. The data presented in this paper were generated by three methods—participant observation in 43 homes, a telephone survey of 309 married women and 24-hour diaries completed by 158 of the respondents. The research findings indicate that women still shoulder most of their traditional responsibilities. As women's labor force participation increases, the number of women carrying a double burden of work also increases because the traditional patterns show little sign of changing.

Before the publication of Lopata's *Occupation: Housewife* in 1971, housework had been virtually ignored as a topic for serious research by sociologists reflecting our cultural denigration of unpaid labor. Since 1971, however, research interest has mushroomed, bringing us Oakley's groundbreaking study of British housewives (1974a, 1974b) as well as Vanek's study of time use by American women (1974), followed by the Berheide et al. (1976) of middle-class women and Ferree's (1976) of working-class women. One important focus of attention in such research has been the division of labor in the home, particularly whether it has changed in response to

Catherine White Berheide is Assistant Professor of Sociology, Department of Sociology, Anthropology and Social Work, Skidmore College, Saratoga Springs, NY.

The research reported was conducted with the aid of a grant from the N.I.M.H. Center for the Study of Metropolitan Problems (#MH27340-01). An earlier version of this paper was presented at the annual meetings of the Society for the Study of Social Problems, September, 1982, San Francisco, California.

I wish to thank my co-workers on the household work research project, Richard A. Berk and Sarah Fenstermaker Berk, without whom these data would never have been collected. I would also like to thank Beth Hess for her significant help in revising this chapter.

women's increased labor force participation (Berk and Berk, 1978; Szinovacz, 1977). Other topics covered have included men's participation in family work (Berk, 1979; Pleck, 1979); the social status of full-time homemakers (Bose, 1980; Nilson, 1978); attitudes towards housework (Ferree, 1980; Iglehart, 1979); and the allocation of time to housework (Berk and Berk, 1979; Robinson, 1977). Recent interest in these questions is not limited to sociology, but may be found in anthropology (Hartmann, 1981), psychology (Andre, 1981), economics (Wales and Woodland, 1977), history (Strasser, 1982), political theory (Malos, 1980), and religion (Rabuzzi, 1981). Throughout the past decade, the study of housework has been a special concern of feminist sociologists with a Marxist perspective (e.g., Sokoloff, 1981; Glazer, 1980), and is increasingly recognized as an important variable in research focused on other issues, especially women's employment (Kessler and McRae, 1982). Now that a critical mass of information is available, we can step back and take stock of the knowledge about household labor accumulated through these many studies. What changes, if any, have occurred in this important area of women's lives?

This chapter examines the nature of household work: time budgets, the division of labor, working conditions, and women's feelings about their labor in the home.

Women's work in the home has been distinguished from work in the labor market primarily by its lack of pay, but there are three other important differences. First, in an industrial capitalist economy, family work is regarded as "private" rather than "public" labor precisely because it is unpaid labor in the private home. Indeed Glazer (1980, p. 258) argues that household labor became more privatized because "before the development of the industrial wage labor force, housework and child care were usually collective household activities." Second, there is neither a spatial nor temporal separation of work and home. In an industrial society, the typical worker does not work in the home. The workplace for household labor is unusual in this respect. Zaretsky (1976) argues that the split between public and private production that occurred with the rise of industrial capitalism separated work from home for all workers except homemakers. In doing so, it obscured the economic functions of women's private production in the home and devalued household labor by relocating the economic reward system outside the home. Finally, household work is a labor of love performed for family members to whom the worker is attached by ties of affection. In short, household work is an occupation where work and family roles are to all intents and purposes indistinguishable. This fusing of work and home has consequences for patterns of time allocation, the household division of labor, working conditions, and women's feelings towards their labor.

RESEARCH METHODS AND CHARACTERISTICS OF THE SAMPLE

This paper is based on data generated in 1975 during a larger study of household work in Evanston, Illinois, an affluent suburb of approximately 80,000 residents on the northern boundary of Chicago (see Berheide et al., 1976). Three data collection methods were used: (1) participant observation; (2) telephone interviews; and (3) 24-hour diaries. Forty-three families chosen through a snowball sample in Chicago, Evanston, and several other northern suburbs of Chicago were studied during the participant observation phase of the research (see Berk and Berheide, 1977). The field work typically involved two three-hour sessions of both observation and open-ended interviews. A forty-minute telephone interview was administered by female interviewers to a random sample drawn from the telephone directory. Three hundred and nine women living with their husbands participated, yielding a response rate of 71%.[1] One hundred and fifty-eight women, self-selected from the participant observation and survey samples completed diaries.[2]

Over half of the employed women in both the survey and diary samples held high-status jobs (frequently in traditionally female professions, such as non-college teaching). Moreover, 63% (196) of the husbands and 50% (153) of the wives in the survey sample have completed college, and 44% (118) of the husbands earned over $20,000 in 1975. In short, as Table 1 indicates, this sample is clearly middle class (by 1975 standards). Therefore, caution should be exercised in generalizing from this sample. On the other hand, the survey and diary samples are more representative of the nation on some other demographic variables. Twelve percent (37) of the survey sample was black which is the equivalent of the national figure. Forty-three percent (133) of the survey respondents worked full time, a proportion only slightly above the national average for married women in 1975. Still, any inferences drawn about "typical" American families have to be constrained by the middle-class character of the sample.

Table 1 presents a comparison between the diary and telephone survey respondents on selected demographic variables. Any differ-

TABLE 1

COMPARISON OF SELECTED BACKGROUND CHARACTERISTICS OF EVANSTON

SURVEY RESPONDENTS (N=309) WITH DIARY RESPONDENTS (N=158)

		SURVEY		DIARY	
		Mean	N	Mean	N
1.	Number in Household	3.4	309	3.3	152
2.	Number of Children per Household	1.3	309	1.3	152
3.	Age of Wife	42.7	309	41.5	151
4.	Age of Husband	45.1	307	43.9	151
5.	Years Married	18.3	308	17.3	151
6.	Wife's Work Hours (Hours/Week)	34.1	163	31.9	71
7.	Wife's Monthly Pay (Dollars)	660.52	138	578.68	60
		%	N	%	N
8.	Wife's Employment Status		309		152
	No Employment	37.2		42.8	
	Part-time Employment	19.7		21.7	
	Full-Time Employment	43.0		35.5	
9.	Wife's Occupation		162		71
	Professional/Technical	45.7		50.7	
	Managers/Officials/Proprietors	9.3		7.0	
	Clerical and Kindred	27.8		28.2	
	Sales Workers	4.3		4.2	
	Operatives	1.9		1.4	
	Private Household Workers	3.1		1.4	
	Service Workers	4.9		2.8	
	Students	3.1		4.2	
10.	Wife's Race		308		151
	White	85.1		90.7	
	Black	12.0		7.3	
	Latin	0.6		0	
	Oriental	1.6		1.3	
	Other	0.6		0.7	
11.	Wife's Education		309		152
	Some High School	8.1		4.6	
	High School Completed	18.1		14.5	
	Vocational	3.6		2.6	
	Some College	20.7		23.7	
	College Completed	28.5		27.0	
	Some Graduate School	13.6		16.4	
	Graduate School Completed	7.4		11.2	
12.	Husband's Income		268		129
	$10,000 or Less	15.3		13.2	
	$10,001 - $20,000	40.7		41.9	
	$20,001 - $30,000	31.0		30.2	
	$30,001 - $40,000	4.1		5.4	
	$40,001 - $50,000	6.0		7.0	
	$50,001 - $75,000	1.9		2.3	
	> $75,000	1.1		0	

TABLE 1 (continued)

		SURVEY		DIARY	
		%	N	%	N
13.	Husband's Occupation		275		138
	Professional/Technical	44.4		42.8	
	Managers/Officials/Proprietors	29.5		37.0	
	Clerical and Kindred	2.2		0.7	
	Sales Workers	6.5		8.0	
	Craftsmen, Foremen and Kindred	5.1		2.9	
	Operatives	3.3		2.2	
	Service Workers	6.5		3.6	
	Students	2.5		2.9	
14.	Husband's Education		309		152
	Some High School	7.4		4.6	
	High School Completed	13.9		11.8	
	Vocational	1.3		2.0	
	Some College	13.9		15.8	
	College Completed	22.7		23.7	
	Some Graduate School	12.6		13.2	
	Graduate School Completed	28.2		28.9	

ences that existed between survey and diary respondents were remarkably small. First, diary respondents were somewhat less likely to hold full-time jobs (only 36%), and, as a result, they earned less money ($579 a month rather than $661). Aside from the lower representation of employed women, the only other important difference was the lower representation of black women in the diary sample (only 7%). The diary subsample, therefore, shows little evidence of systematic self-selection.

HOUSEHOLD LABOR

Once one defines household labor as work, the sociology of work tradition suggests several crucial questions: how is time allocated? who does what? under what working conditions? and with what attitudes?

TIME

Household work is repetitive (65% of the tasks were to be done again the following day or sooner), often following a regular schedule (58% of the tasks were done at their usual time the day the respondent filled out the diary). As a result, household work takes on a routine and almost unfinished quality that many women find frustrating.

Most tasks are simply *repetitive* and not necessarily frustrating by themselves, but frustrating by the nature of their need to be done over and over. By the same token, I don't find most of my work difficult *to do,* but difficult to face on a daily basis.

Housework is not too unpleasant to me unless it is never-ending like "picking up" or "cleaning up" (after meals)—tasks which I seem to be doing and redoing constantly, yet never finishing or never being able to see an end accomplished.

The British housewives in Ann Oakley's research (1974a) expressed similar feelings about the repetitive nature of housework. Unfortunately, the constant redoing of tasks does not mean that women have unlimited discretion in scheduling their work. External constraints (e.g., work and store hours), inflexible needs (e.g., sleeping and eating) and familial demands all limit a woman's ability to plan her workday, especially the timing of a particular task.

The women in this sample, both full-time homemakers and employed women, concentrate household work during the morning and evening meal times. Employed women, however, also used their lunch hours to accomplish such household tasks as fixing lunch for their families, shopping or running errands. They also were more likely to perform household tasks later in the day. Even though employed women get a head start on their household chores before they leave for work—Berk and Berk (1979) found that employed women tended to wake up thirty minutes before nonemployed wives—they still face a multitude of household tasks when they come home from work. Household work is not time bound in the manner of paid employment—it is not a nine-to-five job. Indeed, women with children at home often put in a 24 hour day. The distinction between being at home and being at work blurs for women. While homemaking may provide more opportunities for leisure pursuits during the typical workday, it provides less during the traditional off-work hours.

TASK DURATION

Most common household tasks, such as wiping counters, folding laundry, and diapering, take less than 15 minutes. The modal duration for housework tasks was fifteen minutes, the median was also fifteen minutes, and the mean was 25 minutes. However, despite the fact that 93% of housework tasks took less than an hour, some, such as sewing, painting or wallpapering, and shopping, averaged over an hour thus skewing the distribution. Homemaking appeared to consist of a large number of short tasks. Those tasks which did not require the woman to devote constant attention to them tended to be dovetailed with another task. Women did an average of three tasks at one time. For example, a woman could be fixing dinner, doing a load of wash and supervising children during the same block of time. By dovetailing 66% of the tasks, women were able to get their work done in considerably less time than if they had done only one at a time.

Despite the fact that most of the tasks were of short duration and several were done at the same time, women still spent an average of 6 hours and 49 minutes per day in household labor (see Table 2); full-time homemakers spent the most amount of time (8 hours and 11 minutes), while women with full-time jobs spent the least (5 hours and 5 minutes). Yet, if a seven or eight hour working day is defined as a full-time job, employed women work a day and a half, spending more time on the job *and* at home than either full-time homemakers or employed men. Szalai (1972) reports similar pat-

TABLE 2

SUM OF THE AVERAGE TIMES SPENT ON HOUSEWORK TASKS

IN THE DIARIES

Group	Mean (in hours)
Entire Sample	6.832
Women without a job	8.189
Women with part-time jobs	7.015
Women with full-time jobs	5.088

Group	Mean (in hours)
Entire Sample	6.832
Women without children	5.438
Women with one child	7.547
Women with two children	7.549
Women with three children	7.599
Women with four children	9.224
Women with five children	11.233

terns of time use among urban and suburban populations in twelve countries.

Robinson (1977) found that employment status is the major predictor of women's family care time, with presence of children as the second most important factor. In general, the more children the respondent lived with, the more time she spent on family work. Contrary to popular belief, the more appliances a woman had, the *more* time she spent on household work (see also Vanek, 1974). It appears that appliances either create more household work or that the small amount of time saved is immediately allocated elsewhere, perhaps as a consequence of rising standards of household care. The image of the modern homemaker with hours of free time is not supported by any housework time study (e.g., Walker and Woods, 1976). This is, of course, especially true if the homemaker has a full-time job as well.

DIVISION OF LABOR

While husbands and children are involved in family work, the vast majority of household labor is done by wives—between 74% and 92% of the tasks in eight major areas (meal preparation, cleaning the kitchen, laundry, straightening, ironing, outside errands, child care, and other household tasks). As one woman succinctly put it, "If I don't do it, it doesn't get done." In contrast, husbands did between 12% and 26% of the tasks in each area, except outside errands in which they did 54% and their wives did 74%. (The overlap reflects the degree to which the work is alternated or done together.) Children did between 7% and 13% of the tasks. Respondents' comments made it clear that the household remained their responsibility although other family members sometimes "helped."

> I neither get nor expect too much assistance with household work. However, if I need it my son will help.

> All in all I'm happy and proud that my husband and I share *some* of the work. Which is more than both of our mothers can say.

In fact, help was often a mixed blessing, as 43% of women surveyed said they had to supervise the household work of other family members.

I wish there were some accurate way to record and describe how much work it is to get others to do *their* work—children dressing for school or putting away toys, for example.

It is little wonder, then, that women are reluctant to ask for help when it seems easier just to do it oneself.

Husbands whose wives worked outside the home were slightly more involved in household work than were husbands of full-time homemakers. Berk and Berk (1979, p. 231) also concluded "that husbands of employed wives pick up some of the burden although not nearly enough to reach parity with their employed wives. That is, it is still probably fair to say that employed wives hold down two full-time jobs" (see also Robinson, 1977; Walker and Woods, 1976; Meissner et al., 1975). However, Pleck (1979, p. 487) found "non-trivial increments in husbands' family work associated with wives' employment" that he feels represent the beginning of a major shift in men's family roles.

Whether Pleck's more optimistic conclusion is correct or not, women today continue to carry the main responsibility for household work. Moreover, a wife's employment made the household division of labor more problematic, leading to arguments about who should do what.

In general, the reduction in time spent on household labor by an employed woman was the result of her lowering her housekeeping standards and doing less rather than the result of any significant increase in "help" from other family members or any greater "efficiency" on her part. As one diary respondent described the impact of her employment:

> I'm not a very good housekeeper, at best, and working full time, in addition, means that I have had to lower my standards and cut corners wherever I could. It was very depressing to see how little time I spend on myself in a typical day.

Angrist et al. (1976) and Holmstrom (1973) found that professional women more often purchase household services rather than rely on additional assistance from family members. Alternatives to increased participation by other family members include appliances, friends and neighbors, and paid help. However, only 21% of the housework activities reported in the diaries involved an appliance. No machines are available to aid women with many household chores. Similarly, only 22% of the survey respondents said they got frequent help from friends and neighbors with even a limited set of household tasks such as babysitting and running errands. Only 19% had paid housekeeping help on a regular basis, typically once a week. Even for those women fortunate enough to have these forms of assistance, much of the day-to-day work still remained for the individual woman to perform. One important strategy for reducing a woman's time investment in household work would be to transfer more of it outside the private home rather than to redivide the same amount of work among family members.

WORKING CONDITIONS

One consequence of housework's location in the private home is that the work is done in isolation or only in the company of family members. Women performed 58% of the tasks reported in the diaries while they were alone. Respondents were more likely to have the companionship of their children (22%) than of their husbands (16%) while doing household work. Only 4% of the tasks were performed when unrelated adults were present. Activities done with the husband or another adult present were more enjoyable than those done alone or with children. The presence of children was a mixed blessing—both a source of companionship and a source of work. These data support Oakley's (1974a, p. 98) observation that "loneliness is an occupational hazard for the modern housewife." Both Ferree (1976) and Rubin (1977) found that lack of social contacts within the home is one factor that leads women to seek paid employment. Women had at least two means of combating loneliness. First, some tasks (10%) took place outside the home and thereby provided social interaction. Second, the TV, radio, stereo and telephone were used during 32% of the diary activities to bring the outside world into the home.

Because household work is frequently performed in isolation, women do not experience direct supervision. Seventy-four percent (226) of the survey respondents reported that they were almost never criticized, and 70% (217) rarely or never felt pressure about their household work. Yet something akin to supervision did occur; the wife was expected to fulfill her "responsibility" for household work and would have received complaints if she had not. As Oakley (1974a) also noted, some women became their own supervisors:

> My life is quite easy and my time is pretty much my own—but I feel compelled to do my "housewife" duties. The work is not pressing or difficult, but I always feel better if I get a few things done.

Given the lack of direct supervision and the isolation of family work, women working in the home have more potential for discretion to plan their work than do other workers. However, women's discretion to plan their work and leisure was limited by interruptions—from the telephone and children especially—as well as the family needs and external constraints described earlier. The lack of spatial or temporal separation of work and home made it difficult for some women to stop housework and engage in leisure pursuits, or even to rest when ill. As Oakley (1974a, p. 43) explained, "In the housewife's case autonomy is more theoretical than real. Being 'your own boss' imposes the obligation to see that housework gets done. The responsibility for housework is a unilateral one, and the failure to do it may have serious consequences."

FEELINGS ABOUT HOUSEHOLD WORK

When asked about their feelings concerning household tasks, the majority of survey respondents had neutral feelings about five of six areas of household work (see Table 3). For the survey respondents, "neutral" meant routine, necessary, nondescript, mindless and other similar reactions.

> I'm not sure your categories of "feelings" describe exactly how I felt performing tasks—neutral or numb perhaps would best describe how I operate generally—no strong feelings—just rather doing things because they must be done and I happen to be there to do them.

> Most of my tasks are automatic to me and I do them daily and no longer really ascribe these emotional feelings to a specific task.

> Some things are done so many times a day and for so many years that it is difficult to assess my true reaction to having to do them—they are taken for granted and done without thinking about them.

TABLE 3

PERCENT OF RESPONDENTS (N=309) ATTACHING FEELING TO SIX AREAS OF

HOUSEHOLD WORK

	Enjoyable	Ful-filling	Neutral	Frustra-ing	Tedious or Boring	Physically Tiring	Un-Pleasant	Diffi-cult
Doing the Laundry	38.6	31.2	68.6	11.5	36.9	29.1	15.9	5.1
	(114)	(92)	(203)	(34)	(109)	(86)	(47)	(15)
Straightening	43.6	37.6	62.4	23.9	40.5	26.8	22.2	6.2
	(133)	(115)	(191)	(73)	(124)	(82)	(68)	(19)
Ironing	37.0	25.7	53.0	19.6	49.6	29.6	27.8	5.2
	(85)	(59)	(122)	(45)	(114)	(68)	(64)	(12)
Cleaning the Kitchen	39.0	32.7	61.4	15.7	51.6	35.9	27.1	8.2
	(119)	(100)	(188)	(48)	(158)	(110)	(83)	(25)
Preparing Meals	80.5	58.1	53.2	18.2	26.6	23.1	5.8	4.5
	(248)	(179)	(164)	(56)	(82)	(71)	(18)	(14)
Child Care	96.2	94.2	18.6	52.6	13.5	57.1	18.6	41.9
	(150)	(147)	(29)	(82)	(21)	(89)	(29)	(65)

In this respect household work is not unlike many paid jobs where the employees just "put in time," i.e., do their work without investing much psychic energy. Many women expressed this same reaction to the routine quality of household labor—it has to get done, so they just do it. These women seem to have made a conscious adjustment to their situation as household workers by not thinking about it. Household work seemed to be a potential source of unhappiness which was defused by being accepted as necessary. The diary data confirmed these results; women described 42% of the household tasks recorded in the diaries as neutral. In short, household work was accepted as a necessary and not wholly onerous job with generally few affective reactions one way or the other.

Oakley (1974a, p. 70) hypothesized that "a 'like' or 'don't mind' attitude seems symbolic of a search for satisfaction in housework; the declaration of a 'dislike' appears to indicate the recognition of dissatisfaction." Perhaps these women followed a mindless approach in order to avoid expressing dissatisfaction with household work and by implication with their families, their lives, and their roles as women. As one respondent said,

> I have marked most of them as neutral rather than boring be-
> cause I don't think about what I am doing. If I did I would con-
> sider it all boring, frustrating, tiring and unpleasant.

Still, a sizeable proportion of the respondents were willing to state
that they found doing the laundry, straightening, ironing and cleaning the kitchen tedious or boring. However, since most of the respondents felt strong emotional attachments to the household members for whom they labored, the emotional benefits accruing from
the roles of wife and mother appeared to outweigh the specific costs
of household work.

> I don't hate my work—often I am neutral about it—but it's part
> of how I give to my family.

> I do enjoy taking care of my family and home. At times things
> may seem tiring or boring, but on the whole it is a fulfilling job
> to me. I wouldn't want to do anything else.

> Perhaps I don't mind what I am doing because I know I could
> do anything else I might want to do—I'm educated and compe-
> tent. This is my choice. Love raising kids, pets and plants, too.
> Very creative.

> I have a very helpful family and so I am not dissatisfied—even
> with the boring chores and I love to cook and care for them.

Since most household tasks did not require great skill, the respondents adopted a mindless approach. Only cooking and child care
were rated enjoyable and fulfilling by the majority of survey respondents because they were the "creative" tasks in household work. It
is a mixed blessing, then, that men seem more willing to share these
two tasks than the other less enjoyable ones.

A variety of seemingly contradictory feelings were attached to
child care. Caring for children was enjoyable, fulfilling, tiring, and
frustrating. While child care is the least routine part of a mother's
household work, it is usually the most rewarding part. As one articulate diary respondent put it: "Fortunately, but almost unexplica-
bly, the myriad of small enjoyable tasks performed each day in the
line of 'child care' somehow add up to fulfilling, enjoyable work."
Yet, many mothers also indicated that their children ran them ragged:
"The nicest job is doing things with the kids but they also throw me
for a loop at times." Being totally responsible for another human

being's welfare can be a heavy burden as well as a joy, but it cannot be characterized as "neutral."

DISCUSSION AND CONCLUSION

In sum, with the exception of child care, women had few strong positive or negative reactions to their daily tasks. Moreover, they did not feel especially pressured although they hardly led lives of leisure. The women viewed household work as routine and repetitive. To summarize women's attitudes towards household work as neutral is to obscure a great deal of ambivalence. On the one hand, these women loved the people for whom they were doing household work. On the other hand, they felt frustrated when they were constantly doing the same jobs over again and no one seemed to care. This ambivalence was neatly expressed by one of the field work respondents:

> It doesn't bother me that it's (housework) mindless. I think about other things. I work my tail off and no one notices. It just has to be done all over again. There isn't anything else I can do to have someone say I keep a good house. I never make progress. I have to work so hard to keep even.

The fact that household work is constantly done and redone is also mentioned by women as a source of monotony and dissatisfaction.

> Housework is very frustrating for me. When I do things I like them to stay done—housework doesn't.

> Some chores are enjoyable one day, but maddening when they have to be repeated the next because of carelessness of others, for example.

The reward of lasting accomplishment is not part of household work. As the diaries indicated, the bulk of housework tasks occur over and over again with little or no variation even in the time of accomplishment. The diary data strongly suggest that the routine and repetitive qualities of household work with the resultant sense of frustration of mindlessness diminish any intrinsic enjoyment offered by these tasks. Gove and Tudor (1973) argued that the frustration and lack of rewards associated with being a full-time homemaker or combining homemaking with paid work may help explain why women have higher rates of mental illness than men.

In conclusion, household labor has some rather distinctive features. First, "home" and "work" are inextricably bound for homemakers. Second, family work is not "public" work. Third, the work is done for the family rather than an impersonal boss. Because the work is carried out primarily for loved ones, altruistic rewards, but no monetary or status ones, are likely to be present even for the most tedious work. As one respondent concluded regarding household work, "The rewards and frustrations are often intangible." These intangible rewards are most often in the form of appreciation for being a wife and mother rather than for accomplishing specific tasks. Thus, household labor is largely unrewarded, isolated, routine, and repetitive. It allows for some discretion, little supervision, and many time constraints. It consumes large quantities of time with tasks that women regarded with resigned indifference, at best.

The data reveal that women who join their husbands in the labor market still shoulder most of their traditional household responsibilities. This one-sided division of labor resulted in a long workday for employed women because they devoted a considerable amount of time to household work before and after the hours spent at their jobs. Much of the employed woman's "free" time was devoted to work, particularly family work, rather than to leisure. For her, such necessary activities as sleeping, eating, and grooming might be the only leisure-like activities included in her day. She continued to perform two jobs in part because she viewed paid work as more rewarding and less onerous than household work. As women's labor force participation increases, the number of women carrying this double burden of work also increases because the traditional patterns for assigning household responsibilities show little sign of changing. This double burden forms a serious barrier to women's attainment of equality in employment and within the family.

Feminist writers have often argued that the oppression of women is linked to their family roles. The traditional division of labor in industrial societies still demands that women work as homemakers. In a society whose cultural norms and institutional arrangements still assume the traditional nuclear family with a male breadwinner/female homemaker, families that fail to follow the traditional pattern typically face certain problems in everyday living. For instance, when both husband and wife work outside the home, who goes to the post office, admits the repairperson, accepts deliveries, brings a sick child home from school? Two-earner families develop ad hoc individual solutions to these problems. If women are to attain equality, we must understand how they currently cope with the double burden of household work and paid work in order to determine how to restructure our society so that these tasks are shared with others, either with husbands or the community as a whole.

I concur with Holmstrom (1973) that the problems faced by the two-career family, and the employed wife in particular, are related to the rigidity of the occupational structure and the isolation of the nuclear family within the private home. Both men and women must be able to schedule their job hours flexibly so that they can meet household obligations. Similarly, service facilities related to household tasks, such as stores, restaurants, laundromats, banks, and post offices, schools, should be open during hours when they are accessible to employed men and women. The length of the paid work week could be shortened or part-time work upgraded so that men and women can do both paid work and household work, including parenting if they so choose, without giving up most of their leisure time or the significant benefits of full-time employment. Professional men and women whose jobs demand their total commitment, and blue-collar men and women with mandatory overtime, are in even greater need of having their work weeks reduced. Furthermore, the expectation that women, and especially men, must not take time out of the labor market to be homemakers and child rearers if they wish to be considered "serious" aspirants to occupational success must be changed.

Alternatively, household work could be collectivized or moved into the market sector so that virtually no work remained for the nuclear family to accomplish on its own. Certainly we need more support services such as fast-food restaurants, rental businesses, housekeeping services and, last but not least, child care centers. If at least some housework tasks can be removed from the private home and the remaining ones redistributed among family members according to age, skills and preferences, women would not face such long work weeks when choosing (or being forced by economic need) to work outside the home.

Respondents found it difficult to achieve a more equitable division of labor because to do so would involve arguing with family members they loved about a "trivial" issue—household work. Furthermore, the homemaker (part-time or full-time) does not see herself as part of a group of dissatisfied workers with a common interest in changing their working conditions. If her attempts to adapt and to be a better homemaker fail to increase her work satisfaction, she generally seeks an individual solution outside the home. Often she takes a paid job that she hopes will meet her needs. (Andre, 1981, p. 50)

Many women do not perceive their husband's or family's supervision of their domestic labor as oppressive. Objectively, it may be; subjectively, they do not experience it as such. Thus women may be suffering from a form of false consciousness. The sexual division of labor which makes housework women's work is at least taken for granted and all too often accepted as legitimate in most American families. Domestic labor is women's work in and for the family. As Glazer (1980, p. 253) notes,

For women the family is a "workplace". . . . It is within the marriage and by virtue of the marriage contract that women do the equivalent of what men do in the workplace—meeting basic human needs that allows the continuation of their lives. . . . Marriage (the work that women are responsible for within marriage) remains an essential aspect of how women "earn" their living.

It is difficult for women, therefore, to escape male domination within marriage. To improve their lives, women must fight loved ones who are resisting change in order to protect their privilege not to do housework. The unique relationship women have to their bosses/clients within the home makes their struggle for equality within the family more difficult. However much change the women's movement has brought about outside the home, the traditional division of labor within the home remains relatively untouched.

FOOTNOTES

1. The random sample of names drawn from the telephone book included many households which were not part of the population being studied, that is, which did not include a married woman living with her husband. Twenty-nine percent (410) of the names were determined to be ineligible for participation in the survey because they did not meet the inclusion criteria. Some undetermined additional portion of the 22% (293) who refused to participate in the research were also ineligible. Since 57% of the names whose eligibility status could be determined were ineligible, the 57% figure was used as an estimate of the proportion of the

people who refused to cooperate who were actually ineligible to participate. Using this estimation procedure, the response rate rises from 51% to 71%.
2. Respondents were paid five dollars for completing a diary.

REFERENCES

Andre, R., *Homemakers*. Chicago:University of Chicago, 1981.
Angrist, S.S., J.R. Lave, and R. Mickelsen, "How Working Mothers Manage," *Social Science Quarterly* 56:631-37, 1976.
Berheide, C.W., S.F. Berk and R.A. Berk, "Household Work in the Suburbs," *Pacific Sociological Review* 19(October):491-517, 1976.
Berk, R.A. and S.F. Berk, *Labor and Leisure at Home*. Beverly Hills, CA:Sage, 1979.
Berk, R.A. and S.F. Berk, "A Simultaneous Equation Model for the Division of Household Labor," *Sociological Methods and Research* 6(May):431-68, 1978.
Berk, S.F., "Husbands at Home" pp. 125-58 in K.W. Feinstein (ed.), *Working Women and Families*. Beverly Hills, CA:Sage, 1979.
Berk, S.F. and C.W. Berheide, "Going Backstage," *Sociology of Work and Occupations* (February):27-48, 1977.
Bose, C., "Social Status of the Homemaker," pp. 69-87 in S.F. Berk (ed.), *Women and Household Labor*. Beverly Hills, CA:Sage, 1980.
Ferree, M.M., "Satisfaction with Housework," pp. 89-112 in S.F. Berk (ed.), *Women and Household Labor*. Beverly Hills, CA:Sage, 1980.
Ferree, M.M., "Working-Class Jobs," *Social Problems* (April):431-41, 1976.
Glazer, N., "Everyone Needs Three Hands," pp. 249-73 in S.F. Berk (ed.), *Women and Household Labor*. Beverly Hills, CA:Sage, 1980.
Gove, W. and J. Tudor, "Adult Sex Roles and Mental Illness." *American Journal of Sociology* 78:50-73, 1973.
Hartmann, H., "The Family as the Locus of Gender, Class, and Political Struggle," *Signs* 6(3):366-94, 1981.
Holmstrom, L.L., *The Two-Career Family*. Cambridge, MA:Schenkman, 1973.
Iglehart, A.P., *Married Women and Work*. Lexington, MA:Lexington, 1979.
Kessler, R.C. and J.A. McRae, Jr., "The Effect of Wive's Employment on the Mental Health of Married Men and Women," *American Sociological Review* 47(2):216-227, 1982.
Lopata, H., *Occupation:Housewife*. New York:Oxford University, 1971.
Malos, E. (ed.), *The Politics of Housework*. London: Allison and Busby, 1980.
Meissner, M., E.W. Humphreys, S.M. Meis, and W.J. Scheu, "No Exit for Wives," *Canadian Review of Sociology and Anthropology* 12:424-30, 1975.
Nilson, L.B., "The Social Standing of a Housewife," *Journal of Marriage and the Family* 40(3):541-57, 1978.
Oakley, A., *The Sociology of Housework*. New York:Pantheon, 1974a.
Oakley, A. *Woman's Work*. New York:Vintage, 1974b.
Pleck, J.H., "Men's Family Work," *The Family Coordinator* 28:481-88, 1979.
Rabuzzi, K.A., *The Sacred and the Feminine*. New York:Seabury, 1982.
Robinson, J.P., *How Americans Use Time*. New York: Praeger, 1977.
Rubin, L., *Worlds of Pain*. New York: Basic, 1977.
Sokoloff, N., *Between Money and Love*. New York:Praeger, 1981.
Strasser, S., *Never Done*. New York:Pantheon, 1982.
Szalai, A. (ed.) with P. Converse, P. Feldheim, E. Scheuch, and P. Stone, *The Use of Time*. The Hague:Mouton, 1972.
Szinovacz, M., "Role Allocation, Family Structure and Female Employment," *Journal of Marriage and the Family* 39(November):781-91, 1977.

Vanek, J., "Time Spent in Housework," *Scientific American* (November):116-20, 1974.

Wales, T.J. and A.D. Woodland, "Estimation of the Allocation of Time for Work, Leisure, and Housework," *Econometrica* 45:115-32, 1977.

Walker, K. and M. Woods, *Time Use*. Washington, D.C.:American Home Economics Association, 1976.

Zaretsky, E., *Capitalism, the Family and Personal Life*. New York:Harper and Row, 1976.

Chapter 5

The View from Below: Women's Employment and Gender Equality in Working Class Families

Myra Marx Ferree

Most women workers today are married and most have children. This is in stark contrast to the earlier decades of this century when the female work force was largely composed of young unmarried "girls." Women who work for pay today are less likely to define themselves as daughters and more likely to see themselves primarily as wives and mothers, than at any previous time in our history.

Important as family status—wife, mother or daughter—is in shaping the meaning of paid employment for women, there is really no reason to assume that it is any less important for men. Most workers, male and female alike, participate in the labor force not only as individuals but also as members of families, and both men and women consider their families to be more important than their jobs as sources of satisfaction in their lives (Bernard, 1981; Pleck & Lang, 1979). Paid work is a means to satisfy both individual and family needs, and to improve both individual and family well-being. While

Myra Marx Ferree is Associate Professor of Sociology, University of Connecticut, Storrs, CT.

An earlier version was presented at the National Women's Studies Association meetings, Bloomington, Indiana, May 1980, and some of the material was previously included in a paper jointly done with Carole Turbin entitled "On and Off the Job: Work, Family and Community."

The paper has greatly benefited from the suggestions offered by Katherine Jones-Loheyde and members of the Women and Work Study Group funded by a Problems in the Discipline Grant from the American Sociological Association.

57

this is true for both men and women, the roles of men and women within the family are culturally differentiated. While men are expected to take pride in the family role of "breadwinner" and "good provider," women's work is considered "behind the scenes," supportive and auxiliary to that of the "head of the household" (Bernard, 1981). Subordinated to male authority in the family, women then find their family status used against them in the labor force. The idea that women are or ought to be dependent on a man is used to justify overt discrimination and to give subtle (and not-so-subtle) legitimation to women's subordinate status on the job. Women whose wages are barely adequate to support themselves and totally insufficient to maintain their children are scarcely in a position to bite the hand that feeds them at home. Women's status in the family and women's status at work thus reflect and reinforce each other; so also does the very different family and work status of men (Feldberg & Glenn, 1979).

WORK AND FAMILY: WOMEN'S DOUBLE BIND

In the classic sociological model, the relationship of family and job for women is portrayed as one of conflict and competing demands. Family demands are assumed to have the higher priority, while work performance and satisfaction are influenced by family circumstances, with work commitment and actual labor force participation viewed as contingent upon "prior" home responsibilities. In contrast, the relationship of family and job for men is seen as one of mutual support and complementarity. The family is responsible for keeping the male worker in the state of highest possible fitness for his job; that is, not only fed and clothed, but freed from distractions and given whatever advantages the family can manage. The male worker's performance of family roles and satisfaction with family life are considered contingent upon his work circumstances: A man who is economically disadvantaged is thought to be incapable of filling family roles adequately, while his involvement in the family is limited by the extent and nature of his work (Feldberg & Glenn, 1979; Pleck, 1977; Coser & Rokoff, 1971).

This description exaggerates sex differences and ignores class differences. Work circumstances themselves can account for many of the differences between male and female workers that have classically been attributed to socialization and family roles (Feldberg &

Glenn, 1979; Kanter, 1977; Howe, 1977). Working class people, both male and female, typically give high priority to family roles (Kanter, 1977; Levitan & Johnson, 1982). Family members may reject stereotypes about male and female roles and traits but still be economically constrained to protect or increase the earnings potential of the worker in the family who has the best paying job or the best chance of getting ahead (Benenson, 1983). Since women are rarely the workers with the best opportunities or wages, they may expect their own families to place higher priority on the men's work and accept this as being "no great hardship" to themselves, without necessarily subscribing to general principles about women's second class status or her place at home and hearth. Economic subordination can limit aspirations at home as well as on the job.

The present relationship between job and family is so structured that women bear the brunt of the conflict between the two, a conflict that is not in women's roles or in women's heads but reflects the very different needs and demands of the workplace and the home. Competition for advantages in the family may undermine the willingness to share resources and risks that keep the family together, but competing in the workplace is made easier by holding these family advantages. In light of such structural conflict, achieving gender equality in the workplace demands that family and job be made more mutually supportive for both women and men.

However, the changes we have seen have been much more limited: women are increasingly likely to be in the paid labor force but there has been little change in the division of labor at home (see Berheide, Chapter 4, pp. 37-56). Employed women continue to do 4.8 hours a day of housework compared to 1.6 hours for their husbands (Walker & Woods, 1976). In the absence of significant domestic participation by men, women's employment may not be to their advantage. For paid jobs to benefit women, the relationship between the family and paid work will have to change, so that family members give greater priority to the needs of women workers.

WORK, FAMILY, AND CLASS

When employment is portrayed as a positive experience for women, the implicit model is that of the "dual-career" family. This model pervades both sociological research and the mass media, and it distorts our thinking about the meaning of paid employment for women (Benenson, 1983). In this view, women in elite professions exemplify the "non-traditional" woman, with shared housework and childcare a natural consequence of the couple's mutual commitment to egalitarian principles (e.g., Rapoport & Rapoport, 1971, 1976; Pepitone-Rockwell, 1980). Since dual-career wives have husbands who are also "good providers," they are assumed to have purely non-economic reasons for working. This is then taken, along with the high level of education characteristic of elite couples, to be a prerequisite for an "egalitarian relationship" and thus for a work experience that is beneficial to women.

The premises of the model itself are questionable. I doubt that most women professionals—or their families—are as indifferent to their earnings as the model assumes, and many studies suggest that commitment to egalitarian principles is a relatively weak predictor of actual household behavior (Huber & Spitze, 1981; Hiller, 1980; Ferree, 1979). But while this model may not even accurately represent the work and family relationships of the elite, it greatly distorts perceptions of the two-job families in the working class. Working class women are implicitly compared, not to working class men, but to women who most closely conform to male professionals in their career orientation and commitment. The importance of earnings from employment for working class women is directly contrasted to the "personal" reasons for employment given by dual-career professional women, and to the exclusion of all other motives. Women who "have to" work for financial reasons are assumed not to want to work at all, rather than simply not liking their present jobs (e.g., Wright, 1978). Social policy is directed at ensuring women a "choice" and protecting them from this presumably evil necessity—thus perpetuating the notion that it is the male alone who is responsible for financial support and the woman who is a "natural" dependent. Exploitation is not measured by the characteristics of women's work itself, which is rarely studied, but by the very fact of her employment (Feldberg & Glenn, 1979). The complexities of most workers' love-hate relationship with their jobs (Levitan & Johnson, 1982) are transformed into simplistic categorizations of women as either loving or hating their work, and if the latter, as needing to be "protected" from working (e.g., Kreps, 1972).

In fact, studies of working class women over the past three decades consistently show relatively high levels of actual employment, as well as considerable interest in working for pay among full-time housewives (e.g., Komarovsky, 1962; Berger, 1968; Rubin, 1976;

Ferree, 1976). Even jobs that are monotonous and/or physically taxing may be experienced as a welcome change from social isolation and unrelieved responsibility for young children (Oakley, 1974; Gavron, 1966; Ferree, 1976). This does not mean that working class women necessarily like their particular jobs, although some do, and the idea of "someday" being able to quit, like the prospect of retirement for blue collar men, may help many of them get through the days and years of labor (Eckart et al., 1976). A job is not a career; as Komarovsky (1962, p. 57) put it, "a good job is a means to a good living, but achievement in a specialized vocation is not the measure of a person's worth, not even for a man." Yet blue collar women are proud of their accomplishments on the job and their role as family providers, alone or in conjunction with their husbands (Walshok, 1981), and they are hurt psychologically as well as financially when they lose their jobs (Rosen, 1981). They see their work as something good for them as well as their families (Rubin, 1981), but do not have the work commitment characteristic of professional women, and should not be expected to acquire it to meet a class-biased standard of non-traditionality. Certainly, women who receive psychological rewards from their jobs are more satisfied than those who do not, but there is no reason to assume that family dependence on her income lessens the importance of nonmonetary benefits. For working class women, as for working class men, the job may be both personally and financially important.

Economic need in and of itself does not, of course, transform women's jobs into personally rewarding experiences, but women's work must be defined as an essential contribution to the family, as men's work has been, for family members, in turn, to respect and support women's needs as workers. The definition of women's work as a contribution or a cost to the family shapes the context in which family rights and responsibilities are negotiated, and is reflected in the balance of power and division of labor within the household. While employed women in general report having more decision-making power than full-time housewives (Blood & Wolfe, 1960; Safilios-Rothschild, 1970; Bahr, 1975), women who work because of economic necessity may have *more* power in family decision making than do women whose work is economically optional. The women whose income is significant for meeting the basic household needs has a more legitimate claim upon family resources in support of her paid work. Women who are working for what are often dismissed as "psychological reasons" have no such legitimate

claim, and other members may more willingly put their interests into conflict with the demands of her job. Lacking a right to demand
family support, such women are particularly susceptible to being
cast in the role of supermom and may find themselves feeling grateful for being "allowed" to add a paid job to their other responsibilities. This is scarcely a situation that could be described as optimal
for women.

But this is exactly the outcome inherent in the "dual-career"
model. Since commitment to egalitarian values by both husband and
wife is the only lever by which women can negotiate a more favorable division of labor, the dual career model emphasizes the importance of changing attitudes as a route to equality in the home. Young
women and educated women have more egalitarian sex role attitudes, and are thus heralded as the new wave, but age and education
actually have relatively little to do with the division of household
roles, in comparison to employment status and relative equality of
earnings (Heer, 1958; Ferree, 1979; Hiller, 1980). In fact, sharing
housework and childcare is a result of relative economic equality
more than of either sex role attitudes or social class *per se* (Hiller,
1980). In turn, mental health benefits of employment are associated
with shared responsibility at home rather than with age, education,
or income level of the job (Kessler & McRae, 1982).

Even when working class women are not portrayed as deficient in
the non-traditional attitudes presented by the dual-career model, the
comparison between value systems stressing "equality, individualism and reason" and those of "hierarchy, wholism and morality"
(Harding, 1981) reveals an elitist bias when they are called "egalitarian" versus "hierarchical" strategies rather than, for example,
"individualistic" versus "wholistic." This choice of emphasis con-
ceals the weaknesses of the dual-career ideal; we can agree that
equality is desirable without also accepting the assumption that family relationships ought to be primarily contractual and subordinated
to the whims of the market (cf. Harding, 1981, p. 63).

The emphasis in working class families may be more on protecting its weaker members by pooling limited resources than on achieving the dual-career ideal of maximizing individual opportunities
(Rapp, 1978; Humphries, 1982). In practice, the dynamics of shared
scarcity and mutual sacrifice are different from those of relative advantage and individual fulfillment. To take the risks and incur the
costs of sharing requires a level of commitment beyond that of simply being good friends; indeed, in the working class, the device of

"fictive kinship" brings friends *into* the network of shared resources, while in middle class families, the use of kinship titles is discouraged even among blood relatives (Rapp, 1978). The middle class ideal marriage "is more like friendship, hopefully the best of one's life" (Harding, 1981, p. 64). This protects each "partner's" financial resources from claims made by the other as well as from those of extended family members (Rapp, 1978). Working class families literally cannot afford this level of financial independence; the poorer the family, the more it depends on the circulation of resources outside the market system and on financial and moral support from family members in times of crisis (Humphries, 1982). In the middle class, family claims tend to be experienced as restrictions on individuality and independence; in the working class, family members are more aware of both the supportive and the oppressive aspects of family life because the oppressive nature of the economic system is more salient.

In sum, the dual-career model has, by its idealization of middle class family norms, led to a misunderstanding and denigration of working class women and their families. The distinction between working for financial reasons and for psychological reasons is exaggerated, undermining the legitimacy of employment for women of both affluent and poor families. Women's earnings are seen as less significant than her attitudes, while lip service to a norm of egalitarianism is confused with real equality in the family. An ideal of family life is reinforced that subordinates it to the convenience of the employer and the market rather than insuring its integrity as an alternative value system and source of concrete support. In its view of both work and family life, the dual-career model portrays working class women as deficient and backward rather than as subordinated and actively resisting that subordination within the confines of a class system.

The following analysis focuses on some of the issues confronting working class women as they attempt to reconcile the conflicts between personal needs and family demands and between employment and family life. A key issue is the process by which a family defines women's work as essential or inessential to its well-being, and the consequences of that definition for women and their families. Since the division of domestic labor is, I believe, of central importance in making paid employment more or less advantageous for women, a major focus of this discussion is the meaning of women's employment for the housework done by both women and men. Finally, comparisons are made between working class and middle class families which, though speculative, present a different and hopefully less class-biased view of the process of negotiation between women and their families. Central here is the distinction between the rules and norms that shape these negotiations and the actual bargaining position of husband and wife.

METHODOLOGY

As part of a larger study of working class women's employment and attitudes, I included a few questions designed to tap norms about women's participation in the labor force and men's participation in domestic work. These open-ended questions asked respondents to "advise" a woman who is caught in some familiar binds: She wants to work and her husband is opposed; they need the money and he wants to take a second job; he doesn't want her to tell her friends what he does and doesn't do around the house. To avoid sounding too hypothetical and abstract, the questions were written to present particular scenarios, e.g., "Anita's husband earns a very good living as a plumber, but now that her children are in school she would like to take a job. She was a bookkeeper before she married and has seen ads in the paper for jobs she might get. Even though she doesn't need the money, do you think she ought to take the job if she wants to? . . . Why? . . . Suppose her husband were against the idea. Should she take the job anyway or give up the idea? , . . Why is that? . . . Suppose there were a financial crisis in the family. She would like to get a job to help out, but her husband is opposed. He plans on looking for a second job. Should he take a second job or should she take a job to solve their money problems? . . . Why is that?" The question about housework was: "Betty often meets with some of the women in the neighborhood for coffee after her children are in school. Recently they have been discussing ways to get their husbands to do more housework, like washing dishes. Is it all right for Betty to tell her friends what work her husband does and doesn't do around the house? . . . Why/Why not?"

The interviews from which these questions were taken were conducted with 135 working class wives in a Boston area community. I defined these women as being working class because they resided in a predominantly working class community and sent their children to the local school, thus avoiding definitions based solely on their husband's characteristics or on their own education or paid occupations. Nonetheless, these women would be considered working class by such conventional criteria. Most of the husbands were manual workers and only three of the 135 women had graduated from college, a little over a third had not graduated from high school, and most were in clerical, service, or factory occupations. Even those who would be exceptions on the basis of one or another of these characteristics still seemed very much a part of this working class community. The sample included only married women who were citizens, spoke English, and had at least one child in first or second grade and none younger.

WOMEN'S EMPLOYMENT AS CONTRIBUTION OR COST

Because men's work typically has the family support that women's paid work so often lacks, it is important to consider how men have obtained that support. Rather than directly employing the "resources" of the job (income, skills, etc.) in the negotiating process, as suggested by the conventional exchange framework of family studies (e.g., Blood & Wolfe, 1960), the husbands in these working class families appear to base their claims for family support on the effort they expend and the costs they incur on the job. Because working class jobs are often exhausting, boring, and alienating, the husband who holds such a job is seen as making a sacrifice for the good of the family. In return, his needs are carefully heeded: quiet when he sleeps, time away from the family, leisure in the evening, etc. "He works hard, he's earned it" is the way these women justify the special consideration shown their husbands.

Women who hold paid jobs will be perceived as making a sacrifice for the family only when the family needs the income she earns. For the family to meet an employed woman's needs for quiet, escape, and leisure, a shift in responsibilities is required that is greater than that introduced by her simply taking a job. Such a shift does not happen automatically but is more or less successfully negotiated. In the process of bargaining, an employed woman can appeal to her husband's sense of justice and equity ("I'm tired when I come home, too") but such appeals may be most effective when they carry the implicit warning that she could only continue her job if they were met, and if the loss of her income would have a significant effect on family well-being.

When the family wants her to work but does not create the conditions she finds essential, her quitting may force a change in conditions at home. As one woman put it, "I quit my job in a fit of anger—I was handing over every penny, so why take that? But he [her husband] says no family can survive these days without two people working." Conversely, if family members prefer that she not hold a paid job, and do not accept her definition of the job as a sacrifice for them, they incur no moral obligation to offer any return for her effort. In such circumstances, my respondents suggest that a woman might appropriately drop out of the labor force; then, when the family once again found itself in straitened economic circumstances, attempt to negotiate the conditions of her re-entry. This cycle might recur repeatedly in economically marginal families, until the value of her contribution is recognized and some appropriate acknowledgement made.

In contrast to the situation in which a job is defined as a sacrifice for which there is a legitimate expectation of compensation, a wife's work may be defined as a reward or privilege. While this occurs surprisingly often in working class families, I think it is still more likely to be characteristic of middle class families, where the husband's higher income means that women's earnings can more often be defined as unnecessary. In this case, the family—not always or only the husband—does not see its standard of living as materially improved by the woman's employment. Indeed, her job could interfere with some of their pleasures, and the longer she has been a full-time housewife the more likely it is that these pleasures have solidified into rights. Because women who work for pay generally do less housework, the value of their non-monetary contribution declines, and their "unnecessary" income does not offset this. Paid employment is then defined not as a *contribution* to the family but a *cost* the family bears, more or less willingly, as a consequence of the woman's desire for a job.

In this case the job itself becomes a privilege, and if a woman desires it for "personal" reasons, she will have to pay a price. She may pay by becoming the supermother/superwife who can demonstrate that her job doesn't interfere with her meeting family demands. ("Dinner will still be on the table.") A number of women, in fact, suggested strategies for overcoming opposition by proving that her job did not change "anything" at home, that her level of household production would not drop, nor would she demand additional assistance. Alternatively, the working woman may pay a price in gratitude that her family is so "understanding" of her occasional failure to meet their demands. She may so appreciate the fact that no objection is raised to her paid job that she entirely fails to notice how little a shift in the division of labor has occurred at home. One respondent was overwhelmingly grateful because her husband made her a cup of tea in the evenings when she came home from work.

Even if her gratitude cannot obscure the fact that she is now working twelve to sixteen hours a day, she is not really in a position to do anything about it. She is allowed to work, and if the job becomes too much for her she is allowed to quit, but she has no legitimate basis for recriminations about the division of labor or power in the family, because she, rather than the family as a whole, is presumed to be the primary beneficiary of the arrangement. If her psychic need for the job is great enough, she will continue to work despite the costs in time and energy the family's lack of support imposes; if not, she will quit, and "find other things to do" to make her life more meaningful at less cost.

When a wife's working is perceived as burdensome to the family, her lack of power may be reflected in the way the additional income is handled—trivialized and treated as "pin money" for her to spend or thrown into a common "pot" and used to pay bills, with the surplus used to buy "extras" for other family members in order to coopt their support. Only if—and when—the family is sufficiently accustomed to its new luxuries to consider them necessities, so that her work is vital to the continued satisfaction of their needs, will she have the leverage to negotiate family change.

THE INVISIBILITY OF HOUSEWORK

If the husband's "hard work" earns him respect and consideration from his family, why doesn't housework earn the same rewards for wives? The issue here seems to be the extent to which housework "counts" as a sacrifice on the woman's part and as a contribution to the family's well-being. Being a full-time housewife often appears to be an unattractive alternative for these working class women (cf. Ferree, 1976). It is often described as boring and isolating, while having a paid job is something to "break up the monotony." As another woman said of housework, "you get stagnated if you're in one place. At least if you're out with other people you don't feel like the walls are closing in on you." Full-time housework may even be seen as a source of mental illness. Some respondents advised taking a paid job because a woman "can't be cooped up in four walls, she'd go bats." "There's no point in making yourself crazy by staying home." "A job is healthy." "It's for the emotions." But as much housework is perceived to cost in personal terms, it is not typically perceived as work. "Once the kids are in school, there's nothing to do," women said, "I can't see sitting home." "She needs it to get out to have something to do." "What the heck is there to do?"

While the problem for some women in these working class families is that housework is simply not demanding enough, the basic issue is that women often do not figure in the time spent doing housework when assessing the family division of labor as fair or unfair. In this, the culture cooperates, socially and linguistically defining work as that which occurs in the context of paid occupations. This definition of housework as "non-work" shows up very clearly in women's reactions to the choice between a husband taking a second job or a wife seeking paid employment to meet economic needs.

These women clearly thought it better for a woman to take a paid job in addition to housework than for a man to take a second paid job. Moonlighting creates too extreme a division of labor—he would have no time for the family and she would not be carrying her fair share of the "work"—e.g., "They should both work," "if he did all the work and she stayed home all the time, they wouldn't have anything to talk about." As these arguments reveal, wives' paid employment in working class families is not a matter of absolute economic necessity so much as a preferred strategy for dealing with real economic needs. As family historians have repeatedly pointed out, and as these women clearly recognize, there are alternatives: children, especially older children, can work for pay and contribute their earnings to the family, or husbands can work overtime and/or take a second job (Tilly & Scott, 1978; Cantor & Laurie, 1977). These women's values emphasize ideals of sharing and of companionship in marriage that are sometimes discussed as if they were the exclusive property of the middle class.

There was also a widely shared sentiment that "no man can handle two jobs," "in the long run he ends up sick," the income is eaten up in hospital bills, and the family is no better off if he "ends up dead or in the hospital." Similar concerns were not expressed about women's ability to handle a "double day." Still, a number of wives indicated that when the husband "insists on killing himself," a wife could not prevent it. Though she might be willing to take a paid job, if he insists on "carrying the full burden," she has few alternatives. Because her job at home is not seen as demanding, she may be able to convince him to "allow" her to work rather than overextend himself, but then she has no room in which to negotiate a change in the division of labor at home. If he remains committed to her staying at home and willing to bear the costs of that decision, she is forced to see her own sacrifice for the family in terms of giving up her own preferences for the sake of family harmony. Regardless of her wishes, she is "protected" from having to "work" (cf. Rubin, 1977).

The good of the family in this instance requires that the wife "try to be happy" at home. Insisting on her personal desire for a job "only starts family troubles and you end up with a separation," according to one respondent. The moral obligation is strong: "If [a job] was going to disrupt the home, she should not take it," but there is also a sharp difference of opinion on whether or not husbands can in fact be persuaded to understand their wives' point of view. For some, the criteria for a good marriage include his being able to "see things from her point of view." "A good marriage couldn't be good," some argue, "if this would break it up." Others believe that a husband's opposition can be overridden. One woman suggested, "do what I did, tell him you're bored to death and you have to do something—you'll take a job or have an affair—he can choose." But many women are more resigned to their husband's ability to define the situation as he chooses ("With my husband, I don't win an argument."); they felt that sustained disagreement with or defiance of their husbands would break up the marriage. When the marriage, and thus the welfare of the family itself, is at stake, respondents think the sacrifice of one's desire for a paid job is not too much to ask. In exchange, a wife may receive autonomy and authority within the confines of the home.

HOUSEWORK AND POWER

Although the sharp demarcation of male and female spheres of activity and authority is not uncommon in this working class sample, the effects of changing definitions of sex-appropriate behavior are also apparent. Although the women generally seem to find male participation in household tasks to be acceptable, even desirable, their husbands do not necessarily share this opinion. Employed women have to struggle against their husbands' perceptions of housework as demeaning and unmasculine. The individual man who does not share that perception is nonetheless likely to believe that his buddies do, and all-male social gatherings tend to reflect and reinforce the rejection of housework as unfit for "real men" without fear of contradiction from absent wives. Apparently, the image of a husband wearing an apron conveys a message about family power and authority as much or more than it depicts the family division of labor. For a wife to let other people know what chores her husband does around the house "would make the man seem like he was henpecked," or, "it would make the other women think she had him wrapped around her little finger." "Wearing the apron" means displaying subordinate status just as "wearing the pants" means exercising authority.

While norms are changing to include a positive value placed on egalitarian family relationships, a wife exercising power or authority in the family is still viewed with some ambivalence. While some women said they would be "proud to tell what my husband does," they underlined that this was because "he does it because he wants to" not because they had the power to demand his help. Whenever it might seem that he was doing housework he didn't want to do, there was concern that he would become "a laughing stock." Complaining about how little he does at home was a more acceptable topic of conversation among women than "bragging" about how much housework he does. The danger of the latter was not only that women friends would "tell their husbands and they'll set on him and tease him" but that they would go home and use his "goodness" to "start trouble in other families."

My casual observation of middle class families suggests there is some class difference here, with middle class women seen accepting a norm of household equality that they, too, do not find fully realized in their own families. However, because the norm is that husbands and wives should share housework, "bragging" about the husband's participation is more acceptable than complaining: by careful selection and omission, middle class wives often present an exaggerated picture of their husbands' actual involvement in housework, not only to burnish his image but also to protect their own self presentation as equal and "liberated." As with working class women, middle class wives assume that information about the division of labor conveys information about the distribution of power, crucial evidence of whether or not your family is living up to the ideal of a "good family" and whether or not you yourself are a "good" person. In such a context, it would be expected that such dangerous information would be carefully handled and selectively presented depending on the norms by which credit and discredit are allocated.

These norms differ by class more than does the actual division of labor. Women still do the bulk of the housework in most families (Berk, 1980; Walker & Woods, 1976). Moreover, there are "exceptions" in working class families that would rival those found in the middle class. In one family in this sample, for instance, the husband, who was a firefighter, regularly put in his 40 hours of work on the weekend so that he could take full charge of the house and children the rest of the week while his wife worked a regular nine-to-five job. Another study of men working the night shift found that a major reason for choosing a night job was the opportunity it allowed for men to assume routine childcare while their wives worked, and/or to become more involved with their children. As one worker put it:

> I work nights for the money and to be able to babysit during the day while she is working. I am on third shift now primarily because of our youngest child. . .I would like to go on days in a few years when my youngest child is older and takes care of herself after school. Right now. . .everything is going so well. I don't know whether I want to go on days now. (Robboy, 1983, p. 514)

As usual, such arrangements reflect more than pure economic necessity.

For most working class families, however, both men and women are fearful of the loss of prestige associated with a husband's unwilling participation in housework. This stigma appears to limit women's willingness to press their demands for greater male participation in housework even when their financial leverage makes it probable that such demands would be honored. Thus we find a paradox in that employment may give women power in the family that they do not feel legitimately entitled to use. Particularly if the husband's earnings are low and his "male image" shaky, women may refrain from demanding a more egalitarian division of labor because they might obtain it—at a cost they are not willing to incur (cf. Szinovacz, 1977).

Another way of describing this paradox is to emphasize that power and authority in the family are not interchangeable concepts. Authority, or legitimate power, depends more on the ideals and myths that serve to legitimate it, while power itself reflects resources that can be used to control the behavior of others. Men have for centuries held authority in the family, but their actual power has sometimes declined to the vanishing point when they are unable to support their families. Conversely, even when women's household production and earnings have given them power, this power has not been morally and ideologically legitimated. Illegitimate power is no less real than authority but it has different consequences. While the middle class has espoused values that put male authority in question, middle class women have rarely had the resources to exercise equal power. Thus, male power has gone underground (Bem, 1970; Gillespie, 1971). It may be a point of honor among middle class men "not to boss their wives around," to "let her have a career," and to "consult" her on major decisions precisely because the power exists to do otherwise—there is no honor in necessity. Working class women, who may also possess more power than they are legitimately entitled to use (though still less than men), may similarly take pride in "building their man up," "protecting his ego," and refraining from pressing claims that would "undercut" his authority.

CONCLUSIONS AND FURTHER DIRECTIONS

In summary, both the objective circumstances in which families find themselves and the meanings they give to family life and work are important in shaping their response to women's employment. Women see their jobs through the lens of family life as a contribution to the family or as a cost, or perhaps as a bit of both. The invisibility of housework as work makes it hard for women to take it seriously, which both makes a paid job more important psychologically while makes the burden of combined housework and paid work appear less than two paid jobs. Although norms have changed to make husbands sharing in family life more desirable and their holding two jobs more undesirable, the stigma from housework as a sign of women's power remains a constraining factor. While working class women and middle class women may face different problems and possibilities in reconciling a comfortable family life with their involvement in the labor force, neither can be said to have unalloyed benefit from their paid work.

When we remove the blinders imposed by contrasting an "egalitarian family" with a "hierarchical" one (for neither middle class nor working class women have achieved equality) we can see that the needs women have for paid work go beyond simply being able to use the income. Although the dual career model has polarized financial and psychological rewards to opposite ends of a single continuum, the dichotomy misleads and misinforms us. Not only do we idealize the employment of the few, we apologize for the employment of the many. We point to the poverty of working women's families as the reason why they "desire" their jobs and their paychecks and shy away from suggesting that they have any inherent right to work. We fail to distinguish between the miserable jobs in which they are trapped, on the one hand, and the value of shared labor in all the paid and unpaid tasks that go to constitute social existence, on the other. Working class women themselves, however, affirm the value of sharing labor as a crucial reason for their own paid employment as a strategy for coping with family needs.

Women at all class levels work for a variety of motives, just as men do, and while financial need may bind them to their present jobs and/or work conditions, there are relatively few who would wish to give up the sense of participation and purpose in society which having a job can provide. There is no evidence that most employed working class women would rather do full time housework, or that freeing them from the necessity of "having to work" would be doing them any favor. The need for additional income may free some women from the necessity of staying home and the financial leverage of the job may be an advantage to others, even if norms about family authority make them reluctant to exploit this advantage.

Conversely, an emphasis upon the economic importance of *some* women's work may inadvertently contribute to the de-legitimation of middle class women's desire for a job. Rather than accepting a model of employment that describes some women as working only for personal fulfillment, or only because they want to get out of the house, we need to think about ways of defining work as an objective *and* psychological necessity in people's lives. This means broadening our definition of work to include women's unpaid labor in the home without at the same time undercutting the legitimacy of women's need to do paid work. The removal of meaning from much of the work still left in the home makes a paid job necessary in many instances, and this necessity is no less real for being psychic as well as economic. By legitimating rather than trivializing such motives for women of all classes, we may finally stop apologizing for women's work and begin to create the family and community climate that supports it, a climate in which women's employment may benefit women themselves as well as their families.

REFERENCES

Bahr, S. Effects on power and division of labor in the family. In L. W. Hoffman and F. I. Nye (eds.) *Working Mothers.* New York: Jossey-Bass, 1975.

Benenson, H. Women's occupational and family achievement in the U.S. class system: Dual-career family analysis. *British Journal of Sociology,* forthcoming, September, 1983.

Berger, B. *Working Class Suburb: A Study of Auto Workers in Suburbia.* Berkeley: University of California Press, 1968.

Berheide, C. Women's Work in the Home: Seems like Old Times. *Marriage and Family Review,* 1984, *7*(3/4), 37-56.

Berk, S. *Women and Household Labor.* Beverly Hills: Sage, 1980.

Bernard, J. The Good-Provider Role: Its rise and fall. *American Psychologist,* 1981, *36*(1), 1-12.

Blood, R. and Wolfe, D. *Husbands and Wives.* New York: Free Press, 1960.

Cantor, M. and Laurie, B. (eds.) *Class, Sex and the Woman Worker.* Westport, CT: Greenwood Press, 1977.

Coser, R. and Rokoff, G. Women in the occupational world: Social disruption and conflict. *Social Problems,* 1971, 18, 535-554.

Eckart, C., Kramer, H. and Jaerisch, U. *Frauenarbeit in Familie und Fabrik* (Women's Work in the Family and Factory). Frankfurt: Campus, 1976.

Feldberg, R. and Glenn, E. Male and Female: Job versus gender models in the sociology of work. *Social Problems,* 1979, *26*(5), 524-38.

Ferree, M. M. Working Class Jobs: Paid work and housework as sources of satisfaction. *Social Problems,* 1976, *23*(4), 431-441.

Ferree, M. M. Employment without Liberation: Cuban women in the U.S. *Social Science Quarterly,* 1979, *60*(1), 35-50.

Ferre, M. M. Working Class Feminism: A consideration of the consequences of employment. *The Sociological Quarterly,* 1980, *21*(2), 173-184.

Gavron, H. *The Captive Wife: Conflicts of Housebound Mothers.* London: Routledge and Kegan Paul, 1966.

Gillespie, D. Who Has the Power: The marital struggle. *Journal of Marriage and the Family,* 1971, *33*(3), 445-458.

Harding, S. Family Reform Movements: Recent feminism and its opposition. *Feminist Studies,* 1981, *7*(1), 57-76.

Heer, D. Dominance and the Working Wife. *Social Forces,* 1958, *36*(4), 341-347.

Hiller, D. Determinants of Household and Childcare Task Sharing. Paper presented at American Sociological Assn., 1980.

Howe, L. K. *Pink Collar Workers.* New York: Putnam, 1977.

Huber, J., and Spitze, G. Wives' employment, household behaviors and sex role attitudes. *Social Forces,* 1981, *60*, 150-169.

Kanter, R. M. *Men and Women of the Corporation.* New York: Basic Books, 1977.

Kessler, R., and McRae, J. A. The effect of wives' employment on the mental health of married men and women. *American Sociological Review,* 1982, *42*(2), 216-227.

Komarovsky, M. *Blue Collar Marriage.* New York: Random House, 1962.

Kreps, J. Do all women want to work? In L. K. Howe, *The Future of the Family.* New York: Simon & Schuster, 1972.

Levitan, S. and Johnson, C. M. *Second Thoughts on Work*. Kalamazoo, MI: Upjohn Institute for Employment Research, 1982.

Oakley, A. *The Sociology of Housework*. New York: Random House, 1974.

Pepitone-Rockwell, F. *Dual-Career Couples*. Beverly Hills: Sage, 1980.

Pleck, J. The work-family role system. *Social Problems*, 1977, *24*, 417-427.

Pleck, J. and Lang, L. Men's family role. Wellesley, MA: Wellesley College Center for Research on Women, 1979.

Rapoport, R. N. and Rapoport, R. *Dual-career Families*. Baltimore: Penguin, 1971.

Rapoport, R. N. and Rapoport, R. *Dual-career Families Re-examined*. New York: Harper & Row, 1976.

Rapp, R. Family and Class in Contemporary America: Notes toward an understanding of ideology. *Science and Society*, 1978, *42*(3), 278-350.

Robboy, H. At Work with the Night Worker. In H. Robboy and C. Clark, *Social Interaction: Readings in Sociology* (2nd edition). New York: St. Martin's Press, 1983.

Rosen, E. Between the Rock and the Hard Place: Employment and unemployment among blue-collar women. Paper presented at American Sociological Assn., 1981.

Rubin, L. *Worlds of Pain: Life in the Working Class Family*. New York: Basic Books, 1977.

Rubin, L. Why should women work? Working paper, University of California, Berkeley: Center for the Study, Education and Advancement of Women, 1981.

Safilios-Rothschild, C. The study of family power structure. *Journal of Marriage and the Family*, 1970, *32*, 539-553.

Szinovacz, M. Role allocation, family structure and female employment. *Journal of Marriage and the Family*, 1977, *39*, 781-791.

Tilly, L. and Scott, J. *Women, Work and Family*. New York: Holt, Rinehart and Winston, 1978.

Walker, K. and Woods, M. Time Use: a measure of household production. Paper presented at the Home Economics Association, 1976.

Walshok, M. L. *Blue Collar Women: Pioneers on the Male Frontier*. Garden City, NY: Anchor Books, 1981.

Wright, J. Are working women really more satisfied? Evidence from several national surveys. *Journal of Marriage and the Family*, 1978, *40*, 301-313.

Chapter 6

Working Wives and Mothers

Kristin Moore
Daphne Spain
Suzanne Bianchi

The movement of wives and mothers into the labor force has been accompanied by concerns over possible harmful effects for children, for marriages, for husbands, and for women themselves. Nevertheless, steady increases in employment have been registered not just for women with grown and older children but recently for mothers with preschool children as well. In addition, young women are completing more schooling, marrying later, and delaying childbearing. Such fundamental changes clearly have implications for the roles women have traditionally filled as wives and mothers.

Our purpose in this chapter is threefold: to provide a statistical overview of the employment patterns for women at different stages of the family life cycle, to summarize the major findings on the causes and consequences of employment trends, and to describe some of the important issues which require further research. Our discussion focuses on women as mothers and as wives, for it is the demands of these family roles that so complicate women's employment and which cause such concern for family well-being.

Of the two roles, we propose that motherhood has the most significant effect on women's employment patterns. Few women quit work upon marriage but many women interrupt their employment when their first child is born and others reduce their hours of work

Kristin Moore is Consultant to the Urban Institute and Senior Research Associate, Child Trends, Inc., Washington, D.C. Daphne Spain is on the staff of American Demographics, Ithaca, NY. Suzanne Bianchi is a demographer with the Center for Demographic Studies, U.S. Bureau of the Census.

in response to the demands of motherhood. After a brief overview of trends in female labor force participation, we divide our discussion into three sections. We focus first on women who have not yet had children, then on those who have preschool and school age children, and finally on those whose children have reached adulthood. Within these sections, when possible, data and discussion are presented separately for women who are currently married and women who are not.

TRENDS IN LABOR FORCE PARTICIPATION:
1950 TO 1980

Perhaps no other change has had more far-reaching implications for society, the economy, and the family than the dramatic increase in women's labor force participation. Between 1947 and 1980, the number of women in the labor force increased by 173 percent (from 16.7 to 45.6 million) whereas the number of men in the labor force increased by only 43 percent (from 44.2 to 63.4 million) (U.S. Department of Labor, 1982).

It is difficult to obtain concrete data on the employment of women during World War II but the trend was a surge in female employment during the war years followed by a return to family responsibilities after the war. During the 1950s, most women of childbearing age were at home although a sizable fraction either chose or found it necessary to enter the labor force even during this "familistic" post-war period. But the increase in female employment during the 1950s was disproportionately accounted for by older women who had completed their childbearing and most of their childrearing duties. Oppenheimer (1970) has documented the post-war growth in clerical and service sector jobs which traditionally employ women. Demand for female workers swelled at the very time that early marriage and high fertility created a relative dearth of young single or married women without children. Older women responded to the demand for women workers by entering the labor force.

The increase in women's employment during the 1960s and 1970s was different in a fundamental way from that of the 1950s. During the past two decades it has been younger women with childrearing responsibilities who have dramatically increased their participation in work outside the home. Figure 1 shows labor force participation rates of wives by presence and age of children between 1950 and

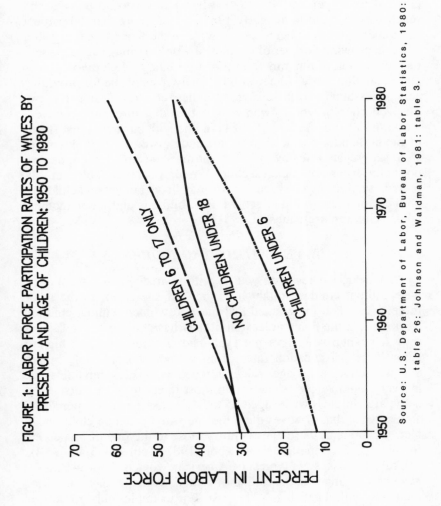

FIGURE 1: LABOR FORCE PARTICIPATION RATES OF WIVES BY PRESENCE AND AGE OF CHILDREN: 1950 TO 1980

CHILDREN 6 TO 17 ONLY

NO CHILDREN UNDER 18

CHILDREN UNDER 6

PERCENT IN LABOR FORCE

Source: U.S. Department of Labor, Bureau of Labor Statistics, 1980: table 26; Johnson and Waldman, 1981: table 3.

79

1980. Whereas in 1950 only 12 percent of married women with preschoolers were in the labor force, by 1960 this proportion had climbed to 19 percent. By 1970 it had jumped to 30 percent and reached 50 percent in the early 1980s. In all, more than 60 percent of mothers of school age children were in the labor force by 1980.

For a growing number of couples, a wife's earnings are an essential component of a family's level of well-being. High divorce rates also mean that many women will be solely responsible for providing economic support to themselves and their children. Table 1 shows the proportion of women who were in the labor force and who were working full-time in June of 1981. In line with our thesis that stages of motherhood are crucial to understanding women's employment, we disaggregate rates by age, current marital status, and, most importantly, by age of youngest child. We refer back to Table 1 in subsequent sections as we discuss wives who have not yet had children, mothers of preschool and school age children, and older mothers whose children are adults.

WIVES WITHOUT CHILDREN

"My dear, whatever do you do with yourself?" is a refrain the wife without children might hear today if she is not in the labor force. It is taken for granted that married women without children work outside the home at least until they have children. As Table 1 shows, women who have not (yet) had children have the highest labor force participation rates of all women, considerably higher than women the same age with children. This relationship holds true in every age category. The group most likely to work outside the home are childless wives aged 25 to 34, whose rate of 85 percent is almost twice that of wives the same age with preschool children. In fact, their rate at these ages is fairly close to the rate of 95 percent for men (U.S. Department of Labor, 1982, Tables A-3 and A-4).

Childlessness is not typical of American women. However, there have been changes in the timing of births. Women today are having their first child later than in the past. For example, only 13 percent of ever-married women aged 25 to 29 were still childless in 1960. Today, 26 percent of such women have not borne any children (Bianchi and Spain, 1983: Table 1). In other words, within the past two decades, the proportion of women remaining childless during traditional family formation years increased from approximately one in ten ever-married women to one in four.

Table 1: Proportion of Women Aged 18-59 in the Labor Force and Proportion Employed Full-Time, by Women's Age, Marital Status and Age of Youngest Child

	Percent in Labor Force		Percent Employed Full-Time		Weighted Sample Size (Numbers in Thousands)	
	Wives	Non-wives	Wives	Non-wives	Wives	Non-wives
Total	57.6	75.5	39.1	53.8	40,981	24,430
18-24	60.3	75.4	40.9	44.1	4,976	9,874
25-34	58.6	79.7	39.3	63.1	12,903	6,450
35-44	61.9	78.6	42.0	62.0	10,040	3,443
45-59	52.4	67.6	36.1	55.3	13,063	4,663
No Children	76.4	82.0	59.7	57.3	6,251	13,314
18-24	77.8	79.9	57.8	47.6	2,153	8,197
25-34	85.0	89.8	69.2	75.7	2,417	3,239
35-44	70.8	87.0	54.7	76.6	657	829
45-59	56.7	70.6	44.1	61.6	1,024	1,050
Children Under Age 6	47.2	57.4	28.4	35.0	11,850	3,531
18-24	46.6	52.6	27.6	25.7	2,753	1,567
25-34	47.2	61.9	28.1	43.0	7,251	1,631
35-44	48.0	57.8	30.4	39.5	1,725	280
45-59	54.5	b	40.3	b	121	53
Children Age 6-17	61.3	74.6	40.1	55.8	13,308	4,586
18-24	b	68.3	b	49.2	69	110
25-34	64.3	77.1	41.9	57.8	3,228	1,578
35-44	63.7	77.7	42.2	58.6	6,594	1,902
45-59	53.7	65.4	34.2	48.1	3,417	996
Children Age 18 and Over	53.2	69.3	37.6	56.9	9,572	3,000
18-24	b	b	b	b	—	—
25-34	b	b	b	b	7	3
35-44	67.6	79.9	51.4	63.5	1,065	433
45-59	51.3	67.4	35.9	55.8	8,501	2,564

b Unweighted sample 75 in age, marital, child status subgroup

Source: Special tabulation, Current Population Survey, June 1981

81

Delayed age at marriage has been an important factor in delayed childbearing. Median age at first marriage for women rose from 20.3 in 1960 to 22.1 in 1980 (U.S. Bureau of the Census., 1981: 1). Demographers, such as Glick and Norton (1979) and Schoen (1983) point to the "marriage squeeze" as a possible factor in the recent delay in marriage of young adults. By marriage squeeze, they are referring to the fact that women tend to marry men older than themselves, and among cohorts of women reaching marriageable ages during the 1970s there has been a relative shortage of males a few years older. The large size of the baby boom cohorts reaching adulthood during the past two decades has also made it difficult for young persons to secure good jobs—another possible factor creating pressure for later marriage and childbearing. The availability of modern methods of birth control and abortion have also contributed to delayed childbearing and marriage (Bauman et al., 1977; Westoff, 1978). In addition, changes in attitudes regarding the desirability of early marriage and timing of the first birth have also occurred (Zelnik et al., 1981; Pebley, 1981) and these changes have affected marriage plans as well. For example, legal changes have improved if not equalized women's access to good jobs and upward mobility. Attitudes toward women's roles have also liberalized (Mott et al., 1980).

The two-year increase in median age at marriage is also significant because it means that a majority of women are not marrying until after the typical age of college graduation. In 1979 for the first time, more women than men were enrolled in college (U.S. Bureau of the Census, 1983). Increases in educational attainment, which in turn create occupational opportunities for women, have been a major factor in the tendency to delay marriage and subsequent decisions to postpone childbearing or to remain childless. Cherlin (1980) has shown that women who plan to be in the labor force at age 35 tend to delay marriage. Data indicate that women at the highest level of education are also most likely to be childless and expect to remain so. Nearly 20 percent of women with five or more years of college anticipated having no children, compared with only 8 percent of women without a high school degree and 10 percent of women with a high school diploma. Women with professional or managerial occupations (typically full-time commitments) were more likely to expect to remain childless (14 percent) than those in sales, service, and clerical work (U.S. Bureau of the Census, 1984, p. 5).

Later marriage means a later age at first birth and tends to result in a smaller completed family size (U.S. Bureau of the Census, 1978; Bumpass et al., 1978). As the biological limits on childbearing are extended, and as divorces and remarriages create new families, women are having children later in life. It has been suggested that in some cases, delaying births may result in infecundity and childlessness by default (Mosher and Pratt, 1982; Veevers, 1973), though this contention is in great dispute (Menken and Larson, 1983). Both delayed childbearing and childlessness have implications for women's labor force participation.

The relationship between women's employment and their marriage and family size decisions is a complex one. The two are inversely related—the smaller the family size, the greater the likelihood a woman is working outside the home—however causality is unclear. Some researchers have found that working wives say they want fewer children and thus limit their fertility (Pratt and Whelpton, 1956; Ridley, 1959; Whelpton et al., 1966). Women who plan to work also anticipate smaller families than those with no work expectations (Blake, 1970; Farley, 1970; Stolzenberg and Waite, 1977). Other researchers have found that the number and ages of children help explain whether a woman chooses to work (Freedman et al., 1959; Sweet, 1973). Studies that allow for reciprocity between labor force and fertility decisions have not fully resolved the controversy. Current research suggests that a birth has a negative impact on employment in the short run but that in the long run childbearing is reduced to accommodate plans for employment (Cramer, 1980; Hofferth, 1981; Smith-Lovin and Tickamyer, 1978; Waite and Stolzenberg, 1976; Hout, 1978). Such a complex decision is inevitably influenced by other factors, such as the attitudes of spouses, family, and community, the health of children, infertility, the labor market, divorce and remarriage. In addition, the impact of different factors probably varies across cohorts. Consequently, the magnitude and causal influence of reduced fertility may never be known exactly.

Labor Force Attachment

Part-time work is one solution to the problem of combining employment with childrearing. Presumably, then, wives without children are more likely to work full-time than wives with children. Data in Table 1 support this conclusion. Among wives 18-59 with no children, 60 percent worked full-time compared to only 28 percent of wives with children under six and 40 percent of wives with school-age children. For wives aged 25 to 34, these percentages are 69, 28, and 42 respectively.

Full-time work varies more by age for childless wives than for those with children, presumably reflecting both age and cohort effects. Among wives with children, the age of the mother has only a slight influence on the proportion employed part-time. Among non-wives with children, full-time work is also less common than among childless non-wives. Given the greater financial needs of most single parents, the proportion of non-wives employed only part-time is strikingly high.

Childlessness and Marital Stability

Many years ago, the belief was that children strengthened a marriage and that childless marriages were more likely to end in divorce (Nimkoff, 1934). It appears, however, that there is little difference in divorce rates for the two types of marriages, although divorce and separation rates are slightly lower for couples with children (Cherlin, 1977, p. 265). Both marital satisfaction and the probability of divorce are higher in the early years of marriage, when there are few if any children. Obviously, childlessness and marriage duration tend to be highly correlated. Hofferth (1981) found couples with one child less likely to divorce than couples with no children or several children. In examining this issue, Cherlin (1977, p. 271) found that children were a deterrent to divorce only when they were preschoolers. He suggests that children may prevent marital disruption not because they lead to stronger bonds between parents, but because they are too expensive for one parent to afford alone. Thus, since childless couples have no such economic ties that bind, they may find it easier to divorce.

Carlson and Stinson (1982, p. 264) also found higher rates of marital dissolution for childless teenaged brides than for those who had children, but young age at marriage is characteristically linked with higher rates of divorce and separation (see Moore and Waite, 1981). Among brides age 20 to 29, childless marriages were actually more stable than those with children. Carlson and Stinson suggest that the argument that childless marriages are less stable applied to a time in which childlessness was most likely to be involuntary. A mutually agreed upon deliberate choice not to have children may actually have a positive effect on marital stability.

MOTHERS WITH CHILDREN UNDER AGE 18

As shown in Figure 1, the proportion of mothers who work has increased dramatically. It is equally the case that the proportion of children who have employed mothers has increased dramatically. Among pre-school children, the proportion with employed mothers has risen from 29 percent in 1970 to 46 percent in 1982. Among children 6-17, 59 percent had mothers who worked in 1982, compared to 43 percent in 1970 (Select Committee on Children, Youth and Families, 1983).

Reasons for Increased Employment Among Mothers

What factors have led to such a dramatic increase in such a short time period?

As with most social phenomena, a multiplicity of causes can be identified and it is very difficult to sort out their independent causal influences. One set of factors are the trends discussed in the previous section—the delays in marriage and childbearing among recent cohorts, who have substituted greater education and employment for early entry into traditional female roles. In addition, more experience in the labor force raises the opportunity costs associated with leaving work, since foregone earnings are higher. Furthermore, development of a life style dependent on two incomes and establishment of an intrinsic attachment to the world of work makes it difficult for many women to give up their employment.

The slow growth of real income for young males in particular during the past decade has provided an incentive for wives to work to augment husband's earnings (O'Neill and Braun, 1981). We also speculate that high rates of unemployment make many young couples unwilling to stake their economic security on just one job. In addition, women may be concerned that if they give up their position in the labor market, not only will they later have to re-enter at a lower lever, they may not be able to locate suitable employment at all.

Changes in the social climate also seem likely to have had an effect. For example, even women who feel happy in their marriages must be affected by the frequency with which marriages break up; maintaining one's position in the labor force provides some insurance against poverty in the event of marital break-up. Women with shaky marriages and mothers who are not married face considerably stronger pressure to be employed. Negative public attitudes toward the employment of wives and mothers have softened in recent decades as well (Mason et al., 1976; Mott, 1982).

Employment Among Mothers

Having noted the many reasons why labor force participation is more common among mothers than in the past, it is crucial to reiterate that employment is nevertheless far less common among women who have young children and that considerably fewer women work full-time while they have young children (see Table 1). Among women aged 25-34, for example, only 47 percent of the wives are employed if there is a child under age six, compared to 64 percent if the youngest child is aged 6-17 and 85 percent if the woman has no children. Moreover, only 28 percent of these wives work full-time if there is a child under six, compared to 42 percent of the wives with children 6-17 and 69 percent of those with no children.

Women's marital status also mediates the probability of employment. Women who are not currently married are slightly more likely to be working if they have children—53 percent versus 47 percent if they have a child under six and 77 percent versus 64 percent if their youngest child is 6-17. Among women with no children, non-wives are somewhat more likely to be employed—90 percent versus 85 percent. However, differences due to the presence and age of children are clearly greater.

CONSEQUENCES OF EMPLOYMENT AMONG FAMILIES WITH CHILDREN

If the determinants of employment are complex, then the consequences of employment are necessarily complex, since women's reasons for working moderate the consequences. An early example of this axiom is provided by the study conducted by Yarrow et al. (1962) who compared satisfied and dissatisfied homemakers and employed mothers. The researchers found that satisfied homemakers scored highest on the measure of adequacy of mothering while dissatisfied homemakers scored the lowest. Satisfied and dissatisfied working mothers obtained intermediate scores. It is to be anticipated that a host of such variables affect the association between maternal employment and outcomes for family members.

Since the well-being of children is of such paramount importance to any society, there has been a great deal of research on the factors that enhance or undermine children's development. Yet, no body of evidence has accumulated identifying any one set of effects that are general, predictable, and clearly related to the fact of the mother's employment rather than some other factor in the child's environment.

After reviewing the research on this topic, the National Academy of Sciences Panel on Work, Family and Community concluded that "Existing research has not demonstrated that mothers' employment *per se* has consistent direct effects, either positive or negative, on children's development and educational outcomes" (Hayes and Kamerman, 1983, p. 221). The Panel called for further research employing more complex paradigms and research methods, with greater attention to intervening variables likely to moderate any relationship that may exist between patterns of maternal employment and outcomes for children.

Social class is an example of a moderating variable that has been found to interact with employment variables. Several researchers report that maternal employment is associated with positive outcomes for children among low status and black households (Milne et al., 1983; Myers et al., 1983; Heyns, 1982; Zill, 1983). Conversely, two recent studies link maternal employment to negative effects on academic achievement among two-parent white families (Milne et al., 1983; Myers et al., 1983). Authors of the latter studies argue that employment has a direct negative effect on children's achievement but that this effect is offset in low-income families by the positive impact of the mother's earnings on the family's economic position. Since data were not available to control for the mother's reasons for being employed, it is not possible to rule out bias due to self-selection into the labor force. Moreover, the effects on achievement, while statistically significant, were substantively rather small. Yet, since it is often presumed that middle class parents arrange for or are able to afford better substitute care, these results raise a host of new issues.

Another intriguing set of issues revolves around effects of the child's sex. While a number of researchers have reported achievement benefits for daughters of working mothers, several researchers have found lowered achievement among sons of middle class working mothers (see Hoffman, 1980). A recent study of infants suggests that the sons of middle class employed mothers may receive less parental stimulation relative to other children (Zaslow et al., 1983). Compared to girls, boys have also been found to show more negative effects after divorce (Hetherington, 1979; Zill, 1983), and, among children born to teenage mothers, boys seem to show more deficits (see Baldwin and Cain, 1980, for a review). Thus it is possible that boys are more vulnerable to stress. On the other hand, Zill (1983) finds that girls are more negatively affected by remarriage, suggesting that different types of stress may have different effects because the experiences of each sex differ in important ways.

Effects of employment might also be expected to vary according to the age of the child. Infant-mother attachment has been a focus of recent concern. Numerous studies have demonstrated, however, that young infants are able to establish normal attachments to their mothers when the mothers work (see Nadelson and Notman, 1981; Etaugh, 1974; Hoffman, 1974). In addition, while working mothers may spend less time in the company of their children, they appear to go to considerable lengths to spend time doing things with their children (Hayes and Kamerman, 1983). Hill and Stafford (1980) report that working mothers, particularly college-educated women, will give up sleep and leisure activities in order to devote time to their children.

Among older children, compared to offspring of nonemployed mothers, daughters of working mothers are more likely to plan to work themselves (unless their mothers had low status jobs) and both sons and daughters tend to be more egalitarian in their sex role attitudes (Bloom-Feshbach et al., 1982). In addition, the self-esteem of preschool children does not seem to be affected by the mother's employment, although the mother's type of employment, work satisfaction, and reasons for working seem to mediate self-esteem among older children (Bloom-Feshbach et al., 1982).

Conspicuously absent from most of these studies is a concern with the effects of the father's work schedule. The review by Bronfenbrenner and Crouter (1982) suggests that the father's occupation and his experience with unemployment does affect the children. It makes considerable sense that the effects of the mother's employment would interact with factors such as the father's work schedule, his supportiveness of his wife, his level of contributions to house-work and child care, and the degree to which he is preoccupied with or exhausted by his own work. This interaction seems like a crucial starting point for future research.

In summary, it is significant how few negative effects have been documented, given the diligence with which they have been pursued. An alert has been raised for middle class families, particularly boys; however, large and consistent differences have not been detected. In addition, positive effects have been noted for daughters and for lower class boys and girls.

In general, it seems important to focus future research on mechanisms associated with positive outcomes for children. The number of working parents, their joint work schedule, their occupation and economic status should be carefully studied. Rather than simply increasing guilt among parents powerless to change their employment status, such research might assist families and employers in managing employment to enhance the development of children.

EFFECTS ON MARRIAGE

Given the heavy work load experienced by families with children (Hofferth, 1981), the addition of paid employment outside the home can result in a class of the "time-poor" (Vickery, 1977). Data indicating that mothers create time for their children by sacrificing sleep and passive leisure (Hill and Stafford, 1980) leaves one wondering whether couples can find time to be together.

Although concern with role overload among working wives has been widespread, Pleck (1982) observes that "employed wives no longer experience 'role overload' relative to the husbands, on the average" because employed wives now spend relatively less time in family roles and because husbands in general are now spending slightly more time in family roles. Employed women still work considerably longer hours than non-employed women, however, and among those who work full time and have young children the burden in absolute terms is quite high (Hill, 1981). However, Pleck (1982) reports that marital dissatisfaction is related to wives' satisfaction with their husbands' level of housework and child care rather than the absolute level of his contributions. This illustrates an important point. Satisfaction is a very subjective concept, and the same activity that is stressful within one relationship can be neutral or a source of satisfaction in another relationship.

The potential benefits of being married to a working woman have been largely overlooked. For example, one might argue that the job experiences of employed women give them something in common with husbands or make them more interesting companions, or it could be the case that having a second earner takes a great deal of pressure off a man's shoulders. Unemployment may be less threatening. A husband may feel less pressure to be promoted, to "make it" on the job. The freedom to return to school, change jobs, work part time, or retire early all exist for men who rely on a wife's earnings, if the wife's earnings are sufficient.

The fact that most women earn relatively little compared to men may explain the lack of evidence that married men are altering their labor force participation in response to their wives' earnings. In addition, many families need the full income of both earners, so neither spouse is in a position to work part time. One might anticipate a greater response among men married to women with relatively high earnings; but since these husbands tend to have relatively high earnings themselves, the opportunity costs associated with cutting back are considerable. Also, if good part-time jobs are difficult to find for women (Kamerman and Kingston, 1982), they are likely to be unavailable to men as well. Moreover, employers may in fact view men seeking part-time employment with even greater suspicion than they view women. Finally, men may not feel comfortable with giving up the provider role or even with sharing it. Thus, instead of expecting to find significant responses on the part of husbands with employed wives, we should look for change at the margins. For example, men with employed wives may be less likely to work more than a 40-hour week. Such men might be more likely to refuse transfers and might be more likely to respond to a poor work situation by changing jobs.

The connection between employment and marital happiness—like that between employment and child development—is undoubtedly complex. For example, data indicating that working women are more likely to become divorced (e.g., Moore et al., 1978) suggests that employment lowers marital satisfaction. However, issues of cause and effect remain to be disentangled. Employment may cause stress in a relationship; on the other hand, women who foresee the need to support themselves may seek employment. Some evidence suggests (see Hofferth and Moore, 1979) that working wives are more satisfied with their marriages if they are relatively well-educated, if they work from choice, if their husbands are favorable toward their employment, and if they work part-time. On the other hand, several studies have found husbands to be less satisfied when their wife works. Most of these studies have become somewhat dated though and are handicapped by reliance on a single measure of marital quality as a dependent variable.

One recent study found that two-earner marriages did not differ from one-worker marriages on a variety of dependent variables measuring marital adjustment and companionship, either for husbands or for wives (Locksley, 1980). It seems important to differentiate components of the independent variable as well. In other words, there is little reason to expect employment *per se* to have a negative impact on marital quality, unless employment takes place under conditions of particular stress, as, for example, when the husband cannot maintain stable employment, when reliable child care is not available, or when spouses disagree about whether the wife should work. In addition, the effects of number and ages of children should be considered. A number of studies have documented slight but statistically significant decrements in marital satisfaction among couples who have children whether the wife works or not (Glenn and McLanahan, 1982; Spanier and Lewis, 1980); however, surprisingly little consideration has been given to interactions between spouses' employment, age and number of children, and marital satisfaction. Future studies might include such measures or sub-divide their sample to take account of these factors in determining marital satisfaction.

WOMEN WITH CHILDREN AGE 18 OR OLDER

Women whose children were grown and those with older children were in the forefront of the trend toward increasing labor force participation (see Figure 1). Considering women aged 35-44 and 45-59, those who have never had children are only slightly more likely to be employed than those whose children are all age 18 or over, though differences in the proportion working full time are more substantial (see Table 1). However, since many women who have raised children took time off from paid employment when their children were younger, their labor market experience and thus their earnings are likely to be somewhat low (Suter and Miller, 1973; O'Neill and Braun, 1981). Thus the effect of being a mother continues to be felt even after children are grown.

Women currently aged 45 to 59 spent a large portion of their adult life raising children, given the levels of fertility that prevailed in the 1950s and early 1960s. As a group, these women have lower educational attainment than younger women, which limits their occupational choices. Women who want to enter the labor force later in life face the prospect of age discrimination. With a large proportion of younger women already in the labor force, employers may perceive older women as too expensive to train for the limited number of working years left before retirement. Hess and Waring (1978) propose that, in the future, employed women who limit their fertility, or remain childless, will have potentially higher retirement income from lifetime work. This will increase the emotional and financial independence of older women in the future.

We expect that there are many ways in which the work lives and marriages of mothers of grown children continue to differ from those of their childless age-peers. For example, the earnings of many of these women may go toward college tuition, weddings, and assistance to children setting up their own households, rather than toward travel and retirement. Their time may also continue to be heavily dominated by the needs of their children or grandchildren. Although it is not known how frequently, how regularly, or under what terms grandmothers provide child care to facilitate their children's employment, evidence suggests that relatives provide care for about one-third of the children of working mothers (U.S. Bureau of the Census, 1982b). Research on teenage mothers suggests that the role of the grandmother can be important (Furstenberg, 1976; Williams, 1977; Miller, 1983) but even in this vulnerable subpopulation the assistance of the grandparent generation is not inevitably or consistently available. Since many older women are also employed, their ability and willingness to be available for child care duties may be limited.

Hofferth (1981) reports that many young couples receive help from their parents, but that few older mothers receive financial assistance from relatives. Research documenting other kinds of assistance among extended family members has only begun.

After their children are grown, women may feel it is their turn to achieve in their own right or to enjoy leisure and recreation activities unencumbered by the demands of children. Couples may define this life cycle stage as a time to focus on one another. As their children grow into adulthood, the reactions of single parents might range from relief to loneliness. There are no systematic data to support or refute these speculations. In addition, whether and how employment patterns interact with marriage and parenting for women whose children are grown is not known. Hoffman (1980) argues that working women are better able to handle the developing independence of their children because their employment provides alternate sources of self-worth.

Much of the research on parental employment and parental influences in general has been conducted on very young children. Parent influences among older individuals are typically measured with proxies, such as "Mother's education," "Family SES," etc. Direct information on both generations is rarely available. One exception is a study based on interviews with both mothers and daughters from families in which a daughter was interviewed for the National Longitudinal Survey of Young Women and the mother was interviewed for the National Longitudinal Survey of Mature Women (Mott et al., 1982). The mother's attitudes toward the employment of young women were found to predict significantly the number of weeks worked by the daughter when she became an adult. In addition, the negative impact of a child under age six was found to be much stronger when the grandmother held traditional attitudes about maternal employment than when she held nontraditional attitudes.

We would hypothesize that the attitudes and experiences of mothers continue to be relevant to their children, even when their children are grown. Such influences may reflect earlier socialization or current mother-daughter interactions. Of course, other influences are likely to be more important when adult children are considered; but parental inputs may nevertheless be substantial. Further research might explore how parental characteristics such as maternal employment affect the attitudes and behaviors of adult children.

Maternal employment seems likely to have different effects at different points in the life cycle. Among mothers with older children the effects of greater income, greater independence for children, and the example of achievement may be of significant benefit to children. On the other hand, the progress of the women themselves in the labor force may continue to be hampered, not only by their lack of labor market experience but by continued demands from and involvement with adult children. Alternatively, it may be that mothers of grown children who have had a diminished involvement with the work force are relatively enthusiastic and committed workers, compared to men and women who have maintained a continuous full-time commitment to the labor force. The lack of research on these issues is striking and suggests an area in need of new studies.

CONCLUSIONS AND PROSPECTS FOR THE FUTURE

The changes that have occurred in women's labor force attachment over the past several decades have been of such magnitude that they have inevitably affected patterns of marriage, childbearing, and childrearing. Women are tending to delay marriage, remain in school longer, postpone childbearing, and continue employment even when they have young children. Of course these changes do not describe all women, but the proportions affected have been increasing. We expect, furthermore, that rather than diminishing or turning around, these trends will become more pervasive and accepted during the next several decades.

Given the magnitude of the changes and the widespread concern over their impact, some find it surprising that only scattered evidence suggests negative consequences for women, for marriages, and for children. However, research on this topic has no timeless validity. As attitudes, behavior patterns, technology, and family structure change, new research is needed to explore the interaction between employment and family functioning. In particular, there is a need for work on fathers and husbands. How do the work schedules, attitudes, and domestic responsibilities of men affect women's employment and children's well being? In addition, research on older women, as wives and as mothers, is lacking.

New studies should avoid the dichotomies so often used in past research. For example, instead of comparing women defined as "employed" or "non-employed" women, variables measuring work history, hours of work, occupation, and work satisfaction should be developed and explored jointly. Mediating processes should be examined. If maternal employment is hypothesized to have a negative impact, then the mechanism by which that effect is expected to be transmitted should be specified, operationalized, and examined. Analyses should be conducted within a framework that controls for other factors that might affect the outcome. For example, life cycle stage and economic status should be controlled in studies of marital satisfaction. In studies of child outcomes, the child's age and sex and the family's socioeconomic status should be controlled.

Finally, we would argue that research questions should be framed so as to be helpful. For example, even if maternal employment were documented to be harmful, most women would not be able to return to full-time homemaking. More useful to working parents would be studies of the effects of work scheduling; the costs and advantages of employer benefits; the effects of different types of child care; school and community adaptations that assist working parents; and effects of varied levels and types of father involvement. Such studies might enhance the lives of working wives and mothers and their families, and this seems a worthy goal for future research.

REFERENCES

Baldwin, W. and Cain, V.S. The Children of Teenage Parents. *Family Planning Perspectives,* 1980, *12,* 34-43.

Bauman, K., Anderson, A., Freeman, J., and Koch, G. Legal Abortions and Trends in Age-Specific Marriage Rates. *American Journal of Public Health,* 1977, *67,* 52-53.

Bianchi, S. and Spain, D. American Women: Three Decades of Change. *Special Demographic Analyses, CDS-80-8,* 1983, Washington, D.C.: U.S. Government Printing Office.

Blake, J. Demographic Science and the Redirection of Population Policy. In T. Ford and G. DeJong (Eds.), *Social Demography,* Englewood Cliffs, N.J.: Prentice-Hall, 1970, 326-347.

Bloom-Feshbach, S., Bloom-Feshbach, J., and Heller, K.A. Work, Family and Children's Perceptions of the World. In S.B. Kamerman and C.D. Hayes, (Eds.), *Families that Work: Children in A Changing World,* Washington, D.C.: National Academy Press, 1982.

Bronfenbrenner, U. and Crouter, A.C. Work and Family Through Time and Space. In S.B. Kamerman and C.D. Hayes, (Eds.), *Families that Work: Children in A Changing World,* Washington, D.C.: National Academy Press, 1982.

Bumpass, L.L., Rindfuss, R.R., and Janosik, R.B. Age and Marital Status at First Birth and the Pace of Subsequent Fertility. *Demography,* 1978, *15,* 75-86.

Carlson, E. and Stinson, K. Motherhood, Marriage Timing, and Marital Stability: A Research Note. *Social Forces,* 1982, *61,* 258-267.

Cherlin, A. Postponing Marriage: The Influence of Young Women's Work Expectations. *Journal of Marriage and the Family,* 1980, *42,* 355-365.

Cherlin, A. The Effect of Children on Marital Dissolution. *Demography,* 1977, *14,* 265-272.

Cramer, J.C. Fertility and Female Employment: Problems of Causal Direction. *American Sociological Review,* 1980, *45,* 167-190.

D'Amico, R.J., Haurin, R.J., and Mott F.L. The Effects of Mothers' Employment on Adolescent and Early Adult Outcomes of Young Men and Women. In C.D. Hayes and S.B. Kamerman, (Eds.), *Children of Working Parents: Experiences and Outcomes,* Washington, D.C.: National Academy Press, 1983.

Etaugh, C. Effects of Maternal Employment on Children: A Review of Recent Research. *Merrill Palmer Quarterly,* 1974, *20,* 71-98.

Farley, J. Graduate Women: Career Aspiration and Desired Family Size. *American Psychologist,* 1970, *25,* 1099-1100.

Freedman, R., Whelpton, P.K., and Campbell, A.A. *Family Planning, Sterility, and Population Growth,* New York: McGraw-Hill, 1959.

Furstenberg, F.F., Jr. *Unplanned Parenthood: The Social Consequences of Teenage Childbearing,* New York: The Free Press, 1976.

Glenn, N.D. and McLanahan, S. Children and Marital Happiness: A Further Specification of the Relationship. *Journal of Marriage and the Family,* 1982, *44,* 63-72.

Glick, P.C. and Norton, A.J. Marrying, Divorcing and Living Together in the U.S. Today. *Population Bulletin,* 1979, *32,* Washington, D.C.: Population Reference Bureau, Inc.

Hanson, S.L. A Family Life-Cycle Approach to the Socioeconomic Attainment of Working Women. *Journal of Marriage and the Family,* 1983, *45,* 323-338.

Hayes, C.D. and Kamerman S.B. (Eds.). *Children of Working Parents: Experiences and Outcomes,* Washington, D.C.: National Academy Press, 1981.

Hess, B.B. and Waring, J.M. Changing Patterns of Aging and Family Bonds in Later Life. *The Family Coordinator,* 1978, 304-314.

Hetherington, E.M. Divorce: A Child's Perspective. *American Psychologist,* 1979, *34,* 851-858.

Heyns, B. The Influence of Parents' Work on Children's School Achievement. In S.B. Kamerman and C.D. Hayes, (Eds.), *Families that Work: Children in A Changing World,* Washington, D.C.: National Academy Press, 1982.

Hill, C.R. and Stafford, F.P. Parental Care of Children: Time Diary Estimates of Quantity, Predictability and Variety. *The Journal of Human Resources,* 1980, *15,* 219-239.

Hill, M.S. Patterns of Time Use. Survey Research Center, University of Michigan, Mimeographed paper, 1981.

Hofferth, S.L. Effects of Number and Timing of Births on Family Well-Being Over the Life Cycle. Final Report to the Center for Population Research, NICHD Contract N01-HD-82850, 1981.

Hofferth, S.L. and Moore, K.A. Women's Employment and Marriage. In Ralph Smith (Ed.), *The Subtle Revolution,* Washington, D.C.: The Urban Institute, 1979.

Hoffman, L.W. The Effects of Maternal Employment on the Academic Attitudes and Performance of School-Aged Children. Paper prepared for the National Institute of Education, 1980.

Hoffman, L.W. and Nye, F.I. (Eds.). *Working Mothers,* San Francisco: Jossey-Bass, 1974.

Hout, M. The Determinants of Marital Fertility in the United States, 1968-79: Inferences from a Dynamic Model. *Demography,* 1978, *15,* 139-159.

Hudis, P., Macke, A., and Hayward, M. A Longitudinal Model of Sex-Role Attitudes, Labor Force Participation and Childbearing. Ohio State University, Center for Human Resource Research, 1981.

Johnson, B. and Waldman, E. Marital and Family Patterns of the Labor Force. *Monthly Labor Review,* 1981, *104,* 36-38.

Kamerman, S.B. and Hayes, C.D. (Eds.). *Families That Work: Children in a Changing World,* Washington, D.C.: National Academy Press, 1982.

Kamerman, S.B. and Kingston, P.W. Employer Responses to the Family Responsibilities of Employees. In S.B. Kamerman and C.D. Hayes, (Eds.), *Families That Work: Children in a Changing World,* Washington, D.C.: National Academy Press, 1982.

Locksley, A. On the Effects of Wife's Employment on Marital Adjustment and Companionship. *Journal of Marriage and the Family,* 1980, *42,* 337-346.

Marini, M.M. Effects of the Number and Spacing of Children on Marital and Parental Satisfaction. *Demography, 17,* 225-242.

Mason, K.O., Czajka, J.L., and Arber, S. Changes in U.S. Women's Sex-Role Attitudes 1964-1974. *American Sociological Review,* 1976, *4,* 573-596.

Menken, J. and Larsen, U. Age and Fertility: How Late Can You Wait? Paper presented at the annual meeting of the Population Association of America, 1983.

Miller, S. *Children as Parents: A Final Report.* New York: Child Welfare League of America, 1983.

Milne, A.M., Myers D.E., Ellman F.M., and Ginsberg, A. Single Parents, Working Mothers and the Educational Achievement of Elementary School Age Children. Revised version of a paper presented at the annual meeting of the American Educational Research Association, New York, 1983.

Moore, K.A. and Waite, L.J. Marital Dissolution, Early Motherhood and Early Marriage. *Social Forces,* 1981, *60,* 20-40.

Moore, K.A. and Hofferth, S.L. Women and Their Children. In Ralph Smith, (Ed.), *The Subtle Revolution,* Washington, D.C.: The Urban Institute, 1979.

Moore, K.A., Waite, L.J., Hofferth, S.L., and Caldwell, S.B. The Consequences of Age at First Childbirth: Marriage, Separation and Divorce. Working Paper 1146-03, Washington, D.C.: The Urban Institute, 1978.

Mosher, W.D. and Pratt, W.F. Reproductive Impairments Among Married Couples, United States. National Center for Health Statistics. *Vital and Health Statistics*, Series 23, No. 11, Washington, D.C.: U.S. Government Printing Office 1982.

Mott, F. *The Employment Revolution: Young American Women in the 1970s.* Cambridge, Mass.: The MIT Press, 1982.

Mott, F.L., Statham, A., and Maxwell, N.L. From Mother to Daughter: The Transmission of Work Behavior Patterns Across Generations. In F.L. Mott, (Ed.), *The Employment Revolution: Young American Women in the 1970s,* Cambridge, Mass.: The MIT Press, 1982.

Myers, D.E., Milne, A., Ellman, F., and Ginsberg, A. Single Parents, Working Mothers and the Educational Achievement of Secondary School Age Children. Revised version of a paper presented at the annual meeting of the American Educational Research Association, April 1983.

Nadelson, C. and Notman, M. Child Psychiatry Perspectives. Women, Work and Children. *Journal of American Academy of Child Psychiatry,* 1981, *20,* 863-875.

Nimkoff, M.F. *The Family.* Boston: Houghton-Mifflin, 1934.

O'Neill, J. and Braun, R. Women and the Labor Market: A Survey of Issues and Policies in the United States. Working Paper, Washington, D.C.: The Urban Institute, 1981.

Oppenheimer, V.K. The Female Labor Force in the United States. *Population Monograph Series,* No. 5, Berkeley, California: University of California, 1970.

Pebley, A.R. Changing Attitudes Toward the Timing of First Births. *Family Planning Perspectives,* 1981, *13,* 171-175.

Pleck, J. Husbands' and Wives' Family Work, Paid Work and Adjustment. Working Paper No. 95, Wellesley: Center for Research on Women, Wellesley College, 1982.

Pratt, L. and Whelpton, P.K. Social and Psychological Factors Affecting Fertility. *Milbank Memorial Fund Quarterly,* 1956, *34,* 1245.

Ridley, J.C. Number of Children Expected in Relation to Non-Familial Activities of the Wife. *Milbank Memorial Fund Quarterly,* 1959, *37,* 227-296.

Rubin, V. Family Work Patterns and Community Resources: An Analysis of Children's Access to Support and Services Outside School. In C.D. Hayes and S.B. Kamerman, (Eds.), *Children of Working Parents: Experiences and Outcomes,* Washington, D.C.: National Academy Press, 1983.

Schoen, R. Measuring the Tightness of a Marriage Squeeze. *Demography,* 1983, *20,* 61-78.

Select Committee on Children, Youth and Families. U.S. Children and Their Families: Current Conditions and Recent Trends. Washington, D.C.: U.S. Government Printing Office, 1983.

Smith-Lovin, L. and Tickamyer, A. Nonrecursive Models of Labor Force Participation, Fertility Behavior, and Sex Role Attitudes. *American Sociological Review,* 1978, *43,* 541-556.

Spain, D. and Bianchi, S.M. How Women Have Changed. *American Demographics,* 1983, 19-25.

Spanier, G.B. and Lewis, R.S. Marital Quality: A Review of the Seventies. *Journal of Marriage and the Family,* 1980, *42,* 825-839.

Stolzenberg, R.M. and Waite, L.J. Age, Fertility Expectations and Plans for Employment. *American Sociological Review,* 1977, *47,* 561-566.

Suter, L.E. and Miller, H.P. Income Differences Between Men and Career Women. In J. Huber, (Ed.), *Changing Women in a Changing Society,* Chicago: The University of Chicago Press, 1973.

Sweet, J. *Women in the Labor Force.* New York: Seminar Press, 1973.

Thornton, A. and Freedman, D. Changing Attitudes Toward Marriage and Single Life. *Family Planning Perspectives,* 1982, *14,* 297-303.

U.S. Bureau of the Census. Fertility of American Women: June 1983 (Advance Report). *Current Population Reports,* Series P-20, No. 386, Washington, D.C.: U.S. Government Printing Office, 1984.

U.S. Bureau of the Census. School Enrollment—Social and Economic Characteristics of

Students: October 1981 (Advance Report). *Current Population Reports,* Series P-20, No. 373. Washington, D.C.: U.S. Government Printing Office, 1983b.

U.S. Bureau of the Census. Fertility of American Women: June 1981 (Advance Report). *Current Population Reports* Series P-20, No. 368, Washington, D.C.: U.S. Government Printing Office, 1982a.

U.S. Bureau of the Census. Trends in Child Care Arrangements of Working Mothers. *Current Population Reports* Series P-23, No. 117, Washington, D.C.: U.S. Government Printing Office, 1982b.

U.S. Bureau of the Census. Marital Status and Living Arrangements: March 1980. *Current Population Reports* Series P-20, No. 365. Washington, D.C.: U.S. Government Printing Office, 1981.

U.S. Bureau of the Census. Perspectives on American Fertility. *Current Population Reports,* Special Studies, Series P-23, No. 70. Washington, D.C.: U.S. Government Printing Office, 1978.

U.S. Department of Labor. *Labor Force Statistics Derived from the Current Population Survey: A Databook,* Volume I. Bulletin 2096. Washington, D.C.: U.S. Government Printing Office, 1982.

U.S. Department of Labor, Bureau of Labor Statistics. *Perspectives on Working Women: A Databook.* Bulletin 2080. Washington, D.C.: U.S. Government Printing Office, 1980.

Veevers, J.E. Voluntarily Childless Wives: An Exploratory Study. *Sociology and Social Research,* 1973, 356-365.

Vickery, C. The Time-Poor: A New Look at Poverty. *The Journal of Human Resources,* 1977, *12,* 27-48.

Waite, L.J. and Stolzenberg, R.M. Intended Childbearing and Labor Force Participation of Young Women: Insights from Nonrecursive Models. *American Sociological Review,* 1976, *41,* 235-252.

Whelpton, P.K., Campbell, A.A., and Patterson, J.E. *Fertility and Family Planning in the United States.* Princeton: Princeton University Press, 1966.

Westoff, C. Some Speculations on the Future of Marriage and Fertility. *Family Planning Perspectives,* 1978, *10,* 79-83.

Williams, P.R. Black Illegitimacy and Social Response. A Research Report prepared in connection with Contract No. NO1-HD-52825, 1977.

Yarrow, M.R., Scott, P., DeLeeuw, L., and Heinig, C. Child-rearing in Families of Working and Nonworking Mothers.'' *Sociometry,* 1962, *25,* 122-140.

Zaslow, M., Pedersen, F., Suwalsky, J., and Rabinovich, B. Maternal Employment and Parent-Infant Interaction. Paper presented at the meetings of the Society for Research on Child Development, 1983.

Zelnik, M., Kantner, J., and Ford, K. *Sex and Pregnancy in Adolescence.* Beverly Hills: Sage Publications, 1981.

Zill, N. *Happy, Healthy and Insecure: A Portrait of Middle Childhood in America,* New York, 1983.

Chapter 7

Dual-Earner Families

Chaya S. Piotrkowski
Rena L. Repetti

The entry of married women into the labor market—particularly white, middle-class mothers—constitutes a major social change in this century. Modern women have always contributed to the support of their families through their unpaid household work and other home-based activities such as taking in boarders or doing sewing and laundry at home. What is a relatively new phenomenon is the widespread emergence of two physically separated and socially distinct work roles for women: one inside and one outside the home. Whereas the male breadwinner family formerly had represented an ideal for working-class and middle-class families, the dual-earner family now is normative and widely accepted (Harris & Associates, 1981). Today, over half of husband-wife families include an employed wife, compared to less than one-third with a male breadwinner only (Hayghe, 1982).

As used here, the term "dual-earner family" refers to those husband-wife families in which both partners participate regularly in paid market work. Two other terms commonly have been used to refer to such families: "dual-worker families" and "dual-career families." The former terminology is limited because it obscures unpaid household work, still performed primarily by women (cf. Aldous, 1981). In reality, there are three jobs performed by mem-

Chaya S. Piotrkowski is Assistant Professor of Psychology, Yale University, New Haven, CT. Rena L. Repetti is a member of the Department of Psychology, Yale University, New Haven, CT.

bers of most dual-earner families: two market jobs and one unpaid job in the household. Since most employed men and women do not have careers, the latter terminology obscures important social class distinctions among families. In contrast to most dual-earner families, dual-career families have material resources to help manage the difficulties inherent in being a dual-earner family in our society. More than others, dual-career families rely on paid domestic help (Safilios-Rothschild, 1970; Angrist, Lave, & Mickelsen, 1976), i.e., the cheap labor of women who themselves may be part of dual-earner families (Hunt & Hunt, 1982).

Any brief chapter on dual-earner families necessarily must be limited in scope. Our perspective is "women-centered" (Rapoport & Rapoport, 1980); that is, we evaluate theory and research for explicit and implicit assumptions about the role of women in the family. The selection of women as the focal point of the chapter reflects the perspective of this volume, the history of research in the field, and our belief that women—more than men—have undergone important changes as a result of their dual work roles. In the interests of parsimony we omit research on maternal employment and individual child outcomes (see Moore et al., this issue), on child care policy (e.g., Kamerman & Kahn, 1981), and on predictors of women's labor market entry and career advancement (e.g., Rallings & Nye, 1979). Instead, we emphasize *relationships* in dual-earner families, focusing on the mother-child and the marital relationship in particular.

The literature on dual-earner families is part of a more general research tradition on work and family life (Piotrkowski, Rapoport, & Rapoport, forthcoming). Two major lines of research on dual-earner families will be discussed. They are distinguished both by the questions addressed and by the methods employed to answer them. The first and more extensive line of research is characterized by efforts to predict the consequences for families of women's participation in the labor force and by the use of relatively large samples and quantitative methods. This body of research has provided relatively generalizable findings but little depth. The second line of research has a more recent history and is characterized by descriptions of the dynamics of dual-earner families and by a reliance on small, convenience samples and qualitative methods. It has provided rich, dynamic descriptions with limited generalizability. An important strength of research on dual-earner families is such methodological diversity. We will note the significant conceptual and methodological shifts that have resulted in a welcomed integration of the two approaches.

PREDICTING THE CONSEQUENCES OF WOMEN'S EMPLOYMENT

Initially, this line of research focused on two fundamental questions: (1) Is women's employment harmful? (2) Does wives' employment result in structural change in families? The first question stems from a problem-orientation and is based on the conception of women's employment as detrimental to children and destructive of families. Consistent with the idea that women's fundamental duty involved support of *others,* early researchers rarely considered the consequences for women of their own employment. Instead, the questions addressed by social and behavioral scientists reflected the debate occurring in the 1950s and early 1960s regarding women's "proper place" (Piotrkowski & Katz, 1982a).

HARMFUL EFFECTS: THEORETICAL AND METHODOLOGICAL PERSPECTIVES

Psychologists were interested in possible detrimental effects on children's development and on attachment between mothers and children. Attachment theory, as well as other psychoanalytic approaches, were used to predict the negative consequences for children of repeated maternal absences, which were presumed to disrupt the crucial tie between mother and child (e.g., Spitz, 1964; Bowlby, 1951). Thus, maternal employment became equated with maternal deprivation.

Sociologists were interested in the negative consequences of wives' employment for marriage. Parsonian structural-functionalist theory posited the necessity of discrete, complementary, gender-based family roles as the basis for marital solidarity (e.g., Parsons, 1949). Wives were the expressive leaders and husbands the instrumental ones. Labor market competition could only introduce tensions into the family, destroying the functional complementarity of spousal roles. If wives were to be employed, marital solidarity required them to have occupations of lower status and to earn less than their husbands. The application of role theory (e.g., Goode, 1960) led to the prediction that the multiple roles of employed wives (but not husbands) would hinder their ability to perform family functions adequately because they simply had too much to do (Gove & Peterson, 1980). Discrepancies between role performance and expectations would cause marital difficulties.

These psychological and sociological theories were based on idealizations of families and women's roles within them. In the case of psychological theories, it was fulltime mothering that was idealized. There was little or no recognition of the tensions created when women alone are responsible for maintaining households while simultaneously caring for their children (Piotrkowski, 1979; Piotrkowski & Katz, 1982a). Parsonian theory embodied the notion of women as emotional supports to men. Theories of role strain were differentially applied to men and women: Only women's participation in the public world of work would hinder their ability to function in their familial roles.

An important consequence of these idealizations was the assumption that a woman's presence in or absence from the home was the critical issue. If she were at home, the family would not face major difficulties, as the traditional male breadwinner family was viewed implicitly as problem-free. Not surprisingly, a typical research design was to compare families in which women were employed to those in which they were not. Yet, static comparisons of nonequivalent groups are not adequate for determining the effects of women's employment (Sussman, 1961; Piotrkowski & Katz, 1982a). Equivalent outcomes in dual-earner and traditional families may result from significantly different mediating processes. Moreover, since dual-earner and male breadwinner families differ on demographic and psychological variables (e.g., Hayghe, 1982; Burke & Weir, 1976b), the comparison of roughly matched groups may result in relatively atypical samples. Despite these methodological difficulties, group comparisons are still a favored method for finding the "effects" on families of women's employment.

While assumptions of the negative effects of women's employment were elaborated, no comparable theories about possible beneficial effects were advanced until recently. As a result, the types of outcomes studied (e.g., marital stability, children's attachment to mothers) were based on the prevailing paradigms. Although many researchers were interested in demonstrating that women's employment was *not* harmful, they also worked within the dominant conceptual and methodological traditions. In other cases, the social problem orientation led to shopping lists of outcome variables without regard for their theoretical relevance.

The assumption that women's employment status is the critical variable in family functioning still dominates much research. As a result, little attention has been directed to what women actually do while at home or at the workplace. The employment conditions of women—even the number of hours they are employed—are rarely considered (Piotrkowski & Crits-Christoph, 1981). Instead, women's employment is typically treated as a simple dichotomous variable, in striking contrast to the way in which men's employment has been studied (Feldberg & Glenn, 1979).

STRUCTURAL EFFECTS: THEORETICAL PERSPECTIVES

Efforts to answer the question of whether or not wives' employment changes family structure focused on two closely related variables—family power and the division of household work, with the latter sometimes treated as an indicator of the former.[1] The possible link between wives' employment and power was elaborated by Blood and Wolfe (1960), who advanced a "comparative resource" theory of marital power. According to this formulation, power spontaneously accrues to an individual according to the resources he or she can make available to the other. Wives' employment increases their marital power because it provides them with economic and other, less tangible, resources. Thus, Blood and Wolfe offered an essentially rational view of the family as a political economic system, with the implied potential for equality between men and women. Gillespie (1971) correctly criticized Blood and Wolfe for treating the distribution of power in marriage as a private, interpersonal event without recognizing the limitations on the acquisition of power by women that stem from societal barriers to gender equality.

Blood and Wolfe also provided a rational basis for predicting increases in men's participation in housework when wives are employed. The concept of "comparative availability," refers to the relative distribution of time resources and—secondarily—the skill to perform housework. When wives are employed, the structure of

---

[1]Treating the division of labor in the family as an indicator of family power rests on the assumption that housework is onerous and necessarily is avoided by those with the power to do so. To make this assumption, without empirically testing it, reflects the general devaluation of housework in our society.

employment time leads directly to a restructuring of time spent doing housework, and tasks are reallocated to the more available partner, who may be the husband. Here Blood and Wolfe recognized the impact of traditional attitudes on the division of household work. Still, they assumed that rational, essentially economic considerations easily overrode the effects of sex role socialization, and they ignored the possibility that the extent of wives' participation in employment itself was shaped by their family roles (e.g., Ewer, Crimmins, & Oliver, 1979; Duncan & Perucci, 1976).

What Have We Learned?

Despite our inability to draw conclusions about the *effects* of wives' employment on families from the static group comparison approach, it is still important to know what differences—if any—characterize relationships in male breadwinner and dual-earner families. But research findings must be interpreted cautiously. Studies done in the 1950s and 1960s are not necessarily comparable to more recent ones because of changing norms and attitudes towards women's employment. Most relevant for our purposes, then is the more recent research. The overwhelming evidence from the group comparison studies indicates that there are few reliable differences in the family relationships of dual-earner and male breadwinner families.

Parent-Child Relations

Researchers have assessed the quality of the mother-child relationship in two ways. In the case of infants and toddlers, they have compared the security of children's attachments to their employed or nonemployed mother, using standard laboratory experimental designs. In the case of school-aged children, researchers have typically asked about their feelings of closeness to their mothers or about their mothers' supportiveness. It should be noted that there are few such studies, and they rarely consider or control for mothers' employment histories in relation to children's ages.

The few studies of the security of infants' and toddlers' attachment to their employed and nonemployed mothers generally have resulted in no reliable differences between groups (Hoffman, in press). Lamb (1982) did find some evidence to support the notion that the infants of employed mothers are less securely attached than those of nonemployed mothers. However, other data indicate that any such differences are not a simple function of maternal employment status. Reviewers generally agree that day care children are as securely attached to their mothers as home-reared children (e.g., Belsky & Sternberg, 1978; Clarke-Stewart, 1982), suggesting that daily maternal absences do not necessarily dilute the mother-infant tie. Thompson, Lamb and Estes (1982) found that a mother's return to work changed the nature of a baby's attachment, but not necessarily to greater insecurity. Some babies became *more* securely attached. Variables that show promise of being able to account for such findings include (a) the congruence between a mother's work status and her attitudes towards the importance of maternal care for infants (Hock, 1980); (b) the extent to which a mother values parenthood relative to her paid job (Lamb, 1982); (c) her role satisfaction (see below).

Studies of the quality of mother-child relationships among school-aged children, in general, have found no associations between children's feelings of closeness to their mothers and maternal employment status (Nye, 1963b; Peterson, 1961; Douvan & Adelson, 1966; Propper, 1972), or between perceived maternal supportiveness and the hours employed mothers work (Piotrkowski & Katz, 1983). While some studies did find more frequent or serious disagreements between children and parents in dual-earner families, such conflict was not accompanied by less closeness (Propper, 1972). Evidence from research on adolescents suggests that such disagreement reflects parental encouragement of autonomy (Douvan & Adelson, 1966), and there is evidence that parents in dual-earner families are more likely than parents in male breadwinner families to encourage independence in their children (Hoffman, 1979).

Interestingly, there are some indications that mothers' employment status may be related to the quality of the father-son relationship. One study found less secure attachment between fathers and sons in dual-earner than in male breadwinner families (Chase-Lansdale & Owen, cited in Hoffman, in press). Moreover, school-aged sons in lower-class and working-class dual-earner families have been found to express greater disapproval of or to admire their fathers less than sons in traditional families (e.g., McCord, McCord, & Thurber, 1963; Propper, 1972). These sons may view their mothers' employment as indicators of their fathers' failure (Hoffman, 1979) or as threats to their parents' marriages (King, McIntyre, & Axelson, 1968). The attitudes of older children towards their mothers' employment status could, therefore, be a crucial variable in understanding any direct and indirect effects of women's employment.

Marital Quality

When adequate controls have been included, several recent studies find no simple relationship between wives' marital adjustment and their employment status (e.g., Staines, Pleck, Shepard, & O'Connor, 1978; Locksley, 1980). Research on husbands demonstrates a similar pattern, with a few early studies favoring male breadwinner families (e.g., Axelson, 1963; Burke & Weir, 1976a), but later ones, with improved controls, showing no differences or favoring dual-earner families (e.g., Staines et al., 1978; Booth, 1977; Simpson & England, 1981). An exception to this pattern of findings appears in lower-income families, where employed wives—but not husbands—still report poorer marital relations than fulltime housewives (e.g., Feldman & Feldman, 1974; Nye, 1974; Staines et al., 1978; cf. Wright, 1978).

When we consider marital stability it is clear that, among white women at least, there is an association between divorce and employment. With cross-sectional studies, it is impossible to say which came first—the divorce or the job. Studies do consistently show that employed women report having contemplated divorce more frequently than housewives, even though the two groups report being equally satisfied with their marriages (e.g., Nye, 1963a; Staines et al., 1978; Booth & White, 1980). Still, the meaning of such thoughts of divorce are not clear. Possibly, increased financial independence and social interaction make employed women more independent of marriage than housewives (Haavio-Manila, 1971).

Power and the Division of Household Labor

In studies of wives' employment, reports of decision-making outcomes generally have been used to indicate family power. Reviewers agree that there is little evidence that employed women play a greater role in family decision-making than nonemployed women (e.g., Smith, 1979; Bahr, 1974). The one difference between groups seems to lie in a specific area of decision-making: Employed wives appear to play a greater role in financial decisions than nonemployed wives (Blood, 1963; Safilios-Rothschild, 1970; Bahr, 1974).

Research regarding the division of household work is conclusive on two points: (1) Employed women spend less time doing housework, particularly routine cleaning and maintenance, than nonemployed wives, and (2) women—employed or not—still do the lion's share of housework. (See, for example, Walker & Woods, 1976; Robinson, 1980; Pleck & Rustad, 1980.) Some controversy remains over whether or not husbands of employed wives participate more in housework than husbands of nonemployed wives (see Stein, this issue). Recent data suggest that husbands of employed wives are doing more, but the increment is slight (Pleck, 1979).

New Directions in Theory and Research

Rallings and Nye (1979) have suggested that the general lack of reliable differences between dual-earner and male breadwinner families is due, in part, to the fact that few married women actually are employed fulltime throughout the year. This explanation is not entirely plausible. In 1978 over half of dual-earner wives worked fulltime at least 40 weeks during the year (Hayghe, 1982), and numerous studies utilized samples of such wives. More compelling to us are four other alternatives. First, it is likely that the importance of a constant maternal or wifely presence has been overestimated. In fact, we do not know how much contact is minimally necessary to ensure adequate relationships between mothers and children or between husbands and wives. In some marriages, for example, lessened contact may enhance individual development (e.g., Douvan & Pleck, 1978). Similarly, as children mature, lessened maternal involvement may facilitate the development of autonomy (Maccoby, 1958; Hoffman, 1974, 1979).

Second, employment status is a gross variable, with little explanatory power, that obscures heterogeneity within groups (Lamb, 1982). For example, maternal employment status is not an adequate indicator of either the quality or amount of direct mother-infant interaction (Hoffman, in press). Third, complex moderators most likely obscure group differences that might exist. For example, when social class or attitudes towards employment are included as moderator variables, differences between groups sometimes emerge (e.g., Orden & Bradburn, 1969). Fourth is the possibility that net outcomes for the two groups may be similar, while the processes linking employment status to outcomes differ significantly. In fact, researchers interested in the consequences of women's employment for families have begun investigating these possibilities, initiating a second phase of research that reflects a greater appreciation of the complex dynamics of dual-career families.

Parent-Child Relations

Especially interesting findings regarding parent-child relations in dual-earner families are emerging from research in developmental psychology. One set of findings suggests that patterns of interaction differ in dual-earner and male-breadwinner families and that such differences are linked to the gender of the child. Pederson, Cain, Zaslow and Anderson (1982) found that fathers in dual-earner families played with their infants less frequently than did fathers in male breadwinner families. Employed mothers showed the most intense interaction. The authors suggested that these mothers were compensating for their return to paid employment and, inadvertently, were crowding out their husbands. Two other studies have found that preschool sons in middle-class dual-earner families receive less parental attention than daughters in such families (Stuckey, McGhee, & Bell, 1982; Zaslow, Pederson, Suwalsky, & Rabinovich, 1983). Coupled with other patterns of gender differences, such findings have led Hoffman (in press) to conclude that child's gender cannot be overlooked as a critical variable in research on maternal employment.

While these efforts still rely heavily on group comparisons, they are notable for several reasons. First, they demonstrate the complexity of dual-earner family dynamics. Second, the use of observational techniques—a commonplace in child development research—represents an important methodological contribution to research on dual-earner families. Third, the results are interesting because the family is viewed at least as a three person system and *father-child* interaction is understood in the context of mothers' employment. Finally, the findings—especially those regarding children's gender—are important in themselves. Unfortunately, these kinds of data cannot lead to clear conclusions regarding the role of maternal employment in "causing" group differences or the differential treatment of boys and girls. Thus, researchers working in this area must be careful not to interpret their findings as an effect of maternal employment.

A second set of studies confirm early findings that the degree of congruence between actual employment status and desired status is a better predictor of maternal behavior than is employment status alone (Yarrow, Scott, DeLeeuw, & Heinig, 1962). Lack of fit between attitudes about maternal employment or desired work status and actual employment status has been related to difficulties in infant attachment (Hock, 1980), to poor adjustment among young children (Farel, 1980) and to parents' expression of negative affect to their pre-school children (Stuckey et al., 1982). Insofar as congruence is an indicator of role satisfaction, such studies are consistent with other research examining employed women's role satisfaction more directly. In general, the more satisfied mothers are with their employment situations, the better relations they have with their children (Hoffman, 1963; Harrell & Ridley, 1975; Piotrkowski & Katz, 1983). More satisfied women may make better mothers, regardless of their employment status (Lamb, 1982).

Marital Quality

Since it has become clear that wives' employment *per se* does not necessarily decrease marital solidarity, several investigators have recently tested directly the proposition that employed wives' status attainment threatens marriage. Results of cross-sectional and longitudinal studies indicate little support for the proposition that a wife's superior occupational status, relative to her husband, reduces marital solidarity (Richardson, 1979; Simpson & England, 1981; Philliber & Hiller, 1983; cf. Hornung & McCullough, 1981). Theories also have been advanced proposing that similarity or consistency in spouses' occupational statuses is beneficial (e.g., Oppenheimer, 1977; Simpson & England, 1981).

Safilios-Rothschild (1976) has suggested that wives' superior occupational status can be tolerated if their incomes are lower than their husbands', because income is a more salient index of status in our culture than occupational prestige. Indeed, there is evidence to suggest that wives' income may have some impact on family relations, but how income operates remains obscure. Simpson and England (1981) found that wives' income was positively related to their marital adjustment but negatively related to husbands' marital adjustment. Piotrkowski and Crits-Christoph (1981) found no association between wives' income and their marital satisfaction and a negative relationship between wives' income and their satisfaction

with family relations in their subsample of women in low status occupations. Using a longitudinal data set, Cherlin (1979) found that
the greater a wife's actual or expected wage relative to her husband,
the greater the probability of marital dissolution. The effect was
small but significant. Since wives' *potential* earnings were also measured, these results suggest the operation of an "independence effect."

Such findings indicate that complex, poorly understood processes
underlie any links between wives' income and marital relations. Recently, Hiller and Philliber (1982) proposed that the effects of wives'
occupational achievements depend on spouses' sex role attitudes.
Marital strain, they predict, occurs when spouses have traditional
gender identities and wives have higher occupational achievement
than their husbands. Marriages between "androgynous" partners,
on the other hand, are not expected to suffer. What is important
about their formulation is that decreased marital solidarity represents but one possible outcome. Others include a wife leaving the
labor force or moving to a lesser job. Recent research and theory on
the family effects of wives' occupational attainment thus reflects the
increasing complexity of thinking in this area.

Multiple Roles and Coping

Research on the effects of multiple roles has begun to move
beyond the "role strain" paradigm to an interest in the possible *pro-
tective* functions of multiple roles (e.g., Sieber, 1974; Gove &
Geerken, 1977; Thoits, 1983; Repetti & Crosby, in press). According to this view, the housebound homemaker—with her limited
status and sources of gratification—is at risk, while the employed
woman—with her multiple sources of gratification—prospers. Although employed women—more than men—report feelings of strain
in performing their many roles (Keith & Schafer, 1980), this growing body of research and theory indicates that multiple roles are not
necessarily detrimental to women and their families. Equally important, it raises questions about the long-standing assumption that
women's multiple roles necessarily interfere with their family role
performance.

Researchers also have begun to study the coping strategies used
by employed women (but not men) to deal with role conflicts and
role overload (e.g., Harrison & Minor, 1978; Gilbert, Holahan &

Manning, 1981; Elman & Gilbert, in press), the supports they require (e.g., Houseknecht & Macke, 1981) and the occupational and familial factors that predict degree of family role strain (e.g., Pleck, Staines & Lang, 1980; Bohen & Viveros-Long, 1981; Katz & Piotrkowski, 1983). What are needed now are studies that link predictors of role strain, the experience of strain and family outcomes.

Power and the Division of Household Labor

The study of family power as the net outcome of decision-making has been repeatedly criticized on conceptual and methodological grounds (e.g., McDonald, 1980). Consistent with general trends in this literature, research on family power and wives' employment is beginning to focus on processes of negotiation between husbands and wives (see Szinovacz, this volume). Scanzoni (1978), for example, has examined the multiple variables that predict outcomes at each stage of the negotiation process in both dual-earner and male breadwinner families. Similarly, Chafetz (1980) has developed a model linking resources, including those from employment, to the strategies used in conflict management. She proposed that employment provides wives with greater "control resources," which may—in turn—lead to both greater egalitarianism and increased conflict.

Research on the division of household labor also is becoming increasingly sophisticated. Researchers have begun to study specific occupational factors that may predict the amount of time men spend in housework. For example, using multiple regression techniques, Fox and Nickols (1983) found that only 2% of the variance in the time husbands spent doing housework was accounted for by the ages of their youngest children and by their wives' employment hours. Some studies have found that husbands' income is negatively related to time spent in housework (Ericksen, Yancey, & Ericksen, 1979) and that husbands do more housework as wives' income approaches theirs (Model, 1981; Scanzoni, 1978). A much needed longitudinal study of time spent in housework (excluding child care) confirms our earlier conclusion: When wives increase their time in market work, husbands minimally increase their time in housework. More dramatic, however, is the decrease in husbands' housework when their wives reduce their employment hours (Nickols & Metzen, 1982).

Contextual Variables

Finally, there is a growing interest in identifying the variables that moderate relationships between wives' employment and family outcomes. Gender of child, social class, role satisfaction, and attitudes towards women's employment have been mentioned already. Other moderators that have received some attention include the fit between husbands' and wives' attitudes towards women's employment, women's commitment to the employment role, and the presence and age of children (e.g., Staines et al., 1978; Geerken, cited in Gove & Peterson, 1980; Eiswirth-Neems & Handel, 1978; Safilios-Rothschild, 1970; Ridley, 1973; Orden & Bradburn, 1979; Locksley, 1980). Systematic conceptualization and research on the role of such variables is needed to further our understanding of the familial consequences of women's employment.

Summary

There have been two notable shifts in this first line of research, directed at predicting familial effects of women's employment. The first is a lessened concern with harmful consequences of women's employment. The second is the use of increasingly sophisticated designs and methods of data analysis, including longitudinal studies, precise and direct measures of theoretically important predictors and within-group analyses. This latter design shift is especially significant. It reflects the recognition of within-group diversity, the realization that findings of no differences between dual-earner and male breadwinner families do not mean that wives' employment is unimportant, and an interest in illuminating mediating processes. A drawback of these most recent research efforts is that, at times, we appear to be at sea in a mass of empirical data without a theoretical rudder. We believe this to be an inevitable by-product of the new complexity in the field, from which we can anticipate the development of new explanatory theories.

DESCRIPTIVE STUDIES OF DUAL-EARNER FAMILIES

A second, more recent, line of research on dual-earner families differs from the one described above in several ways. First, researchers initially adopted a sympathetic stance towards women's employment and career involvement. Not only was the dual-earner family acceptable and viable, it even was viewed as a desirable reflection of the movement towards greater equality of the sexes. Less interested in the negative consequences of wives' employment, researchers tried to identify the satisfactions and difficulties inherent in balancing work and family lives in modern societies. Not surprisingly, researchers were themselves often dual-earner couples (Aldous, 1981). Second, researchers sought complexity, rather than isolating single predictor and outcome variables. For example, the pioneering work of Rapoport and Rapoport (1979; 1971; 1977) described the interactions of husbands' and wives' occupational and family careers as these influenced the integration of work and family roles. Third, researchers have built on the work of the Rapoports and have adopted an explicitly developmental orientation, so that the interaction of family, individual and occupational careers could be studied (e.g. Handy, 1978; Poloma, Pendleton, & Garland, 1981). Finally, this research tradition is marked by the use of qualitative methods of data collection and analysis and a reliance on small, non-representative samples.

Two significant omissions, however, characterize this body of research. With a few exceptions (e.g., Working Family Project, 1978; Hood, 1983), there has been an almost exclusive focus on the families of managers and professionals, i.e., *dual career* families (e.g., Rapoport & Rapoport, 1971; Epstein, 1971; Holmstrom, 1972; Poloma, 1972; Garland, 1972). Aldous (1981) has proposed that the emphasis on dual-career families represents both a narcissistic bent among dual-career researchers and the invisibility to researchers of working-class women, who have long been part of two paycheck families (see Ferree, this volume). Rapoport and Rapoport (1969; 1971), however, developed a theoretical rationale for this focus that has been accepted by those who followed them: Dual-career families represent a pioneering lifestyle, offering researchers an unique opportunity to look into the future. Yet it is clear that comparatively few employed adults in dual-earner families have "careers," nor will they do so in the near future. Hunt and Hunt (1982) have argued that dual-career families represent a minor variant. Without empirical evidence to the contrary, we cannot assume that the particular patterns of strains and satisfactions common to dual-career families can readily be generalized to other types of dual-earner families.

A second significant omission in the research tradition on dual-career families is any consideration of the children in them. While intensive interview data have provided a close look at the experience of men and women in such families—both as spouses and as parents—children have not been included explicitly. Consequently, most research on dual-career families is more accurately described as studies of dual-career marriages.

What Have We Learned?

The case study approach, commonly utilized in this research tradition, emphasizes particular problems and complex solutions, thereby making generalization difficult. Still, there are at least two broad conclusions that can be drawn from the early studies of dual-career families. First, the allocation of family role responsibilities in dual-career families is remarkably traditional, despite egalitarian ideologies. Even though they have demanding, high-level careers as doctors, academics, architects, lawyers, and so forth, the women in such families still tend to retain primary responsibility for child care and other household matters. The men interviewed by Garland (1972), for example, were uniformly supportive of their wives having careers. Still, most of them expected their wives to place families above jobs in case of a conflict between them, and the wives did just that (Poloma, 1972). This lack of congruence between attitudes and behavior is not simply due to the period in which the early research was done. Later studies have confirmed this pattern (e.g., Yogev, 1981; Bryson, Bryson, Licht, & Licht, 1976; Poloma et al., 1981).

Second, the dual-career lifestyle is not without difficulties for which couples and individuals evolve complex adaptations, such as the purchase of domestic help, careful scheduling of leisure time, and the creation of clear priorities. Women give children priority over a clean house and their careers, often compensating for time spent on the job by planning special activities with their children. Family and work roles, in general, are given priority over leisure time with friends and kin. (See Rapoport & Rapoport, 1971; Herman & Gyllstrom, 1977; Poloma, 1972; Poloma et al., 1981; Epstein, 1971.)

Interestingly, descriptions of coping generally have emphasized women's adaptations in dual-earner families. Is this emphasis due to the feminist orientation of researchers? Or does it reflect the fact that women have made the major adaptations in such families? An adequate answer to this question requires a similar attention to the coping strategies used by men and children in dual-earner families.

New Directions in Theory and Research

One of the major drawbacks of the early studies of dual-career families derived from their strength: The case analytic approach, suited to the study of complex processes, led to the introduction of constructs which were difficult to operationalize, and to descriptions of multiple interactions among many variables. Subsequently, dual-career researchers have begun to investigate more delimited, focused questions (Rapoport & Rapoport, 1980). A notable early effort was that by Bailyn (1970), who examined the interaction of family and career orientations of husbands and wives in upper middle-class families. She found that the greatest marital difficulty occurred when both spouses had strong career orientations. The development of predictive typologies also represents a significant trend (e.g. Handy, 1978; Hall & Hall, 1980). Another important focus involves attention to specific coping strategies used by dual-career couples, such as job sharing, commuting, implicit contracts, and so forth (e.g., Gerstel, 1979; Gross, 1980; Douvan & Pleck, 1978; Bailyn, 1978; Gowler & Legge, 1978; Arkin & Dobrofsky, 1978). As yet, this latter work has led to few systematic empirical investigations, but we anticipate that such further work will be forthcoming. The recent development of coping inventories specifically designed for dual-earner families (e.g. Skinner, 1982) will facilitate these efforts.

Conclusion

The two lines of research on dual-earner families are now converging. The convergence is evident in the Rapoports' (1978) overview of the dual-career research tradition, in which they include studies we would more readily identify as part of the research on the consequences of women's employment. The convergence also is evident in two of the most recent collections of papers on dual-earner families, which include a range of methodologies and family types (see Pepitone-Rockwell, 1980; Aldous, 1982). Whether they utilize qualitative or quantitative methods, large samples or small, researchers now are focusing on some common questions: What are the particular strains associated with the dual-earner family? Under what conditions is marital solidarity enhanced and when is it threatened? What coping strategies are being used? Researchers are sharing a common sympathy for the dual-earner family and an interest in the family over the course of its development. Of note also is the convergence in findings regarding the role of men and women in dual-earner families: In all types of dual-earner families studied, women still have primary responsibility for "family work" (Pleck, 1977), irrespective of ideology and social class. Roles may be changing, but the pace remains slow.

COSTS AND BENEFITS IN DUAL-EARNER FAMILIES: LAST REMARKS

Despite two decades of research on dual-earner families, we are just now beginning to understand their dynamics. Most three job families lack sufficient resources to avoid some strain. The question is not so much which family type wins and which loses, but what the pattern of "costs and benefits" (Rapoport and Rapoport, 1971) is and how it varies. We expect the differing resources, attitudes and coping strategies of various ethnic and social class groups to affect the balance of costs and benefits, so that extending research beyond the white middle-class is imperative (Ybarra, 1982). More important, the processes linking jobs to families may vary *within* groups. Attention to societal change also is necessary. We cannot assume that any particular balance of costs and benefits will persist as social norms and attitudes change. And only an explicitly developmental approach can take into account the interaction of family and occupational "careers" and individual development (see Voydanoff, 1980).

This chapter has focused on interpersonal subsystems within dual-earner families. It is clear, however, that individuals and families-as-wholes must also be considered simultaneously. Why do some studies indicate that working class employed women exhibit higher self-esteem and lower depression than fulltime housewives (e.g., Ferree, 1976), while other studies find them less satisfied with their marriages? Why do husbands of employed women appear psychologically distressed in some studies (Burke & Weir, 1976a; Kessler & McRae, 1982; cf. Booth, 1977), while not necessarily reporting less marital satisfaction? We need to verify and make sense of such disparate findings. We are advocating systematic attention to underlying processes and inclusion of outcomes that can represent the balance of long-term and short-term costs and benefits in various parts of the family system and at different points in the family life cycle (see also, Walker & Walston, in press). Only a sensitivity to such dynamics can move us beyond the simple question with no answer.

We also propose a reconsideration of the meaning we attach to traditional outcome variables. The simultaneous consideration of multiple outcomes would, for example, allow us to assess the negative consequence of divorce for children and its potential *positive* meaning for some employed wives. Similarly, the expression of marital dissatisfaction on the part of working class employed women may represent a willingness to admit dissatisfactions as a function of increased independence. Just as the meaning of women's employment has changed, so must our conception of the critical family variables we study be reconsidered (also see Laws, 1971).

Even an emphasis on costs and benefits is probably too narrow. For example, there is some empirical evidence that job conditions serve as socializing forces for both men and women (e.g., Kohn & Schooler, 1978; Miller, Schooler, Kohn, & Miller, 1979). It would be useful to look at family processes and individual outcomes as the products of such socialization (e.g., Gold & Slater, 1958; Piotrkowski & Katz, 1982b). The results of research on maternal employment are consistent with the idea that the dual-earner structure may produce different *types* of families and *types* of children than the male breadwinner family. Longitudinal studies are needed to address this issue properly.

If we consider the current pattern of costs and benefits in dual-earner families, it is clear that women shoulder a disproportionate share of the difficulties inherent in the three-job family. A woman's family benefits from the paycheck she brings home, as most families require two incomes to maintain themselves adequately. Society benefits from the unpaid services she provides in caring for the young and the old. Yet, it is women—more than men—who complain of too much to do and too little time to do it (National Commission on Working Women, 1979). The research on employed women's coping strategies indicates their resourcefulness. Yet there are limits to adaptation. The potential danger in over-emphasizing the benefits of multiple roles lies in the obfuscation of such limits and the glorification of the woman who can "have it all" (e.g., Gabriel & Baldwin, 1980). Offering the "male perspective" on wives in dual-career couples, Nadelson and Eisenberg (1977) have described how their professional wives brought them "gentle courage, soft strength, selfless individuality." Thus, social scientists themselves contribute to such a myth. In fact, some women do seem to be trying to do it all (Elman & Gilbert, in press).

The solutions to this dilemma include a more equitable division of family work, greater equality between men and women at the workplace, and social policies that assist *all* families. However, such changes are not likely to occur rapidly. While men are reporting greater psychological involvement with their families than with their jobs (e.g., Glenn & Weaver, 1981; Pleck & Lang, 1978), traditional gender arrangements remain. Some business leaders and managers still hold relatively traditional attitudes towards female employment (Harris & Associates, 1981; Rosen, Jerdee, & Prestwich, 1975), and our social policies are, at best, ambivalent towards the dual-earner family. As long as there are not enough hands to do all the work in two paycheck families, the costs will be borne by individuals in such families, and by some individuals more than others.

But perhaps the most enduring dilemma stems from the internal conflicts of the employed woman herself. Such conflicts have not been studied much, but Gilligan's (1982) research on female moral development suggests that the greatest difficulty faced by the employed married woman may not lie in her inability to do everything but in a private, *moral* dilemma. Where "goodness is service," the judgment of selfishness looms large in women's thoughts, for—as Gilligan argues—meeting one's obligations and responsibilities to others is the central theme in female morality. Thus, employed women facilitate their husbands' job performance more than their husbands help them (e.g., Lopata, Barnewolt & Norr, 1980). Where virtue lies in self-sacrifice, the employed married woman— especially if she has children—gives up her personal time (Harris & Associates, 1981; Yogev, 1982). While the difficulties of balancing multiple roles can be minimized, the moral dilemma persists. The management of internal conflict and moral guilt may remain an ongoing psychological task for employed women in dual-earner families.

REFERENCES

Aldous, J. From dual-earner to dual-career families and back again. *Journal of Family Issues,* 1981, *2,* 115-125.

Aldous, J. *Two paychecks.* Beverly Hills, CA: Sage, 1982.

Angrist, S. S., Lave, J. R., & Mickelsen, R. How working mothers manage: Socioeconomic differences in work, child care, and household tasks. *Social Science Quarterly,* 1976, *56,* 631-637.

Arkin, W. & Dobrofsky, L. R. Job sharing. In R. Rapoport & R. Rapoport (Eds.), *Working couples.* New York, Harper and Row, 1978.

Axelson, L. J. The marital adjustment and marital role definitions of husbands of working and nonworking wives. *Marriage and Family Living,* 1963, *25,* 189-195.

Bahr, S. J. Effects on power and division of labor in the family. In L. W. Hoffman & F. I. Nye (Eds.), *Working mothers.* San Francisco: Jossey-Bass, 1974.

Bailyn, L. Career and family orientations of husbands and wives in relation to marital happiness. *Human Relations,* 1970, *23,* 97-113.

Bailyn, L. Accommodation of work to family. In R. Rapoport & R. Rapoport (Eds.), *Working couples.* New York: Harper & Row, 1978.

Belsky, J., & Sternberg, L.D. The effects of day care: A critical review. *Child Development,* 1978, *49,* 929-949.

Blood, R. O., Jr. The husband-wife relationship. In F. I. Nye & L. W. Hoffman (Eds.), *The employed mother in America.* Chicago: Rand McNally, 1963.

Blood, R. O., Jr., & Wolfe, D. M. *Husbands and wives.* New York: Free Press, 1960.

Bohen, H. H., & Viveros-Long, A. *Balancing jobs and family life.* Philidelphia: Temple University Press, 1981.

Booth, A. Wife's employment and husband's stress: A replication and refutation. *Journal of Marriage and the Family,* 1977, *39,* 645-650.

Booth, A. & White, L. Thinking about divorce. *Journal of Marriage and the Family,* 1980, *42,* 605-616.

Bowlby, J. A. *Maternal care and mental health.* Geneva: World Health Organization, 1951.

Bryson, R. B., Bryson, J. B., Licht, M., & Licht, B. The professional pair: Husband and wife psychologists. *American Psychologist,* 1976, *31,* 10-16.

Burke, R. J. & Weir, T. Relationship of wives' employment status to husband, wife and pair satisfaction and performance. *Journal of Marriage and the Family,* 1976a, *38,* 279-287.

Burke, R.J., & Weir, T. Some personality differences between members of one-career and two-career families. *Journal of Marriage and the Family,* 1976b, *38,* 453-459.

Chafetz, J.S. Conflict resolution in marriage: Toward a theory of spousal strategy and marital dissolution rates. *Journal of Family Issues,* 1980, *1,* 397-341.

Cherlin, A. Work life and marital dissolution. In G. Levinger and O.C. Moles (Eds.), *Divorce and Separation* New York: Basic Books, 1976.

Clarke-Stewart, A. *Daycare.* Cambridge, MA.: Harvard University Press, 1982.

Douvan, E. & Adelson, J. *The Adolescent Experience.* New York: John Wiley & Sons, 1966.

Douvan, E., & Pleck, J.H. Separation as support. In a Rapoport & R. Rapoport (Eds.), *Working Couples.* New York: Harper & Row, 1978.

Duncan, R.P., & Perucci, C.C. Dual occupational families and migration. *American Sociological Review,* 1976, *41,* 252-261.

Eiswirth-Neems, N., & Handel, P. Spouses' attitudes toward maternal occupational status and effects on family climate. *Journal of Community Psychology,* 1978, *6,* 168-172.

Elman, M.R. & Gilbert, L.A. Coping strategies for role conflict in married professional women with children. *Family Relations,* in press.

Epstein, C.F. Law partners and marital partners: Strains and solutions in the dual career family enterprise. *Human Relations,* 1971, *24,* 549-563.

Ericksen, J., Yancey, W.L., & Ericksen, E.P. The division of family roles. *Journal of Marriage and the Family,* 1979, *41,* 301-314.

Ewer, P.A., Crimmins, E., & Oliver, R. An analysis of the relationship between husband's income, family size and wife's employment in the early stages of marriage. *Journal of Marriage and the Family,* 1979, *41,* 727-738.

Farel, A. M. Effects of preferred maternal roles, maternal employment, and sociodemographic status on school adjustment and competence. *Child Development,* 1980, *51,* 1179-1186.

Feldberg, R. L., & Glenn, E. N. Male and female: Job versus gender models in the sociology of work. *Social Problems*, 1979, *26*, 524-538.

Feldman, H., & Feldman, M. The relationship between the family and occupational functioning in a sample of urban women. Unpublished manuscript, Cornell University, Department of Human Development and Family Studies, Ithaca, NY, 1974.

Ferree, M. M. Working class jobs: Paid work and housework as sources of satisfaction. *Social Problems*, 1976, *23*, 431-441.

Fox, K. D., & Nickols, S. Y. The time crunch. *Journal of Family Issues*, 1983, *4*, 61-82.

Gabriel, J.B., & Baldwin, B. *Having it all.* New York: M. Evans & Co., 1980.

Garland, T.N. The better half? The male in the dual professional family. In C. Safilios-Rothschild (Ed.), *Toward a sociology of women.* Lexington, MA: Xerox Publishing, 1972.

Gerstel, N.R. Marital alternatives and the regulation of sex. *Alternative Lifestyles*, 1979, *2*, 145-176.

Gilbert, L. A., Holahan, C. K., & Manning, L. Coping with conflict between professional and maternal roles. *Family Relations*, 1981, *30*, 419-426.

Gillespie, D. Who has the power? The marital struggle. *Journal of Marriage and the Family*, 1971, *33*, 445-458.

Gilligan, C. *In a different voice: Psychological theory and women's development.* Cambridge, MA: Harvard University Press, 1982.

Glenn, N. D., & Weaver, C. N. A multivariate, multisurvey study of marital happiness. *Journal of Marriage and the Family*, 1978, *40*, 269-282.

Gold, M., & Slater, C. Office, factory, store and family: A study of integration setting. *American Sociological Review*, 1958, *23*, 64-74.

Goode, W. J. A theory of role strain. *American Sociological Review*, 1960, *25*, 483-496.

Gove, W., & Geerkin, M. The effect of children and employment on the mental health of married men and women. *Social Forces*, 1977, *56*, 66-76.

Gove, W. R., & Peterson, C. An update of the literature on personal and marital adjustment: The effect of children and the employment of wives. *Marriage and Family Review*, 1980, *3*(3/4), 63-96.

Gowler, D., & Legge, K. Hidden and open contracts in marriage. In Rapoport & R. Rapoport (Eds.), *Working Couples.* New York: Harper & Row, 1978.

Gross, H.E. Dual-career couples who live apart: Two types. *Journal of Marriage and the Family*, 1980, *42*, 567-576.

Haavio-Mannila, E. Satisfaction with family, work, leisure and life among men and women. *Human Relations*, 1971, *24*, 585-601.

Hall, D.T. & Hall, P.S. Stress and the two-career couple. In C.L. Cooper & R. Payne (Eds.) *Current Concerns in Occupational Stress.* New York: John Wiley & Sons, 1980.

Handy, C. The family: help or hindrance. In C.L. Cooper & R. Payne (Eds.), *Stress at Work.* New York: John Wiley & Sons, 1978.

Harrell, J., & Ridley, C. Substitute child care, maternal employment and the quality of mother-child interaction. *Journal of Marriage and the Family*, 1975, *37*, 556-564.

Hock, E. Working and nonworking mothers and their infants: A comparative study of maternal caregiving characteristics and infant social behavior. *Merrill-Palmer Quarterly*, 1980, *26*, 79-101.

Hoffman, L. W. Women's enjoyment of work and effects on the child. In F. I. Nye & L. W. Hoffman (Eds.), *The Employed Mother in America.* Chicago: Rand McNally, 1963.

Hoffman, L. W. Effects of maternal employment on the child: A review of the research. *Developmental Psychology*, 1974, *10*, 204-228.

Hoffman, L. W. (1979). Maternal employment: 1979. *American Psychologist*, 1979, *34*, 859-865.

Hoffman, W.L. Maternal employment and the young child. *Minnesota Symposium on Child Psychology.* St. Paul: University of Minnesota Press, in press.

Holstrom, L. *The Two-Career Family.* Cambridge, MA: Schenkman, 1972.

Hood, J. *Becoming a Two-job Family.* New York: Praeger, 1983.

Hornung, C.A., & McCullough, B.C. Status relationships in dual-employment marriages: Consequences for psychological well-being. *Journal of Marriage and the Family,* 1981, *43,* 125-141.

Houseknecht, S.K., & Macke, A.S. Combining marriage and career: The marital adjustment of professional women. *Journal of Marriage and the Family,* 1981, *43,* 651-661.

Hunt, J.G. & Hunt, L.L. Dual-career families: Vanguard of the future or residue of the past? In J. Aldous (Ed.), *Two Paychecks.* Beverly Hills: Sage, 1982.

Kamerman, S. B., & Kahn, S. J. *Child Care, Family Benefits and Working Parents.* New York: Columbia University Press, 1981.

Katz, M. H., & Piotrkowski, C. S. Correlates of family role strain among employed black women. *Family Relations,* 1983, *32,* 331-339.

Keith, P. M., & Schafer, R. B. (1980). Role strain and depression in two-job families. *Family Relations,* 1980, *29,* 483-488.

Kessler, R.C. & McRae, J.A., Jr. The effect of wives' employment on the mental health of married men and women. *American Sociological Review,* 1982, *47,* 216-227.

King, K., McIntyre, J., & Axelson, L.J. Adolescents' views of maternal employment as a threat to the marital relationship. *Journal of Marriage and the Family,* 1968, *30,* 633-637.

Kohn, M.L., & Schooler, C. The reciprocal effects of the substantive complexity of work and intellectual flexibility: A longitudinal assessment. *American Journal of Sociology,* 1978, *84,* 24-52.

Lamb, M.E. Maternal employment and child development: A review. In M.E. Lamb (Ed.), *Nontraditional Families: Parenting and Child Development.* Hillsdale, N.J.: Erlbaum, 1982.

Laws, J.L. A feminist review of the marital adjustment literature: The rape of the Locke. *Journal of Marriage and the Family,* 1971, *33,* 337-346.

Locksley, A. On the effects of wives' employment on marital adjustment and companionship. *Journal of Marriage and the Family,* 1980, *42,* 337-346.

Lopata, H.Z., Barnewolt, D., & Norr, K. Spouses' contributions to each others' roles. In F. Pepitone-Rockwell (Ed.), *Dual-career Couples.* Beverly Hills: Sage, 1980.

Maccoby, E. Effects upon children of their mothers' outside employment. In *Work in the Lives of Married Women.* Proceedings of the National Manpower Council. New York: Columbia University Press, 1958.

McCord, J., McCord, W., & Thurber, E. Effects of maternal employment on lower-class boys. *Journal of Abnormal and Social Psychology,* 1963, *67,* 177-182.

McDonald G.W. Family power: The assessment of a decade of theory and research, 1970-1979. *Journal of Marriage and the Family,* 1980.

Miller, J., Schooler, C., Kohn, M. L., & Miller, K. A. Women and work: The psychological effects of occupational conditions. *American Journal of Sociology,* 1979, *85,* 66-94.

Model, S. Housework by husbands. *Journal of Family Issues,* 1981, *2,* 225-237.

Nadelson, T., & Eisenberg, L. Successful professional women: On being married to one. *American Journal of Psychiatry,* 1977, *134,* 1071-1076.

National Commission on Working Women. *Perceptions, Problems, and Prospects.* Washington, D.C.: National Manpower Institute, 1979.

Nickols, S.Y., & Metzen, E.J. Impact of wives' employment upon husband's housework. *Journal of Family Issues,* 1982, *3,* 199-216.

Nye, F.I. Adjustment of the mother: Summary and a frame of reference. In F.I. Nye and L.W. Hoffman (Eds.), *The Employed Mother in America.* Chicago: Rand McNally, 1963a.

Nye, F.I. The adjustment of adolescent children. In F.I. Nye & L.W. Hoffman (Eds.), *The Employed Mother in America,* Chicago: Rand McNally, 1963b.

Nye, F. I. Husband-wife relationship. In L. W. Hoffman & F. I. Nye (Eds.), *Working Mothers.* San Francisco: Jossey-Bass, 1974.

Oppenheimer, V. K. The sociology of women's economic role in the family. *American Sociological Review,* 1977, *42,* 387-405.

Orden, S. R., & Bradburn, N. M. Working wives and marriage happiness. *American Journal on Sociology,* 1969, *74,* 391-407.

Parsons, T. The social structure of the family. In R. N. Anshen (Ed.), *The Family: Its Function and Destiny.* New York: Harper & Bros., 1949.

Pedersen, F. A., Cain, R. L., Jr., Zaslow, M. J., & Anderson, B. J. Variation in infant experience associated with alternative family roles. In L. Laosa & I. Sigel (Eds.), *Families as Learning Environments for Children.* New York: Plenum, 1982.

Pepitone-Rockwell, F. *Dual-career Couples.* Beverly Hills, CA: Sage, 1980.

Peterson, E. T. The impact of maternal employment on the mother-daughter relationship. *Marriage and Family Living,* 1961, *23,* 355-361.

Philliber, W.W. & Hiller, D.V. Relative occupational attainments of spouses and later changes in marriage and wife's work experience. *Journal of Marriage and the Family,* 1983, *45,* 161-170.

Piotrkowski, C. S. *Work and the Family System.* New York: Macmillan, 1979.

Piotrkowski, C. S., & Crits-Christoph, P. (1981). Women's jobs and family adjustment. *Journal of Family Issues,* 1981, *2,* 126-147.

Piotrkowski, C. S., & Katz, M. H. Women's work and personal relations in the family. In P. W. Berman & E. R. Ramey (Eds.), *Women: A Developmental Perspective.* NIH Publications, No. 82-2298, 1982a.

Piotrkowski, C. S., & Katz, M. H. Indirect socialization of children: The effects of mothers' jobs on academic behaviors. *Child Development,* 1982b, *53,* 1520-1529.

Piotrkowski, C. S., & Katz, M. H. Work experience and family relations among working-class and lower middle-class families. In H. Z. Lopata & J. H. Pleck (Eds.), *Research in the Interweave of social roles* (Vol. 3). *Families and jobs.* Greenwich, CT: JAI Press, 1983.

Piotrkowski, C.S., Rapoport, R., & Rapoport, R. Families and work: An emerging field. In M.B. Sussman & S.K. Steinmetz (Eds.), *Handbook of Marriage and the Family,* 2nd edition. New York: Plenum, forthcoming.

Pleck, J. H. The work-family role system. *Social Problems,* 1977, *24,* 417-427.

Pleck, J. H. (1979). Men's family work: Three perspectives and some new data. *The Family Coordinator,* 1979, *28,* 481-488.

Pleck, J. H., & Lang, L. *Men's Family Role: Its Nature and Consequences.* Wellesley, MA: Wellesley College Center for Research on Women, 1978.

Pleck, J.H., & Rustad, M. *Husbands' and Wives' Time in Family Work and Paid Work in the 1975-76 Study of Time Use.* Wellesley, MA.: Wellesley College Center for Research on Women, 1980.

Pleck, J. H., Staines, G. L., & Lang, L. Conflicts between work and family life. *Monthly Labor Review,* 1980, *103,* 29-32.

Poloma, M. M. Role conflict and the married professional woman. In C. Safilios-Rothschild (Ed.), *Toward a Sociology of Women.* Lexington, MA: Xerox Publishing, 1972.

Poloma, M. M., Pendleton, B. F., & Garland, T. N. Reconsidering the dual-career marriage. *Journal of Family Issues,* 1981, *2,* 205-224.

Propper, A. M. The relationship of maternal employment to adolescent roles, activities, and parental relationships. *Journal of Marriage and the Family,* 1972, *34,* 417-421.

Rallings, E. M., & Nye, F. I. Wife-mother employment, family, and society. In W. R. Burr, R. Hill, F. I. Nye, & I. Reiss (Eds.), *Contemporary theories about the family.* (Vol. 1). New York: Macmillan, 1979.

Rapoport, R., & Rapoport, R. The dual-career family: A variant pattern and social change. *Human Relations,* 1969, *22,* 3-30.

Rapoport, R., & Rapoport, R. *Dual-career Families.* Baltimore: Penguin, 1971.

Rapoport, R., & Rapoport, R. *Dual-career Families Re-examined.* New York: Harper Colophon Books, 1977.

Rapoport, R., & Rapoport, R. (Eds.). *Working Couples.* New York: Harper & Row, 1978.

Rapoport, R., Rapoport, R. Three generations of dual-career family research. In F. Pepitone-Rockwell (Ed.). *Dual-Career Couples.* Beverly Hills: Sage, 1980.

Repetti, R. L., & Crosby, F. Gender and depression: Exploring the adult role explanation. *Journal of Social and Clinical Personality,* in press.

Richardson, J.G. Wife occupational superiority and marital troubles: An examination of the hypothesis. *Journal of Marriage and the Family,* 1979, *41,* 63-72.

Ridley, C.A. Exploring the impact of work satisfaction and involvement on marital integration when both partners are employed. *Journal of Marriage and the Family,* 1973, *35,* 229-237.

Robinson, J.P. Housework technology and household work. In S.F. Berk (Ed.), *Women and Household Labor.* Beverly Hills, CA: Sage, 1980.

Rosen, B., Jerdee, T.H., & Prestwich, T.L. (1975). Dual-career marital adjustment: Potential effects of discriminating managerial attitudes. *Journal of Marriage and the Family,* 1975, *37,* 565-572.

Safilios-Rothschild, C. The influence of the wife's degree of work commitment upon some aspects of family organization and dynamics. *Journal of Marriage and the Family,* 1970, *32,* 681-691.

Safilios-Rothschild, C. Dual linkages between the occupational and family systems: A macro-sociological analysis. *Signs,* 1976, *1,* 51-60.

Scanzoni, J.H. *Sex Roles, Women's Work, and Marital Conflict.* Lexington, MA: D.C. Heath, 1978.

Sieber, S.D. Toward a theory of role accumulation. *American Sociological Review,* 1974, *39,* 567-578.

Simpson, I.H., & England, P. Conjugal work roles and marital solidarity. *Journal of Family Issues,* 1981, *2,* 180-204.

Skinner, D.A. The stressors and coping patterns of dual career families. In H.I. McCubbin, A.B. Cauble, & J.M. Patterson (Eds.), *Family Stress, Coping and Social Support.* Springfield: Charles C. Thomas, 1982.

Smith, R.E. (Ed.). (1989). *The Subtle Revolution.* Washington, D.C.: Urban Institute, 1979.

Spitz, R.A. Hospitalism. In R.L. Coser (Ed.), *The Family: Its Structure and Functions.* New York: St. Martin's Press, 1964.

Staines, G.L., Pleck, J.H., Shepard, L.C., & O'Connor, P.C. Wives' employment status and marital adjustment. *Psychology of Women Quarterly,* 1978, *3,* 90-120.

Stuckey, M.F., McGhee, P.E., & Bell, N.J. Parent-child interaction: The influence of maternal employment. *Child Development,* 1982, *18,* 635-644.

Sussman, M.B. Needed research on the employed mother. *Marriage and Family Living,* 1961, *23,* 368-373.

Thoits, P.A. Multiple identities and psychological well-being: A reformulation and test of the social isolation hypothesis. *American Sociological Review,* 1983, *43,* 174-187.

Thompson, R.A., Lamb, M.E., & Estes, D. Stability of infant-mother attachment and its relationship to changing life circumstances in a representative middle-class sample. *Child Development,* 1982, *53,* 144-148.

Voydanoff, P. *Work-family Life Cycle.* Paper presented at workshop on Theory Construction and Research Methodology, National Council on Family Relations, 1980.

Walker, L.S., & Wallston, B.S. Social adaptation: A review of dual earner family literature. In L.L'Abate (Ed.), *Handbook of Family Psychology.* Homewood, Ill.: Dow Jones-Irwin, in press.

Walker, K.E., & Woods, M.E. *Time Use: A Measure of Household Production of Family Goods and Services.* Washington, D.C. American Home Economics Association, 1976.

Working Family Project. Parenting. In R. Rapoport & R. Rapoport (Eds.), *Working Couples.* New York: Harper & Row, 1978.

Wright, J.D. Are working women really more satisfied? Evidence from several national surveys. *Journal of Marriage and the Family,* 1978, *40,* 301-313.

Yarrow, M.R., Scott, P., DeLeeuw, L., & Heinig, C. child-rearing in families of working and non-working mothers. *Sociometry,* 1962, *25,* 122-140.

Ybarra, L. When wives work: The impact on the Chicano family. *Journal of Marriage and the Family,* 1982, *44,* 169-178.

Yogev, S. Do professional women have egalitarian marital relationships? *Journal of Marriage and the Family,* 1981, *43,* 865-871.

Yogev, S. Are professional women overworked? Objective versus subjective perception of role loads. *Journal of Occupational Psychology,* 1982, *55,* 165-169.

Zaslow, M., Pederson, F.A., Suwalsky, J., & Robinovich, B. *Maternal Employment and Parent-infant Interaction.* Paper presented at meeting of the Society for Research in Child Development, Detroit, MI, 1983.

Chapter 8

Afro-American Women and Their Families

Doris Y. Wilkinson

The nature of the Black American family as a system interrelated with others in the larger sociocultural milieu has required articulation for some time. . . . In the analysis of any family constellation, a variety of theoretical perspectives is possible ranging from symbolic interactionism, structural-functionalism to. . . conflict theory and combinations of Freudianism-Marxism. Unfortunately, in the majority of instances where Black families have been examined by social scientists, they have been evaluated primarily from the frame of reference of social problem analysis. (Wilkinson, 1969, 810-819)

While there has been considerable modification in the descriptions and interpretations of Afro-American life and culture, there has been minimal systematic attention devoted to the study of Black women and the interplay of their multiple familial and work roles. Their economic statuses juxtaposed with their expressive and instrumental functions within family contexts have not been thoroughly examined. Nor have these been analyzed with regard to diverse lifestyle and role enactments that are a consequence of social class and political distinctions. Rather, historical placement, despite prevailing economic differences, has dominated the study of the variations between and among American families of African ancestry.

In this essay, I shall concentrate on the social and income characteristics of the families of Afro-American women. It is assumed, on

Doris Y. Wilkinson is Professor in the Department of Sociology at Howard University, Washington, D.C.

the basis of relevant sociological evidence, that familial values, modes of child rearing, patterns of socialization, husband-wife relationships, family life cycle events, forms of intergenerational continuity, and mutual aid with relatives, are directly correlated with labor force participation and hence social class. No attempt will be made to compare and contrast non-Black families at the various economic levels. The primary reason for this is that there are caste-like disparities in occupational, educational, and income statuses between Black and White women which place them in relatively fixed sectors of the stratification hierarchy and consequently in distinct political classes (Almquist, 1975; Beal, 1970; Bell, 1974; Dill, 1979; Downs, 1975; Hudis, 1977; Jackson, 1973; Lewis, 1977; Sorkin, 1972). Their labor force participation rates are also dissimilar.

My basic objective is to provide a synthesis of selected research findings on Afro-American women, especially as these apply to their relative socioeconomic positions. Data pertinent to understanding the multiple roles enacted by these women in their families and in their communities will be incorporated. In this connection, it is recognized that "Black women workers, moreso than white women have had a dual role as contributors to family income, often as primary earners" (Wallace, 1980, p. 2). Of particular interest will be the ideas and conceptions of Black women behavioral and social scientists.

A brief discussion of the historical and political forces that have affected contemporary roles of Black women in family milieux is warranted (Cade, 1970; Davis, 1971; Hale, 1977; Ladner, 1981; Lerner, 1972; Staples, 1973). Primarily, however, the literature presented will center on socioeconomic status variables as these relate to family functioning and organization as well as to lifestyles. It is assumed that beliefs, customs, and behaviors vary substantially by economic class and that these distinctions in turn affect family life (Bell, 1965; Billingsley, 1969; Davis, 1981; Jackson, 1975; Martin and Martin, 1978; Lewis, 1967; Radin and Kamii, 1965).

HISTORICAL CONTEXT

The economic and political history of the relationships between women of African heritage and their families has been markedly different from that of all other ethnic women in America. Their roles as wives, mothers, and workers are anchored in a slave and servant background (Davis, 1971; Malveaux, 1980) and their socioeconomic conditions have been defined and molded accordingly. The foundation and the traditions of Afro-American families, however, have revolved around the centrality of women, giving rise to a matricentric arrangement (Staples, 1972). In fact, despite the early disruption of their nurturing units under enslavement, the women of the plantation era managed to provide some modicum of stability to their households.

> Unlike the status of contemporary middle-class feminists, "ex-slave women everywhere dealt with a legacy that viewed them as dependent sexual objects" (Gutman, 1976, p. 390). During slavery, many women were forced to live with a slave husband whom they did not have a role in choosing. After emancipation, ex-slave husbands and fathers found it impossible to protect their daughters and wives from conventional ex-slave holder sexual abuse and insults. The psycho-cultural impact of this on slaves and ex-slaves. . . has not been analyzed by any historian or social scientist. In addition to the aforementioned events, concubinage did not terminate with emancipation. (Wilkinson, 1978, p. 832)

The systematic practice of family dissolution by slave holders "undermined the family as the fulcrum of the social order that blacks had known in West Africa, from which most slaves came, even though it never completely destroyed marriage and the family as important social institutions" (Blackwell, 1975, p. 36). In fact, "the institution of slavery only acted to reinforce the close bond that had already existed between mother and child in African society" (Ladner, 1981, p. 279). This sexist structural legacy gave rise to a distinct political experience on the part of Afro-American women— one which is at variance, for the most part, with the philosophy of the women's liberation movement (Dill, 1979; Gilliam, 1983; Hare and Hare, 1970; Kane and Wilkinson, 1974; LaRue, 1970; Morrison, 1971; Murray, 1971a, 1971b).

It is important to note here that before the Civil War the "opportunities for relatively stable sexual unions outside the institution of marriage not only varied from region to region but also depended upon the willingness of slaveowners to adhere to the laws regarding these unions" (Blackwell, 1975, p. 36). In the state of my mother's and father's families of origin—Kentucky—Black family life was intricately linked to that of White families by patterns of residence and by kinship. While my maternal grandmother was the daughter of an African slave, my paternal great-great-great grandfather was a white slave holder and the ancestor of my father's family and relatives. My paternal great-great grandfather and his wife were thus freed by their slave-holding fathers long before the Emancipation Proclamation. They are listed in the 1850 U.S. Census as free mulattoes. In addition, from the 1850s up to the early 1900s, they were given property which was passed on from one generation to another. This pattern of familial ties between slaves and those who owned, bought, sold, and exchanged them, was prevalent throughout the South. It resulted in differentiating slaves and free persons not only on the basis of paternity but also in terms of land—property. Class and color distinctions were thus formed early in the history of slavery. Further, several families in Casey County, Kentucky (named after the great-grandfather of Mark Twain) who had slaves bequeathed their names (Watkins, 1939). The surnames provide clues into the consanguinal ties and the primary group relationships between Euro-American families and those of African descent,

> The Coffeys, the Riffes, the Wilkinsons, the Walls, the Sweeneys, the Pattons, the Elliots, and the Burdetts all owned slaves. . . .The Burdett family of colored people were off-springs of Enoch Burdett, the eccentric white man who lived in Indian Creek. . .and who collected some thirteen thousand acres of land in Casey county. . .Enoch Burdett of color was a descendant of the white Enoch Burdett who died in 1875. (Watkins, 1939, p. 93)

During the eras of slavery and pre-Reconstruction, the roles of African women involved maintaining two households: their own and those of their masters or former owners. Many of the women, like Patsy Riffe, a former slave and one of my ancestors in Casey County for whom a school was named, purchased their husband's freedom with the money inherited from their masters (Thomas, 1978, p. 16, 209). Women in the deep South bore children fathered by their slave masters (Hine, 1981); yet they managed to display a strong sense of familial and maternal responsibility and a dedication to the survival of their households (Davis, 1971). Further, they worked, not only under the system of slavery, but after its dissolution as servants, cooks, chaperons, nurse maids, mid-wives, and "therapists" for white families.

It has been aptly observed, in this connection, that "the history of black women as domestic workers is rooted in the slave legacy of Black Americans" (Malveaux, 1980, p. 85). Their responsibilities to households other than their own were many and varied. Most of these domestic workers have always been female and poor.

A STEREOTYPE IN CHILDREN'S TOYS

Despite the multiplicity of roles, a single image was captured and sustained in American culture—in art, folklore, the social and behavioral sciences, the contemporary mass media until recently, and even in the market place with children's toys (Wilkinson, 1980). That prominent image was the one of the "Mammy," a caricature of the matriarch. The portrayals in the universe of dolls, manufactured in American and European countries between the mid 1800s through World War II, have been of particular research interest to me because of their importance as instruments of socialization and political indoctrination (Andreas, 1969; Parker, 1980; Wilkinson, 1974; Wilkinson, 1980).

Like other cultural artifacts, play objects document psychocultural eras and offer retrospective accounts of societal beliefs. Values and customs of the larger political order filter through the technical make-up, design, form, and characteristics of material products. The shape and features of dolls are especially illuminating as graphic evidence of the social history and collective psychology of a society. As cultural objects, they provide significant archaeological clues to a people—their shared ideas, folkways, and norms for behavior (*Newsweek*, 1968; Pantovic, 1974; Wilkinson, 1980).

From the 1890s up to the Depression years, the most well-known and economically profitable play artifact was the classic Aunt Jemima. Typically, dolls of this type, reflecting toy makers' perceptions of Afro-American women, were fat with round faces, attired in a servant's outfit. Historical interpretations indicate that this classic figure was perceived as the "ideal good Negro" woman servant. Similar artifacts were labeled "Darky Nurse Rag Doll" and "Southern Mammy." Each of these portrayals, originating in a system of enslavement, was perpetuated with the institutionalization of domestic servant occupations (Guzman, 1938). In this connection, contemporary feminists have recognized the political and psychological consequences of stereotyped language and definitions for women's opportunities in the economic sphere.

Actually, the names for black dolls constituted status differentiating labels very much like the designations of women and men of African ancestry in Casey County and elsewhere in the South as "Aunt" and "Uncle." This was the custom in the South (Thomas, 1978, p. 16). Such labels, however, are important for the information they provide about macro-structural forces and the matrix of societal beliefs. They also function to mold perceptions and attitudes. "Some. . .are exceedingly salient and powerful. They tend to prevent alternative classification or even cross-classification. Ethnic labels are often of this type. . ." (Allport, 1958, p. 175). Throughout the nineteenth and early to mid-twentieth centuries, the purposefully distorted conceptions of the Black female reinforced family stereotypes (King, 1973).[1]

Despite the economic and social influences which were antithetical to the survival of families of Americans of African descent, the women in their roles as mothers, grandmothers, aunts, and sisters served as expressive and instrumental role providers (Bernard, 1966; McCray, 1980; Rodgers-Rose, 1980). Yet, they may be "the only ethnic or racial group which has had the opportunity to be women. . . . This freedom, as well as the tremendous hardships from which Black women suffered, allowed for the development of a personality that is rarely described in the scholarly journals for its obstinate strength and ability to survive" (Ladner, 1972, p. 280). The socio-economic contexts out of which contemporary Afro-American families have evolved gave rise to a unique "interplay between the black woman's family role and her work role" (Wallace, 1980, p. 100).

SOCIODEMOGRAPHIC VARIABLES

In addition to political and economic forces, sociodemographic variables as well as differences in regional location have affected Afro-American family composition and structure. The latter represent two dimensions which have dominated the sociological literature for four decades. In the early U.S. censuses, most Black families were clustered in the rural south. This geographic locus was associated both with the organization of family life as well as with the types of work performed by men and women. Two-parent house-holds were dominant. Families were stable and the mothers worked as domestic servants in the households of whites, an economic status arrangement giving rise to distinct modes of constructing political realities.

Data on Black family composition available since 1940, reveal a trend of increasing proportions of households maintained by women (McEaddy, 1976; Ross and Sawhill, 1975; Stein, 1970). For at least three decades, between 1940-1970, the majority were husband-wife families. But by 1980, Black women experienced exceptionally high divorce rates (257 per 1,000) (U.S. Bureau of the Census, 1980). With the decline in the proportions of husband-wife families, there has been an accompanying decrease in the proportion of own children living with both of their parents (U.S. Bureau of the Census, 1978). By 1982, more than half of the estimated 6.4 million Black families were intact, while 41 percent were maintained by women.

Changes in the structure and function of Afro-American families are related to a number of political variables and sociodemographic processes such as emergence of a color caste, property ownership, patterns of internal mobility and geographic settlement, decline in agrarian way of life, high unemployment rates, a highly technologi-cal society, and the aftermath of World Wars I and II. All of these have affected the employment status of Black males (Wilkinson and Taylor, 1977) in the wider society and hence the entire family con-figuration. One consequence is that among the lower and working strata, a large number of females, out of necessity, have had to sup-port their families without the assistance of a male wage-earner.

In addition to these social and political events, Black families con-tinue to be disproportionately affected by business cycles in the na-tional economy. That is, the dual impact of recessions and inflation have a devastating impact on the stability and functioning of Afro-American families. As the income levels of family units have been altered so have the instrumental and expressive roles of women within them.

SOCIAL CLASS DETERMINANTS OF FAMILY ORGANIZATION

Afro-American women assume numerous diverse roles in their families—as mothers, grandmothers, aunts, and workers. But these vary depending on family economic origins, residential location, and income status, as well as on their own marketable skills and hence employability. Families of African heritage that live in poverty have quite different generational histories, family organizations, and life styles from those in the working or blue collar strata, the middle and upper income strata, and even those in the lower but working group. Values and beliefs of the mother and her attitudes toward child bearing and rearing, the presence of husbands and fathers, the employment status of either or both parents, the numbers of children, the modes of socialization—all of these vary by social class position (Billingsley, 1969; Davis, 1981; Kamii and Radin, 1967).

THE STRUGGLING POOR

The struggling poor are engaged in a perpetual "struggle for existence" (Willie, 1976, p. 94). As a result, their aspirations, wants, and achievements are more restricted than those of middle and working-class family members (Jackson, 1975). Women's roles within them also vary. Understandably, parenting among the poor is secondary to the struggle for survival, thus women must invest considerable energy finding ways to feed and clothe their children. Often even the search for a place to live is rendered difficult by the absence of adequate financial resources. This is especially problematic for those single-parent mothers in poverty (Kriesberg, 1970). The economic status of the impoverished female-headed household is a critical variable which determines many facets of family life (McEaddy, 1976; Stein, 1970) over successive generations.

In many fatherless families from the "struggling poor" sector, grandmothers and grandfathers often assume major responsibilities for childrearing. In addition, cooperation among siblings is common. There are strong customs of mutual support between sisters and brothers. Thus, the mothers who don't have husbands in the poor or low income strata may have alternative networks from which to seek aid. Often, however, their siblings and their parents are unable to provide any meaningful financial support. What is important is the degree of loyalty and the emotional strength of these consanguinal ties.

Those in the lower economic classes who are employed have a somewhat different outlook than the chronically unemployed; i.e., those comprising an "underclass." Yet, receiving public assistance or welfare makes it difficult for many mothers to seek employment since wages for unskilled work are often not equal to assistance payments. Further, non-working or economically poor women frequently have more children than can be maintained on such wages. At the end of the 1970s, it was estimated that "half of the 2.1 million black female heads of families were in the labor force, employed mostly in low-paying, low skill jobs" (Wallace, 1980, p. 80). Nearly half of these had not completed high school and most were below the designated poverty threshold at the time.

Despite difficulties in meeting basic survival needs, mothers in the lower strata have positive aspirations for their children (Bell, 1965; Jackson, 1975; McMillan, 1967, Radin and Kamii, 1965; Webster, 1965). They are concerned about economic and health needs of their offspring and are aware of the impact of their class-status and family culture on the children's lives and futures. There is a close interaction between class and culture among those in the lower social classes (Lewis, 1967), but this association exists for families at any income level. In fact, one of the basic premises of stratification theory is that a direct correlation exists between family socioeconomic status and its structure and functioning.

Similar to those in the working class, families designated as among the struggling poor do not participate in community activities, although for parents who work, church attendance assumes an important function. Among Afro-Americans, the church is a family social and religious institution. Further, women in households with inadequate financial resources tend to have a fatalistic world view. "Such a *weltanschauung* is related to the economic structure in which the poor are situated. Although in a subordinated position in the larger society, lower-class black families are cognizant of societal goals and institutional means for their acquisition" (Wilkinson, 1978, p. 834). Frequently, retreatist or withdrawal behavior is manifested. But, this is primarily a reaction to a social and political milieu to which "they cannot commit themselves" (Willie, 1976, p. 133). The plight of these poor families in a land of "plenty" represents a serious contradiction in America's value scheme (Stewart, 1974).

WORKING CLASS FAMILIES

Unlike the "struggling poor" and more like their middle class counterparts, working class households tend to be married-couple families, although the traditional structural features are changing.

These changes coincide with those occurring for all American families. In this economic stratum, dual employment of parents is a necessity since husbands often are unskilled, and even if skilled, have low paying jobs. Black women play strategic roles when neither parent has college training and neither is in an economically viable position. They share many of the child rearing and socialization values of middle class mothers. Yet, childhood is supervised not only by mothers, but by maternal kin as well. Husbands typically work long hours and thus do not have the time to devote to their children's upbringing as do fathers in the middle and upper classes.

In working class families, Afro-American women lack the educational attainments of women in the middle income groups. Many are unskilled and their occupational statuses are low and hence the families have lower economic levels. "Although working-class parents tend to be high school drop-outs, they desire more education for their children than they have achieved" (Wilkinson, 1978, p. 834). This point has been emphasized in studies of the social organizational characteristics of Black families of working class origin.

Although internal strength is characteristic, "black working class family life involves a continuous struggle for survival" (Willie, 1976, pp. 13-14) which affects significantly the aspirations of family members. Yet, children are viewed with a special pride as a contribution to society, a factor which might account for larger family sizes among the working than the middle strata. Parenting roles and work responsibilities are assumed earlier in working class family units than in middle class families (Wilkinson, 1978, p. 834; Willie, 1976, p. 66).

Among family members in this stratum, consistent parental roles and the durable nature of the nuclear household represent salient organizational features. Parents and children constitute a closely knit group which insulates its members from external economic and psychological stresses as much as possible. Although both spouses assume appropriate parenting behaviors, mothers are the fulcrum around which household functions revolve. They are responsible for inculcating basic values and rules, always anticipating a better life for their offspring. In their parental roles, women prefer egalitarianism. Yet, they expect their husbands to have an equal responsibility or at least "an equal say" in raising the children. The male role model in the stable working-class family is highly important for maintaining internal stability. Where the mother is absent through divorce or death, fathers may be found serving as single parent householders. However, "the proportion of male-headed families varies markedly from city to city and from region to region" (Blackwell, 1975, p. 41). Understandably, in terms of economic and socio-historical forces, a single male-headed household is an infrequent structural form.

THE MIDDLE CLASS

Simultaneously with the growth of a large black "under-class," there is an increasing "better educated, younger, and highly qualified middle class" (Wallace, 1980, p. 83). Distinctions among the families of African heritage, as previously indicated, are a consequence of their differential economic histories and disparate positions in the stratification system (Barrett and Morgenstern, 1970; Bock, 1959; Bryant, 1971; Davis, 1981; Hare and Hare, 1970; Wallace et al., 1980). While the "matriarchy" has an economic and political basis and has been traditionally associated with lower and working class families (Lincoln, 1966; Mack, 1971), women in the middle income strata have quite different family organizations, work ethics, political beliefs, and behaviors from those in the "struggling poor" or in working nonpoor families. Yet, they encounter comparable forms of discrimination in the occupational sphere as women and men in the other socio-economic groups, although it is difficult to extricate the effects of race from those of gender (Almquist, 1975; Beal, 1970; Bryant, 1971; Epstein, 1973; Green, 1969; Malcolm et al., 1976; Sorkin, 1972).

Middle class mothers are not only more likely to be married and in stable nuclear households, they are also a part of functional mutual aid and intergenerational networks (McAdoo, 1975; McAdoo, 1980). However, "middle class values are more compatible with a nuclear than an extended family" (Martin and Martin, 1978, p. 76). Further, their patterns of child care differ substantively from those of mothers in the lower and working classes (Billingsley, 1968; Comer and Pouissant, 1975). Typically, men in these families are the heads of the household. With respect to work status, usually, both spouses are employed. "Well-educated black women have learned how to balance the demands of the work environment. . . and the demands of their home" (Wallace, 1980, p. 101).

Among middle class families, children reside with their parents. The mothers in these nuclear units not only work to supplement household income, they also serve as occupational role models. In the middle class, clerks, postal workers, and school teachers are disproportionately represented. Predictably, family norms revolve around higher education for children, being thrifty; requiring them to be obedient to their fathers and grandparents, to attending Sunday school, and to associate with peers who are in the same social class—an expectation which parents cannot completely control, especially if their children attend large heterogeneous public schools. There is a tendency for those in the middle stratum "to feel under pressure not only from the expectations family members have of them, but sometimes from what is expected from them by the black community" (Martin and Martin, 1978, p. 78).

Conventionally, Black women in middle economic class families participate actively in church events and in the social functions of their clubs or college sororities. Although significant proportions must work, some find the time to participate in voluntary organizations, although many of these are social clubs.

In Black middle income families, there appears to be a synthesis or blending of spousal and occupational roles (Himes, 1960). Decision-making is a joint responsibility, particularly with regard to major expenditures such as buying a new car, a home, or sending the children to private schools or to college. Often grandmothers and aunts are important in this area and frequently babysit during childrearing years when the mother works. Further, in times of financial exigency, extended kin networks are vital in the support system (McAdoo, 1975). They are also essential when the family is disrupted by children deviating from basic parental values or in case of divorce or death.

Overall, middle class families are characterized by: (1) relatively sufficient family income, (2) conformity to American norms of morality, (3) close supervision of childhood, (4) dual employment of husband and wife, (5) at least one spouse with a college education, (6) belief in upward mobility, (7) close attachment and involvement with children's goals and lives and (8) expectation that offspring will use their parents as role models (Willie, 1976). Parents in this economic stratum anticipate that their children will reflect the values which they have acquired during childhood and adolescence (Gurin and Gaylord, 1976). One of the basic concerns of mothers as well as fathers is that the children go to college. Maternal and paternal grandparents and siblings adhere to the same goals, reinforcing those in the family of procreation.

THE UPPER CLASS

According to the limited literature on the small population of upper class families of African lineage, women lead an entirely different life from those in the economically poor and in the working classes. They devote much of their energies to the home and child-rearing and in later stages of the life cycle to participating in service and voluntary associations. Some of them hold professional degrees (Epstein, 1973). Children, ordinarily planned for, are viewed with special pride. However, women in upper class Black families, like their white counterparts, have fewer offspring at slightly later ages than do women in the working and lower socio-economic classes. On the other hand, also like higher status whites, one may find large families—three or more children. They are well-bred and usually attend the best private schools, often with few blacks. Sacrifices, made early in life, are solely for the purpose of perpetuating the family-heritage and its values.

With respect to specific life style behaviors, mothers in Black upper class families make frequent visits to doctors to ensure the health of themselves and their family members. Costs are not major concerns since most upper class families of African ancestry have a solid background in this economic class. In 1968, when the classic study of *Black Families in White America* was published, it was pointed out that the "new upper class" families contrasted with those in the "old" upper stratum. The established group was "much more likely to be highly educated for the professions, to have reached the peak of their fame at older ages than the new upper classmen, more likely to be light in complexion, and to have grown up in nuclear families with strong fathers" (Billingsley, 1968, pp. 129-130; Wilkinson, 1969). Intergenerational continuity among traditional upper class families is reflected in family customs, behavioral styles, and role models rather than in help patterns or kin relationships based on mutual aid.

Upper class Black women are well integrated in their communities, churches, and in local political and service organizations. Their involvement is primarily a consequence of the status of their husbands but may result from their own achievements, especially in the "new" upper class. Families in this economic stratum live in the best homes in suburban or rural-urban fringe communities and are often referred to as members of an "elite" (Freeman, 1976). This designation has also been applied to established middle-class families. Some of the enduring dimensions of the structure and functions of upper class families include: (1) inherited wealth, (2) sufficient economic security, (3) home ownership, (4) inherited property, (5) long history of stability, (6) middle to upper class life style background, (7) organizationally-oriented rather than church centered, (8) sharing the customs and habit of the wealthy, and (7) wives, if employed, are in high status occupations.

Interestingly, in the late forties, three social scientists captured the general attitudes, beliefs, and folkways of Afro-American women in the upper class (Drake and Cayton, 1945; Frazier, 1958). Many of their observations are applicable today. In fact, it was noted that because of their heritage and property status, women at the higher socio-economic levels share a value perspective which converges with that of members of a "wealthy leisure class" (Frazier, 1958, p. 330). However, today most Black wives who are unemployed or "who do not work represent an impoverished class which is significant within the Black population but rather small within the white population. . . . White wives who do not work represent an enriched class" (Bell, 1974, pp. 472-474)!

Using oral history and ethnography, three decades ago, Black sociologists found that upper class families tend to be basically egalitarian. Despite the tendency of wives not to work, they enjoy a position of equality in decision making as well as considerable freedom in their social and community activities. Even if the wife is financially dependent on the husband, she plays a significant role in determining how family income is distributed, how the household is to be organized, and how the children are to be reared.

SUMMARY

In America, the central figure in Afro-American families is the mother. This is so regardless of the family's rank in the social stratification hierarchy. As wives, mothers, aunts, sisters, daughters, and grandmothers, Afro-American women have always been the primary resources for the maintenance of family stability and intergenerational continuity. They are also the basic agents for the rearing and socialization of children. Regardless of their economic positions, however, they have higher levels of aspiration for their children than they may have held for themselves. It is only in the lower and working classes that "there is an expectation that offspring will not use parents as role models" (Willie, 1976). As this discussion has shown, a behavioral emphasis such as this is at variance with the expectations characteristic of those families with sufficient or substantial incomes.

Since the arrival of their ancestors in the United States, women of African/European descent have functioned in a variety of roles in their families. They have been important and dependable linkages between fathers and their children, grandparents, and maternal and paternal relatives. In the two-parent working or middle income extended family, "it is unusual for a male to be groomed for the role of dominant figure" (Martin and Martin, 1978, p. 25). Pertinent social science literature has revealed the overriding importance of women in giving strength to the family system (Hill, 1971) and in integrating it with the larger community. As mothers and kin liaisons on whom others have relied for guidance and emotional support, these women have given cohesiveness to the family institution among Americans of African lineage (McAdoo, 1980; Myers, 1975; Myers, 1980; Reid, 1972; Rutledge, 1980).

If our society can create the social, economic, and political means to meet the survival needs of those who are chronically unemployed, the unemployable, and those comprising the "struggling poor," then the extra burdens on Black women in the lower socioeconomic strata could be relieved (Barrett and Morgenstern, 1970). While this is unlikely on a grand scale in a nation that is endemically and permanently stratified, it is important to indicate that since the arrival of their ancestors, Afro-American women have served as exemplary models in their families, a fact which has transcended economic status distinctions. Yet, the reciprocal influence of familial and work roles has been characterized by strains in the past. It is not certain that this will be alleviated "as employment discrimination against black males is diminished" (Wallace, 1980, p. 100). What is needed at the national level in the decade ahead, is "a set of pro-family policies in employment, ownership, housing. . .and other external systems, which are vital to the support of the internal workings of Black families" (Billingsley, 1981).

BIBLIOGRAPHY

Allport, W. *The Nature of Prejudice.* Garden City, New York: Doubleday & Co., Inc., 1958.
Almquist, E. M. Untangling the effects of race and sex: The disadvantaged status of black women. *Social Science Quarterly,* 1975, 56, 129-142.

Andreas, C. War toys and the peace movement. *Journal of Social Issues*, 1969, 25, 83-99.
Barrett, N. and Morgenstein, R. Why do blacks and women have high unemployment rates? *The Journal of Human Resources*, 1974, 9, 452-464.
Beal, F. Double jeopardy: To be black and female. In Toni Cade (Ed.), *The Black Woman: An Anthology*. New York: New American Library, 1970, 90-100.
Bell, D. Why participation rates of Black and White wives differ. *The Journal of Human Resources*, 1974, 9, 465-479.
Bell, R. The lower-class Negro mother's aspirations for her children. *Social Forces*, 1965, 43, 493-500.
Bernard, J. *Marriage and Family Among Negroes*. Englewood Cliffs, New Jersey: Prentice-Hall, 1966.
Billingsley, A. *Black Families in White America*. Englewood Cliffs, New Jersey: Prentice-Hall, Inc., 1968.
———. Family functioning in the low-income Black community. *Social Casework*, 1969, 50, 563-572.
———. Black families in White America: A challenge for the 80's. *Black Family*, 1981, 1, 14-18, 22-23.
Blackwell, E. The Black family in American Society. In James Blackwell, *The Black Community: Diversity and Unity*. New York: Dodd, Mead and Co., 1975, 35-64.
Bock, E. W. Farmer's daughter effect: The case of the Negro female professionals. *Phylon*, 1959, 30, 17-26.
Bryant, W. C. Discrimination against women in general: Black southern women in particular. *Civil Rights Digest*, 1971, 4, 10-11.
Cade, T. *The Black Women: An Anthology*. New York: New American Library, 1970.
Comer, J. P. and Poussaint, A., Jr. *Black Child Care: How to Bring Up a Healthy Black Child in America*. New York: Simon and Schuster, 1975.
Davis, A. Reflections on Black women's role in the community of slaves. *The Black Scholar*, 1971, 3, 2-15.
———. *Women, Race and Class*. New York: Random House, 1981.
Dill, B. T. The dialectics of Black womanhood. *Signs*, 1979, 4, 543-555.
Downs, J. Black/White dating. In D. Wilkinson (Ed.), *Black Male/White Female: Perspectives on Interracial Marriage and Courtship*. Morristown, New Jersey: General Learning Press, 1975, 159-170.
Drake, S. C. and Cayton, H. R. *Black Metropolis*. New York: Harcourt, Brace and Co., 1945.
Epstein, C. F. Positive effects of the multiple negative: Explaining the success of Black professional women. *American Journal of Sociology*, 1973, 78, 912-935.
Frazier, E. F. *The Negro in the United States*. New York: The Macmillan Company, 1958.
Freeman, R. *Black Elite*. New York: McGraw-Hill, 1976.
Gilliam, D. Shortsighted. *The Washington Post* November 7, 1983, 1.
Green, B. M. Upgrading Black women in the supervisory ranks. *Personnel*, 1969, 46, 47-54.
Gurin, P. and Gaylord, C. Educational and occupational goals of men and women at Black colleges. *Monthly Labor Review*, 1976, 99, 10-16.
Gutman, H. *The Black Family in Slavery and Freedom: 1750-1925*. New York: Pantheon Books, 1976.
Huzman, J. P. The role of the Black mammy in the plantation household. *Journal of Negro History*, 1938, 23, 349-369.
Hale, J. The Woman's Role: The Strength of Black Families. *First World*, 1977, 1, 28-30.
Hare, N. and Hare, J. Black woman 1970. *Transaction*, 1970, 8, 65-68, 90.
Hill, R. *The Strengths of Black Families*. New York: National Urban league, Inc., 1971.
Himes, J. S. Interrelation of occupational and spousal roles in a middle class Negro neighborhood. *Marriage and Family Living*, 1960, 22, 262-263.
Hine, D. and Wittenstein, K. Female slave resistance: The economics of sex. In F.C. Steady (Ed.), *The Black Woman Cross Culturally*. Cambridge, Mass.: Schenkman Publishing Co., 1981.

Hudis, P. M. Commitment to work and wages: Differences of Black and White women. *Sociology of Work and Occupations,* 1977, 4, 123-146.

Jackson, J. Black women in a racist society. In C.V. Willie, B. Kramer, and B. Brown (Eds.), *Racism and Mental Health.* Pittsburgh: University of Pittsburgh Press, 1973.

Jackson, R. H. Some aspirations of lower class Black mothers. *Journal of Comparative Family Studies,* 1975, 6, 171-181.

Kamii, C. K. and Radin, N. L. Class differences in the socialization practices of Negro mothers. *Journal of Marriage and the Family,* 1967, 29, 302-310.

Kane, P. and Wilkinson, D. Survival strategies: Black women in *Ollie Miss* and *Cotton Comes to Harlem. Critique: Studies in Modern Fiction,* 1974, 16, 101-109.

King, M. C. The politics of sexual stereotypes. *Black Scholar,* 1973, 4, 12-23.

LaRue, L. Black liberation and women's lib. *Transaction,* 1970, 8, 59-64.

Ladner, J. A. *Tomorrow's Tomorrow: The Black Woman.* Garden City, New York: Doubleday & Company, Inc., 1971.

Racism and tradition: Black womanhood in historical perspective. In F. C. Steady (Ed.), *The Black Woman Cross-Culturally,* Cambridge, Mass.: Schenkman Publishing Co., Inc., 1981, 269-288.

Lerner, G. (Ed.), *Black Women in White America: A Documentary History.* New York: Pantheon Books, 1972.

Lewis, D.K. A response to inequality: Black women, racism, and sexism. *Signs,* 1977, 3, 339-361.

Lewis, H. Culture, class and the behavior of low-income families. In H. Lewis (Ed.) *Culture, Class and Poverty.* Washington, D.C.: Health and Welfare Council of the National Capital, 1967, 13-42.

Lincoln, C. E. A look beyond the matriarchy. *Ebony,* 1966, 21, 111-114, 116.

Mack, D. E. Where the Black matriarchy theorists went wrong. *Psychology Today,* 1971, 24, 86-87.

Malcolm, S., Hall, P. Q. Brown, J. W. *The Double Bind: The Price of Being a Minority Woman in Science.* Report No. 76-R-3. Washington, D.C.: April, 1976.

Malveaux, J. From domestic worker to household technician: Black women in a changing occupation. In Phyllis A. Wallace, et al. (Eds.), *Black Women in the Labor Force.* Cambridge, Mass.: The MIT Press, 1980.

Martin, E. P. and Martin, J. M. The dominant family figure. In E.P. Martin and J.M. Martin, *The Black Extended Family.* Chicago: The University of Chicago Press, 1978.

McAdoo, H. P. The extended family. *Journal of Afro-American Issues,* 1975, 3, 291-296.

———. Black mothers and the extended family support network. In La Frances Rodgers-Rose (Ed.), *The Black Woman.* Beverly Hills, Cal.: Sage, 1980.

McCray, C.A. The Black woman and family roles. In La Frances Rodgers-Rose (Ed.), *The Black Woman.* Beverly Hills, Cal.: Sage, 1980.

McEaddy, B. J. Women who head families: A socio-economic analysis. *Monthly Labor Review,* 1976, 99, 3-9.

McMillan, S.R. Aspirations of low-income mothers. *Journal of Marriage and the Family,* 1967, 29, 282-287.

Morrison, T. What the Black woman thinks about women's lib. *The New York Times Magazine,* 1971, August 22: 14-15, 63-64, 66.

Murray, P. The liberation of Black women. In *Voices of the New Feminism,* M. L. Thompson (Ed.), Boston: Beacon Press, 1971a.

———. The Negro women's stake in the equal rights Amendment. *Harvard Civil Rights— Civil Liberties Law Review,* 1971b, 6, 253-259.

Myers, L. W. Black women and self esteem. In M. Millman and R.M. Kanter (Eds.), *Another Voice.* Garden City, New Jersey: Doubleday, 1975.

Black women: Do they cope better? New Jersey: Prentice-Hall, 1980.

Newsweek. Black Christmas. Newsweek, 1968, 72, December 9, 79-80.

Pantovic, S. Black antiques reveal history of stereotypes. *Sepia,* 1974, 23, 44-48.

Parker, P. Contemptible collectibles. *Perspectives: The Civil Rights Quarterly,* 1980, 12, 19-23.

Radin, N. and Kamii, C.K. Child-rearing attitudes of disadvantaged Negro mothers and some educational implications." *Journal of Negro Education,* 1965, 34, 138-146.

Reid, I. S. *Together Black Women.* New York: Emerson Hall Pub. Co., 1972.

Rodgers-Rose, L. F., (Ed.), *The Black Woman.* Beverly Hills, California: Sage Publications, Inc., 1980.

Ross, H. L. and Sawhill, I. V. *Time of Transition: The Growth of Families Headed by Women.* Washington, D.C.: The Urban Institute, 1975.

Rutledge, E. Marital interaction goals of Black women: Strengths and effects. In La Frances Rodgers-Rose (Ed.), *The Black Woman.* Cal.: Sage Publications, Inc., 1980, 145-159.

Sorkin, A.L. Occupational status and unemployment of nonwhite women. *Social Forces,* 1971, 44, 393-398.

Staples, R. (ed.), *The Black Woman in America: Sex, Marriage and the Family.* Chicago: Nelson-Hall Publishers, 1973.

Stewart, C. T. *Low-Wage Workers in an Affluent Society.* Chicago: Nelson-Hall, 1974.

Thomas, G. C. *Casey County, Kentucky: 1806-1977.* Casey County, Kentucky: Bicentennial Heritage Corporation, 1977.

U.S. Bureau of the Census. *The Social and Economic Status of the Black Population in the United States: An Historical View, 1700-1978.* Current Population Reports. Special Studies. Series P-23. No. 80, 1978.

Wallace, P. A., Datcher, L. and Malveaux, J. *Black Women in the Labor Force.* Cambridge, Mass.: The MIT Press, 1980.

Watkins, W.M. *The Men, Women, Events, Institutions and Lore of Casey County, Kentucky.* Louisville, Kentucky: The Standard Printing Co., 1939.

Webster, S.W. Some correlates of reported academically supportive behaviors of Negro mothers toward their children. *Journal of Negro Education,* 1965, 34, 114-120.

Willie, C. V. *A New Look at Black Families.* Bayside, New York: General Hall, Inc., 1976.

Wilkinson, D. Review: *Black families in White America. Journal of Marriage and the Family,* 1969, 31, 810-811.

――――. Racial socialization through children's toys: A sociohistorical examination. *Journal of Black Studies,* 1974, 5, 96-109.

――――. *The Black Male: Perspectives on His Status in Contemporary Society.* Chicago: Nelson-Hall Publishers, 1977.

――――. Toward a positive frame of reference for analysis of Black families: A selected bibliography. *Journal of Marriage and the Family,* 1978a, 40, 707-708.

――――. The Black family: Past and present: A review Essay. *Journal of Marriage and the Family,* 1978b, 40, 829-835.

――――. Minority women: Social-cultural issues. 285-304 In A. Brodsky and R. Hare-Mustin (Eds.), *Women and Psychotherapy.* New York: The Guilford Press, 1980a, 285-304.

――――. Play Objects as Tools of Propaganda: Characterizations of the African American Male. *The Journal of Black Psychology,* 1980b, 7, 1-16.

Chapter 9

Men in Families

Peter J. Stein

OVERVIEW

Culture, history, and social structure generate systematic differences in access to and exercise of power, prestige, and privilege among and between men and women. This background reality is the basis for our examination of the role of men in the contemporary American family.

Although a substantial amount of the research literature suggests that the more things change, the more they remain the same, there is in fact evidence of some change, but just how much and in what areas is a matter of considerable disagreement. Far less problematic is the continued dominance of traditional patterns.

Due to space limitations we will focus only on intact heterosexual families and men's roles within that constellation, including the interface between family and work.

Our data come from national surveys, regional samples, and published and unpublished interviews with couples and individuals. We pay particular attention to dual-earner and dual-career families because these are the structures within which most gender role changes are occurring.

Further, we will treat men as a social category and statistical aggregate, but not as a self-conscious social group sharing collective goals. Men are a superordinate stratum, having greater power, prestige, and privilege than women, although there are critical within-group differences by class, race, and age. In addition, there is con-

Peter J. Stein is Associate Professor in the Department of Sociology, William Paterson College, Wayne, NJ.

The author gratefully acknowledges the invaluable editorial support provided by Beth Hess and Ellen Rope and the manuscript preparation support provided by Yvonne Chilik.

The chapter is dedicated to the memory of my father, Victor Stein.

siderable overlap between men and women in terms of access to and control of scarce resources.

THE SOCIAL CONTEXT OF GENDER ROLES

There are, of course, substantial variations in gender roles across cultures as well as within cultures. Family and peer group expectations, socialization experiences, and cultural influences are important determinants of the rigidity or openness of gender role definitions. Despite the new flexibility in gender role, whatever men do tends to be more highly valued than what women do, setting the basis of gender stratification.

Explanations of gender inequality have been offered in terms of sociobiological factors (Tiger and Fox, 1978); of functional theory (Parsons, 1951; Gilder, 1973); of conflict theory (Collins, 1975; Blumberg, 1978; Sanday, 1981); and even of sex ratios (Guttentag and Secord, 1983). Since the research evidence suggests very few biologically based differences that could support a system of gender stratification, one must examine economic and political system factors, ideology, and socialization practices. In our society, boys appear to be under particularly strong pressures to conform to a cultural ideal of masculinity. In addition, as both boys and girls develop, they organize their self-perceptions around gender identity and thus become active in their own socialization. The result is that most young people enter adulthood more or less adequately conforming to societal expectations.

What about those men who reject, rebel, or simply fail to follow the appropriate norms? The dominant paradigm blames such "problems" on the individual's failure, usually with the help of faulty socialization agents, to acquire a "masculine sex-role identity." The main focus in the study of male sex roles up to now has been the understanding and remediation of the *lack* of culturally desirable levels of masculinity; that is, the research question is "what went wrong?" In his critique of the MSRI model, Pleck (1981) proposes an alternative model—"sex role strain." This model focuses on the socio-cultural definitions of masculinity and femininity, and the strains placed on men and women who attempt to live up to these ideal norms. This shifts attention from the individual to the roles themselves: "what is being learned?" "what behavior is taking place?" and "what are the consequences of such learning and behavior?"

CONSTANCY AND CHANGE
IN GENDER ROLE ATTITUDES

Recent national surveys of gender role attitudes reflect both good news and bad: attitudes are becoming more liberal, but at an exceedingly slow rate (Pleck, 1983). Only a minority (between 10 to 40 percent) of respondents in various studies believe that men should do more housework and childcare than they currently perform. But when asked specifically about husbands of employed women, half the men in a recent survey supported equal sharing of domestic tasks. In addition, the attitudes of both men and women, particularly the younger and more educated cohorts, are becoming increasingly similar. Of the five major studies reviewed by Pleck (1983), two showed no difference between female and male respondents' opinions on men's involvement in the home, while three found more support for increased involvement among the men. It appears that some women have a vested interest in maintaining control over the domestic sphere, perhaps as threatened by their husbands' encroachment on their territory as many men feel by women's increased occupational participation and opportunities.

The general trend toward liberalized sex-role perceptions is also reported by Cherlin and Walters (1981) in their re-analysis of national opinion data between 1972 and 1978. Among white men and women, the major attitudes shift occurred between 1972 and 1975, with little subsequent change. Among blacks, egalitarian attitudes were already common in 1972 and have remained constant throughout the decade. Black women continue to be more supportive of nontraditional sex-role attitudes than black men. Increasingly large percentages of all respondents support employment for married women, as well as high political office for women.

Changes in sex-role attitudes are related to age and to birth cohorts. In one longitudinal study of women and their children spanning 18 years from the children's birth in 1962 to 1980, Thornton, Alwin, and Camburn (1983) found a clear trend toward egalitarian perceptions of gender roles. Sons and daughters were more egalitarian than their mothers had been as young adults, suggesting that young couples today will enter cross-sex relationships and begin married life with more flexible role expectations than in the past. Further, attitudes can also change to meet new situations, so that many traditional couples may find it necessary to change their expectations and behaviors in response to new realities.

Additionally, a recent study of over 14,000 students at seven elite women's colleges (two of which also enroll men) found that students increasingly support shared work and family roles (Zuckerman, 1983). More than one-third of the women planned careers in fields formerly restricted to men, and more than one-third of the men expressed a preference for part-time work while their children were pre-schoolers. Similarities in the responses of women and men students were striking: 90 percent planned to go to graduate school, 93 percent wanted to get married, and 88 percent wanted to have children.

It is difficult to predict future behavior from the current beliefs of college men, particularly those in elite schools where there are many sanctions against holding "old-fashioned" attitudes. We cannot know how many and which of these men will revert to conventional attitudes as they enter adulthood. Conversely, other men may become more egalitarian through the influence of the women they date, live with and marry, particularly if the men can continue to believe that their masculinity is intact. Much depends on economic and cultural factors, supportive social environments, the norms of friendship groups, and the interaction between the women and men involved.

Men have no monopoly on contradictions; women's expectations of men's roles are also marked by ambivalence. To summarize data from a *Psychology Today* survey (a sample of 28,000 adults biased in the direction of young, well-educated, and affluent respondents): women "don't just want a man who is merely sweet, thoughtful, loving, gentle, and faithful; they also rate being successful at work more heavily than men do. . . . The ideal men are strong but gentle, tough on the outside and soft on the inside, able to express emotions but not be a slave to them" (Tavris and Offir, 1977, 39). The study also found that a majority of all respondents valued emotional competence and disclosure in men and rejected extreme "macho" traits.

CONSTANCY AND CHANGE
IN GENDER ROLE BEHAVIOR

While there is extensive evidence, reported in this issue of *Marriage and Family Review* and elsewhere, of dramatic changes in women's behavior in the areas of work, education, and politics, data on men's behaviors are less clear. According to Fox (1983); ". . . for men, in sum, we see only the most tentative of steps beyond their traditional sex-role prescriptions. While some men are exploring their "expressive" side and others are enlarging the father role, most men continue to experience changes in sex roles only indirectly—through their wives who now work, their daughters and granddaughters who join sports teams and aspire to careers as well as marriage, through their lovers who will not give up their futures for men, through women at work who pay for their own lunches and do not flirt" (1983, 155).

The research available and reviewed here indicates a more complex situation. Men's behavior is changing, although not quickly enough for some.

MEN'S FAMILY ROLES

Joseph Pleck, who has done the most extensive research on many aspects of men's roles, suggests that while at a more superficial level there are increasingly positive social values about men being more highly involved in their family roles, at a deeper level there is continued social ambivalence toward such changes. Pleck notes little support for active institutional-level change to support men in their family roles.

Conceptually Pleck (1977) suggests thinking in terms of a work/family role system, interrelated and interdependent. Rather than analysing family roles *per se,* his research indicates that men's family role conflicts with their breadwinner role and women's family role.

TIME SPENT IN FAMILY ROLES

One way to examine men's family roles is through studies of time allocation. Several techniques for measuring time spent in housework and child care exist. Using completed time diaries, Pleck (1983), in a 1975-76 national study, found that employed husbands spend nearly two hours a day on family work, household and child care, compared to four hours for employed wives and six and three-quarter hours for nonemployed wives. Husbands do about 32 percent of the couple's total family work when the wife is employed and about 21 percent when the wife is not employed. Husbands do somewhat less family work when there are pre-schoolers in the house and somewhat more when there are no children (which for a majority of couples is when they are newly married) (Pleck, 1983:132). In addition, when asked for estimates of time spent, husbands as well as wives thought they spent substantially more time on household and childcare tasks than their time budgets indicated. Yet even with these higher figures, husbands still do less than wives.

In a 1975-76 national study of time use the researchers conclude that ". . .despite the historically high rate of labor force participation of women, the proposed ERA amendment and the women's liberation movement—all presumably interacting to raise public consciousness about equal treatment for individuals of both sexes—time use patterns in the mid-1970s clearly indicate sex differences within all ten broad categories of activities'' (Hill et al., 1983, 19). Women spent approximately twice as much time as men in household work, particularly cooking, cleaning, and laundry, while men spent most of their time on upkeep and repairs of the house, car, and lawn. Married women in full-time employment spent an average of 39 hours a week on the job and 25 hours on housekeeping, for a total of 64 work hours. The total for married men was 61 hours a week—48.5 on the job and 12.6 at home.

A major result of this household work imbalance is the role overload experienced by employed wives. Although the entire family benefits from the wife's employment, she bears most of the costs of increased work load (Feree, 1984, this issue). From his review of studies of the family adjustment of dual-earner couples, Pleck concludes that the more family work done by the wife, the greater her role overload and the poorer her emotional adjustment and sense of well-being though the effect is not strong (1983, 146).

Yet a number of studies indicate an increase in husbands' family work associated with wives' employment and the fact that husbands of working wives do more family work than the husbands of nonemployed wives. The 1977 Quality of Employment Study, indicates that "husbands of employed wives perform about a half-hour per day more family work" (Pleck, 1983, 136).

Further evidence of change comes from a comparison of time use data between 1975-6 and 1981-2. Juster (1983) reports that the master trend is for men to spend less time in paid employment and more in housework than before, while women have moved in the opposite direction. Moreover, within the household, tasks are becoming less sex-stereotyped. These trends toward greater equality were most marked among younger adults, and suggest changes that will accelerate in the future.

In summarizing the studies, Pleck cautions that though "husbands of employed wives clearly perform a higher proportion of the couple's total family work. . .the increase is small in absolute magnitude, and employed wives continue to do the bulk of the family work" (1983, p. 138).

MEN'S ROLES IN DUAL-EARNER AND DUAL-CAREER FAMILIES

The family structure within which most gender role changes are occurring are dual-earner and dual-career families. With more than 50 percent of wives employed in the labor force and with a dramatic increase in two-career couples, dual-earner families are the new American family norm. They enjoy substantially higher median incomes than single-earner families, but also experience unique problems. There is much evidence that despite their role overload, employed wives and mothers derive many benefits in mental health and self-esteem (Booth and Edwards, 1980; Kessler and McRae, 1981). In contrast, Kessler and McRae (1982) report that husbands of employed women showed slightly higher levels of depression and lower self-esteem than did men whose wives were not in the labor force. But husbands' dissatisfaction was not due to their increased burdens of home and child care. Men who are sufficiently supportive of their wives to take on added domestic tasks are the most comfortable in such roles. Nor was the wife's income a major threat; indeed, there was a slight positive correlation between wives' earnings and husbands' self-esteem. Rather, the men who did the least family work and who held the most traditional attitudes were the most likely to experience distress.

In addition, Kessler and McRae (1982) found that the impact of wives' employment on husbands' mental health varied by age cohort, with younger men least affected. Other research indicates that younger people display a "new breed" value constellation of cooperation, equality, and tolerance (Yankelovich, 1981). As summarized by Zick Rubin, men who hold these new values may not only accept their wives' employment with equanimity, but may even demand it, suggesting a future in which more men will be upset by wives who do *not* work than by wives who do (1983).

In an increasing proportion of dual-earner families, both husband and wife pursue individual careers with relatively equal commitment, focus, and vigor (Pepitone and Rockwell, 1980). As the number of such couples increases, so do the analyses of their stresses and strains (Holmstrom, 1972; Rapoport and Rapoport, 1976; Rice, 1978; Aldous, 1982). While the chief advantage reported by such couples is their high income and range of life-style choices, wives complain of having "too much to do" and husbands of not having "enough time together" (Catalyst, 1981).

Among a sample of couples with graduate degrees in business administration and full-time jobs, the wives more often assumed responsibility for household management and child care, and worried about these while at work (Matthews and Matthews, 1980).

In a study of physicians, one-third of the women, but none of the men, reported that marriage and family responsibilities led them to change career directions (Nadelson et al., 1980). Similarly, a study of women in law, medicine, and college teaching found that more than one-half of these women coped with parental and work roles by temporarily lowering their career ambitions and saw their career involvement as having a lower priority than their husbands' (Poloma, 1972). In yet another study, of 200 pairs of psychologists, the researchers found the husbands "did very little at home to help their wives" (Bryson, Bryson, Licht, and Licht, 1976). In addition, to the husbands' low participation, the researchers found institutional constraints which cause the wife's career to be subordinated to that of her husband.

While both wives and husbands experience role overload in dual-career marriages (Hall and Hall, 1979), a review of the literature indicates that women experience greater stress (Skinner, 1980; see also Piotrkowski and Repetti, this issue). The adoption of a dual-career life-style involves greater departure from traditional social and marital role patterning for women than for men (Rice, 1978). When scheduling conflicts occur, it is most often the wife who rearranges her time. All the available research clearly indicates that wives experience greater role overload and role conflict (Martorella and Stein, 1983).

Other inequities are also evident. Two different studies indicate that in almost every case, the couple relocated in response to the husband's career needs even though most respondents claimed both careers were of equal importance (Catalyst, 1981; Poloma et al., 1982).

Adding to the problem are discrepancies in perceptions regarding household role-sharing; several studies indicate that husbands thought they were helping more than their wives thought they were. Husbands tended to see the outcome of their participation as positive, while their wives judged the results as less satisfactory or negative. Husbands generally underestimated their wives' overload and stress.

But the husbands themselves faced a lack of external support. Some of the husbands wished to increase their family involvement, but sometimes experienced negative sanctions from relatives and business colleagues who felt that sharing child care is "cute" but basically "unprofessional" and even "unmanly" (Martorella and Stein, 1983). Poloma et al. (1982) conclude that the current structure of the American family makes it virtually impossible for women to pursue career lines similar to those of men, or at least not without extreme role conflict, despite the help of supportive husbands.

MEN'S FAMILY ROLES AND SOCIAL CLASS

The reports cited earlier are primarily based on middle- and upper middle-class men. Are these generalizations true for men from other classes? Curiously, little research has been done on variations in the male role by class, race, ethnicity, or age. Most of the findings contradict each other: one study indicates that older men do more housework while another shows that younger men do more; newlywed husbands do more housework, but so do retired husbands; high-income earners do the least housework in one sample and they do the most in another (Pleck, 1983).

In an often-cited study of working-class couples, Rubin (1976) noted the persistence of traditional behavior among the men. Her working-class male respondents felt confused and threatened by their wives' new demands for companionate relationships; unable to communicate effectively, husbands and wives talked past one another.[1]

But Rubin also notes the discrepancy between what men say and what they do. It appears that the working-class men who find it so difficult to express themselves actually do more to help their wives around the house than do the middle-class husbands who can "talk a better line" about sharing but whose career commitments may limit involvement in family work (Blood and Wolfe, 1960; Ericksen et al., 1979). For example, Model (1982) found that low-income husbands shared 19 percent of the household chores in contrast to 6 percent for men with incomes above the median. Of course, higher income men and couples can hire household help and can spend time sharing other activities.

Studies indicate that husbands' participation is greatest when the income differential between the spouses is smallest, which is more typical of low-income earners than of high earners. And in a five-year study, Farkas (1976) found that the propensity of husbands and wives to share household tasks is "barely responsive to wage ratio, more strongly influenced by children, and most strongly influenced by educational level" (p. 482).

Of the seven studies that examine racial differences, two report that black husbands do more household work than white husbands, and two studies show the precise opposite; one found that black husbands increase their family work in response to their wives' employment, another showed a lowering of involvement, and the seventh reported no effect. The research record is similarly inconsistent with respect to men's participation in child care (reviewed by Pleck, 1983).

But Charles Willie (1981), in a more qualitative examination of black fathers than those reviewed by Pleck, reports substantial equality within black families. With respect to affluent black families, Willie notes that the economic success of such families is due to the "cooperative work of the husband and wife. . .a genuine team effort" (1981, 48). Similarly, with respect to black working-class families, Willie notes that the economic reality of trying to survive is so basic "that relationships between the husband and wife take on an equalitarian character" (1981, 53). Yet here, as with white families, there is an identifiable division of labor so that husbands are concerned primarily with finances, the maintenance and repair of the home, and as "the chief adviser for the boys." Wives tend to be responsible for cooking and cleaning, act as the chief advisor to the girls, and maintain contact with the school and the church (Willie, 1981, 53).

WHY DON'T MEN DO MORE?

Scanzoni and Fox (1980) suggest that men do not do more household work because they get little support from women or from other men. Other researchers contend that men's paid work is so demanding that there is little time or energy left for housework. Still another argument is based on traditional socialization and ideological supports for the breadwinning role to the exclusion of other involvements. Pleck's evaluation of these hypotheses concludes that ". . . the demands of men's jobs clearly have a limiting effect on their family roles, and account for some variation in male's family time (but) this variation occurs around a low baseline that is *not* determined by the demands of the male breadwinner role" (1983, 140). Even when work demands on men are reduced, as in Sweden's paternity leave policy, few choose to use the time to increase family work.

Yet work demands are real and constitute a major source of strain for men. Based on their national sample of 1,084 adults, Pleck et al. (1978, 1980) identified three major forms of work-family conflict: excessive work hours, schedule conflicts, and psychological spill-over, namely fatigue, irritability, and preoccupation with work while with the family. Surprisingly, the researchers found that men and women experience work-family conflict in about the same degree, with about 35 percent of all married workers with children reporting moderate or severe conflict. Parental status was the major background characteristic affecting conflict. These findings correspond with earlier studies that indicate that work-related problems are more severe among working parents (Keith and Schafer, 1980; Bohen and Viveros-Long, 1981; Voydanoff, 1982). Keith and Schafer's (1980) study of 135 dual-earner families indicated that hours worked per week, age, and the number of children at home are major sources of work-family strain among husbands. For wives, all the same variables, plus husbands' hours worked per week, were significant. In a study of two federal agencies, Bohen and Viveros-Long (1981) found that men scored higher on one of two indices of work-family stress while the women scored higher on the other. Flextime, a policy in one of the agencies, reduced the reported stress felt by the workers.

Though both women and men experience the problem of balancing the demands of work and family, and both report the same frequency of conflict, men experience it primarily as "excessive work time," while women experience it as primarily involving "schedule problems" and "psychological spillover."

Working parents must perform several roles: worker, parent, and in most cases, spouse. Each role involves stressors including normative events, normative transitions, and on-going role problems (Boss, 1980; Pearlin et al., 1981).

For both men and women, work-family conflict was associated with long work hours, high psychological involvement with work, frequent overtime, working other than day shifts, inflexible work schedules, and psychologically demanding work (Pleck, 1983, 156). The two other negative outcomes of such conflicts are lowered family adjustment, lessened happiness with one's marriage, and decreased overall well-being.

However, here as in other studies, Pleck notes contradictory results in studies of both frequency and adjustment to conflict. Results seem to depend primarily on sample characteristics. Moreover, Pleck suggests that the crucial predictor may not be the level of conflict, but the "feeling that one has not coped with the conflict well" (Pleck, 1983, p. 156).

MEN'S SATISFACTION WITH FAMILY ROLES

One of the more intriguing findings of survey research is the high degree of satisfaction men derive from their family roles. The research evidence indicates a seeming contradiction: men do less housework and are less involved with child care and yet claim to gain substantial satisfaction from family roles. Indeed, "men who are more involved in their work than their family are still a minority" (Pleck, 1983, 153). This may say more about the nature of most men's work than about their family life, but several researchers have remarked on this "unexpected finding." For example, interviews with working- and lower middle-class husbands found that the men spoke with great pride and emotion about their children, their wives, and the quality of their marriages (Lein, 1974). Farrell and Rosenberg (1981) were impressed with the importance of family relationships in helping men deal with problems of midlife. And Glenn and Weaver (1979) conclude from their review of major national survey data that men derive as much satisfaction from their marital and parental roles as do women, rating these even above work as a source of well-being. The implications for increasing men's involvement in housework and child care are important. Men's high degree of psychological involvement should make the task of changing their behavior easier (Pleck, 1982).

MEN AND FATHERING

How does men's lower family work participation affect father-child relationships and the children's development? Traditionally fathers were viewed in terms of their instrumental functions. Though much more is known about motherhood, a substantial literature demonstrates the important influence of fathers on children's development from infancy to adolescence, particularly the potential negative effects of low father involvement with their sons (Biller, 1971, 1974; Lamb, 1981).

Pleck (1983) notes a confluence of arguments that greater male involvement in the family is desirable and should have beneficial effects on children. Yet some of these arguments are contradictory, particularly on fathers' effect on children's gender roles. Greater father involvement in the rearing of children has been urged by both those who see it as encouraging the development of appropriate "sex role identity" since boys need male role models, and by those who see such behavior as encouraging more flexible gender roles by showing that men can be nurturant and by breaking down traditional sex role stereotypes (Pleck, 1983, p. 147). Pleck suggests that the consequences for specific personality development in children will depend on the nature of paternal involvement.

While it is fashionable to support greater involvement by fathers in child care, the full effects of such participation are not yet clear. A substantial literature argues that children, especially sons, need strong sex-role models in order to develop appropriate gender identities. Yet more recent work challenges the notion that father involvement leads to traditional sex-typing. Rather, there is evidence that children who interact frequently with their fathers display lower levels of sex-role stereotyping and higher levels of cognitive development (Lynn, 1974; Baruch and Barnett, 1981; Radin, 1981). Both effects are probably the consequence of seeing the father in nontraditional activities.. As Pleck (1983) notes, much more systematic data are needed before any firm conclusions about the benefits to children of enhanced interaction with their fathers can be reached.

The *Fatherhood Project* (Levine et al., 1982; Klimmer and Kohl, 1984) is a growing network of researchers and activists concerned with promoting a more active role by fathers in the care and nurturing of their children. A small but growing number of men—typically young professionals married to professionally successful women—are increasingly involved in family work and some are even deliberately assuming the role of househusband (Beer, 1983). In general, young men today, in contrast to their fathers, hold more "nurturing" views of fatherhood and place less emphasis on the provider role (Eversoll, 1979). Russell (1978) found that fathers with less rigid sex role orientations were more involved in the day-to-day care of their children than were traditionally "masculine" fathers. Russell (1981) also notes that the fathers involved in child care were likely to have attended childbirth preparation classes, to have assisted at the birth, and to have read books on child development.

Men's increased involvement with parenting will also have positive effects on husbands and wives who want more father involvement. For example, there is evidence that mothers perform better in their parenting role when they have the help and support of their husbands (Pederson, 1976). Studies conducted by Michael Lamb and his associates (Lamb, 1981) show that fathers of infants can be as effective and nurturant as mothers. Similarly, Parke and Sawin (1976) found fathers to be as "sensitive and responsive to infants' cues" during feeding sessions as mothers. One longitudinal study of parents who shared childcare responsibilities equally found that parents reported improved family relationships and personal happiness as a result (Defrain, 1979).

SOCIAL FORCES IMPEDING
AND SUPPORTING CHANGE

In the final section of this paper we examine the major factors impeding change (namely men's more privileged social status) and the major sources of change (the impact of the women's movement, and changes in women's roles). We conclude by outlining ways in which men's involvement in families can be supported.

Why Should Men Change?

In a recent essay, William J. Goode (1982) asks why any superordinate group should willingly share power. He notes that while in the short run men may perceive the women's movement to have little direct effect on their lives, in the long run they will have to adjust to women who want more equality. What bothers men most, claims Goode, is their "loss of centrality" as the focus of attention has shifted to women, who are less exclusively available to meet men's needs for solace and intimacy. No longer is the male role indispensible or of such intrinsic value to women that it warrants extra rewards of power, prestige, and privilege.

This loss of centrality and attendant confusions are also documented by Robert Lewis (1981) in an aptly titled book, *Men in Difficult Times*. The difficult times come from the questioning of traditional images of masculinity, and from the greater costs in physical and mental health imposed by men's superior status. Scanzoni (1979) identifies two themes in the literature on men's roles: first, men should want to change because that is what is right, fair and best for the entire family unit (the "altruistic" strategy), and second, men themselves would be better off in egalitarian relationships (the "self-interest" strategy). Changes in family roles are achieved through negotiation over "emergent concerns." Not surprisingly, men have been slower than women to renounce their traditional privileges.

Goode also notes that our family laws still assume husbands are "good and kindly men" and are assured of their own generosity, protectiveness, and wisdom. In this sense, men may feel threatened by the women's movement and its challenge to their "family coalition," but also angered at the discrimination experienced by their wives and daughters at the hands of less trustworthy men. They may be particularly hurt and angered that their "gifts" to and support of other family members are no longer gratefully received, or their sacrifices fully appreciated.

The Impact of Women's Changing Roles on Men

There can be little disagreement that the changes in women's roles as a result of the feminist movement have had a dramatic impact on men and men's roles in the family and society. By challenging the assumptions of appropriate gender behavior, the feminist movement has led women—outside as well as inside the movement—to re-examine their roles and relationships. In the process, many men have been forced to confront similar questions.

The accepted wisdom has been that any changes in men's roles would come as a result of pressure from women, but Barbara Ehrenreich (1983) argues that the realization of the dilemmas and difficulties of masculinity actually preceded, rather than followed, the women's movement. It was the earlier weakening of husband's commitment to wives and children, she suggests, that provided the impetus for both feminism and anti-feminism. Men were already rejecting the breadwinner ideology and its burdensome responsibilities in the 1950s in favor of the "free spirit" image so well projected by

Playboy magazine. She claims that with a shift toward self-indulgence couched in the jargon of personal growth and human potential, the male "revolt" against maturity in general and women in particular has been underway for three decades. This male flight from domesticity left women with two choices: struggle for self-sufficiency via the route of feminism, or struggle to bind men more tightly to the family unit via the route of anti-feminism.

Others have criticized this cause and effect sequence, suggesting that the historical evidence indicates simultaneity. Tavris (1983) notes Ehrenreich is not certain if the male revolt is just a "childish flight from responsibility, an accommodation to the consumer culture, or a liberation movement for social change." Given the diversity of our society, all these factors may be at work. Our reading of the research indicates that for a sizable number of men, there is evidence of genuine struggles for change.

SUPPORTING MEN'S INVOLVEMENT WITH THEIR FAMILIES

Our knowledge of how social change comes about suggests a complex interaction between changes at the level of individual values and behavior and changes in institutions. Change in personal values is not sufficient since individuals are constrained by social structures. Institutional change alone may not be sufficient because individuals do not always take advantage of even limited institutional changes. For example, most men do not use paternity leaves when they are available and most men do not use flextime to spend it with their families.

Pleck (1982) offers a three-stage model of change. First, a number of factors are likely to make men want to be more involved with their families. Among these are women's participation in the labor force and the attendant family demands caused by employment, the birth of children, men's career changes, midlife transitions, and a re-examination of their own values. Secondly, many men who want to be more involved in child care and housework may feel limited by their lack of skills and supports. They might experience low self-confidence stemming from the changes mentioned above, or lack peer group support or encouragement from their own wives. Thirdly, men who want greater family involvement and manage to overcome skills and support barriers could then experience the constraint of institutional barriers. Among these constraints are the demands and inflexibility of work schedules, career timing that requires the greatest investments of energy and time in the earlier stages of career development—a period when family demands are also greatest—and the trade-offs involved in balancing men's family involvement and total family income, since men's earnings are, on the average, greater than women's. Added to these institutional barriers are (1) the still-powerful belief that men's work is generally more important than women's work, (2) the cultural support of the centrality of the breadwinner role, and (3) the continuing, though diminishing, emphasis on women's mothering and family roles.

Each of these three areas of change suggests certain interventions. Men's increasing desire for family involvement could be supported through "mass-based" educational programs. Men's skills, self-confidence, and support can be increased through workshops, educational programs, and greater mass media coverage. As one example, the Fatherhood Project offers a series of courses and workshops both locally and nationally. Men's support groups are targeted to smaller, self-selected groups of husbands and fathers.

Decreasing the effect of structural barriers may be the most difficult of all interventions. The major way to reduce the trade-off between men's family involvement and total family income would be to increase women's earnings. Increasing the availability of public child care centers and on-site day care centers would ease the strain on two-wage families. Among more obvious intervention strategies are flexible work schedules, institutional support for paternity leaves, benefits for part-time work, and counseling for couples. Such policy changes would affect all employees, even though not all would take advantage of them. The assessment, development, and implementation of needed policies could help reduce the unnecessary conflict between work and family roles. Through such interventions men would be able to achieve equal participation in family roles by both women and men would be supported.

NOTE

1. Friedman and Sarah (1982) argue that working-class "machismo" or inexpressiveness is a posture that men must present to management in their class struggle over wages and control of the work process. It is a class-related behavior and personality pattern.

REFERENCES

Aldous, J. 1982. *Two paychecks: Life in dual-earner families.* Beverly Hills, CA: Sage Publications Inc.

Baruch, G. and R. Barnett. 1981. Father's involvement in the care of their preschool children. *Sex Roles,* 7, 1043-1055.

Beer, W. 1983. *Househusbands: Men and housework in American families.* New York: Praeger Publishers.

Biller, H. 1971. *Father, child, and sex role.* Lexington, MA: Heath.

———. 1974. *Paternal deprivation: Schools, sexuality, and society.* Reading, MA: Heath.

Blood, R. and D. M. Wolfe. 1960. *Husbands and wives: The dynamics of married living.* New York: Free Press.

Blumberg, R. 1978. *Stratification: socioeconomic and sexual inequality.* Dubuque, IA: Brown.

Bohen, H. and A. Viveros-Long. 1981. *Balancing jobs and family life: Do flexible work schedules help?* Philadelphia: Temple University Press.

Booth, A. and J.N. Edwards. 1980. Fathers: The invisible parent. *Sex Roles,* 6, 445-456.

Boss, P.G. 1980. Normative family stress: Family boundary changes across the life span. *Family Relations,* 29, 445-450.

Bryson, J., R. Bryson, M. Licht, and B. Licht. 1976. The professional pair: Husband and wife psychologists. *American Psychologist,* 31, 10-16.

Corporations and two-career families: Directions for the future. New York: Catalyst, 1981.

Cherlin, A. and P. Walters. 1981. Trends in United States Men's and Women's Sex Role Attitudes. *American Sociological Review,* 46, 453-460.

Collins, R. 1975. *Conflict sociology.* New York: Academic Press.

deFrain, J. 1979. Androgynous parents tell who they are and what they need. *Family Coordinator,* 28, 237-243.

Ehrenreich, B. 1983. *The hearts of men: American dreams and the flight from commitment.* New York: Anchor Press.

Ericksen, J., W. Yancey, and E. Ericksen. 1979. The division of family roles. *Journal of Marriage and the Family,* 41, 301-312.

Farkas, G. 1976. Education, wage rates, and the division of labor between husband and wife. *Journal of Marriage and the Family,* 38, 473-484.

Farrell, M. and S. Rosenberg. 1981. *Men at midlife.* Boston: Auburn House Publishing Co.

Friedman, S. and E. Sarah (Eds.). 1982. *On the problem of men: Two feminist conferences.* London: The Women's Press.

Fox, G. 1983. Sex roles. In R. Hagedorn (Ed.), *Sociology.* Dubuque, IA: Brown Co. Publishers.

Gilder, G. 1973. *Sexual suicide.* New York: Quadrangle.

Glenn, N. and C. Weaver. 1979. A note on family situation and global happiness. *Social Forces,* 57, 960-967.

Goode, W. 1982. Why men resist. In B. Thorne and M. Yalom (Eds.), *Rethinking the family.* New York: Longman.

Guttentag, M. and P. Secord. 1983. *Too many women? The sex ratio question.* Beverly Hills: Sage Publishers.

Eversoll, D. 1979. A two-generational view of fathering. *Family Coordinator,* 28, 503-508.

Hall, F. and D. Hall. 1979. *The two-career couple.* Reading, MA: Addison-Wesley.

Hill, M. 1983. *Patterns of time use.* Unpublished manuscript, University of Michigan.

Holmstrom, L. 1972. *The two-career family.* Cambridge: Schenkman.

Juster, F. 1983. *A note on recent changes in time use.* Unpublished manuscript, University of Michigan.

Keith, P. and R. Schafer. Equity in marital roles across the family life cycle. *Journal of Marriage and the Family,* 43, 359-367.

Kessler, R. and J. McRae. 1981. Trends in the relationship between sex and psychological distress: 1957-1976. *American Sociological Review,* 46, 443-452.

Kessler, R. and J. McRae. 1982. The effect of wives' employment on the mental health of married men and women. *American Sociological Review*, 47, 216-227.

Klinman, D. and R. Kohl. 1984. *Fatherhood U.S.A.: The first guide to programs, services, and resources for and about fathers.* New York: Garland Publishers, 1984.

Komarovsky, M. 1976. *Dilemmas of masculinity.* New York: W. W. Norton.

Lamb, M. (Ed.). 1981. The role of the father. In *Child Development,* 2nd edition, New York: Wiley.

Lein, L. 1974. Male participation in home life: Impact of social supports and breadwinner responsibility on the allocation of tasks. *Family Coordinator, 28,* 489-495.

Levine, J., J. Pleck, and M. Lamb. 1982. The fatherhood project. In M. Lamb and A. Sagi (Eds.), *Fatherhood and Social Policy.* Hillsdale, NJ: Erlbaum.

Lewis, R. (Ed.). 1981. *Men in difficult times.* Englewood Cliffs, NJ: Prentice Hall.

Lynn, D. 1974. *The father: His role in development.* Monterey, CA: Brooks/Cole.

Martorella, R. and P. Stein. 1983. *Corporations and dual-career couples.* Unpublished manuscript, William Paterson College.

Matthews, J. and L. Matthews. 1980. Going shopping: The professional couple in the job market. In F. Pepitone-Rockwell (ed.) *Dual-career couples.* Beverly Hills, CA: Sage.

Nadelson, C. and T. Nadelson. 1980. Dual-career marriages: Benefits and costs. In F. Pepitone-Rockwell (Ed.), *Dual career couples.* Beverly Hills, CA: Sage Publishers.

Parke R. and D. Sawin. 1976. The father's role in infancy. *Family Coordinator, 25,* 365-372.

Parsons, T. 1951. *The social system.* New York: Free Press.

Pearlin, L., E. Menaghan, M. Lieberman, and J. Mullan. 1981. The stress process. *Journal of Health and Social Behavior, 22,* 337-356.

Pederson, F. 1976. Does research on children reared in father-absent families yield information on father influences? *Family Coordinator, 25,* 459-464.

Pepitone-Rockwell, F. 1980. *Dual career couples.* Beverly Hills, CA: Sage Publishing.

Pleck, J. 1977. The work-family role system. *Social Problems, 24,* 417-424.

———. 1980. The work-family problem: Overloading the system. In B. Forisha and B. Goldman (eds.), *Outsiders on the inside: Women in organizations.* Englewood Cliffs, NJ: Prentice Hall.

Pleck, J., H. Staines and L. Lang. 1978. *Work and family life.* In the 1977 Quality of Employment Survey. Wellesley, MA: Wellesley College Center for Research on Women, Working Papers.

———. 1980. Conflict between work and family life. *Monthly Labor Review,* March, 29-32.

Poloma, M. 1972. Role conflict and the professionally employed woman. In C. Safilios-Rothschild (ed.), *Toward a sociology of women.* Lexington, MA: Xerox Publishing.

Poloma, M., B. Pendleton, and T. Neal Garland. 1982. Reconsidering the dual-career marriage: A longitudinal approach. In J. Aldous *Two Paychecks.* Beverly Hills, CA: Sage Publishing.

———. 1981. *Myth of masculinity.* Cambridge, MA: MIT Press.

———. 1982. Male sex roles and midlife transition. Paper presented at the NJCFR annual conference on Men's Changing Roles, William Paterson College, October 1, 1982.

———. 1983. (In press.). Husband's paid work and family roles: Current research issues. In H. Lopata and J. Pleck (eds.), *Research in the interweave of social roles,* Vol. 3: *Families and jobs.* Greenwich, CT: JAI Press.

———. 1983. Theory of male sex role identity. In M. Lewin (ed.), *In the shadow of the past: Psychology portrays the sexes.* New York: Columbia University Press.

———. 1983. Men's power with women, other men, and society: A men's movement analysis. In *The American Man* and *Feminist Frontiers,* 1983. Englewood Cliffs, NJ: Prentice Hall.

Radin, N. 1981. The role of the father in cognitive, academic, and intellectual development. In M. Lamb (ed.), *The role of the father in child development.* New York: Wiley.

Rapaport, R. and R.N. Rapaport. 1976. Dual-career families re-examined. New York: Harper.

Rice, D. 1978. *Dual-career marriage: Conflict and treatment.* New York: Free Press.

Rubin, L. 1976. *Worlds of pain.* New York: Harper and Row.

Rubin, Z. 1983. Are working wives hazardous to their husband's mental health? *Psychology Today,* 17, 70-72.

Russell, G. 1978. The father role in relation to masculinity, femininity, and androgyny. *Child Development,* 49, 1174-1181.

———. 1981. *A multivariate analysis of fathers' participation in child care and play.* Unpublished manuscript, Marquette University.

Sanday, P. 1981. Female power and male dominance: On the origins of sexual inequality. *Sex Roles,* 8, 1157-60.

Scanzoni, J. 1979. Strategies for changing male family roles: Research and practice implications. *Family Coordinator,* 28, 435-442.

Scanzoni, J. and G. Fox. 1980. Sex roles, family, and society: The seventies and beyond. *Journal of Marriage and the Family,* 42, 743-756.

Skinner, D. 1980. Dual-career family stress and coping: A literature review. *Family Relations,* 29, 473-481.

Tavris, C. and C. Offir. 1977. *The longest war.* New York: Harcourt, Brace, Jovanovich.

Tavris, C. 1983. Who started this? review of *The hearts of men. New York Times,* June 5, 1983, p. 12, 19-20.

Thornton, A., D. Alwin, and D. Camburn. 1983. Causes and consequences of sex-role attitudes and attitude change. *American Sociological Review,* 48, 211-227.

Tiger, L. and R. Fox. 1978. *The imperial animal.* New York: Dell.

Voyandoff, P. 1982. Work roles and quality of family life among professionals and managers. In B. Hirschlein and W. Brown (eds.), *Families and Work.* Stillwater, OK: Oklahoma State University.

Willie, C. 1981. *A new look at black families,* 2nd edition. Bayside, NY: General Hall.

Yankelovitch, D. 1981. *New rules: searching for self-fulfillment in a world turned upside down.* New York: Random House.

Zuckerman, D. Career and life goals of freshman and seniors. *Radcliffe Quarterly,* Sept. 1982, 17-19.

Chapter 10

Changing Family Roles and Interactions

Maximiliane E. Szinovacz

Popular literature and textbooks depict an image of family relationships undergoing rapid change. Slogans such as "Changing
Families," "Families in Transition," or "Marriage and Alternatives" increasingly replace the simple "Marriage and the Family"
titles of previous textbooks. In contrast, feminists insist that women's
position in the family is still subject to traditional role expectations
and behaviors. At the center of this critique are analyses of the division of labor between spouses and power asymmetries between the
sexes (Thorne, 1982; Bernard, 1982; Freedman, 1979; Richardson
and Taylor, 1983).

In this paper, evidence of changes in family roles and interaction
within the last two to three decades is reviewed, emphasizing issues
at the center of the feminist critique, namely, the division of labor
between spouses, power and decision-making processes, and sexual
relations.[1] In the first section of the chapter, models of family
change are outlined and criteria for the assessment of change are
presented. Subsequent sections depict changes in selected role domains, and appraise available empirical evidence as well as theoretical contributions. The chapter concludes with an overall evaluation
of familial role changes over time and some speculations on future
trends.

Maximiliane E. Szinovacz is Associate Professor in the Department of Sociology at the
Florida State University.

I would like to express my special thanks to Beth Hess for her comments and extensive
editorial work.

MODELS OF FAMILY CHANGE

Several writers contend that families are becoming more egalitarian with greater sharing of family roles. Already three decades ago, Burgess (1973, originally 1954)[2] projected a movement from the "institutional" to the "companionship marriage," a change characterized by increased equality in marital relations, an emphasis on affection and personal happiness rather than the fulfillment of prescribed roles and duties, and enhanced attention to the personality development of family members rather than to common family objectives (p. 157). A similar perspective is evident in the concept of the "symmetrical" family" (Young and Willmott, 1973), defined as a shift toward less sex segregation in familial roles.

Another model developed by Scanzoni (Scanzoni and Scanzoni, 1976; Scanzoni, 1980) focuses on the balance of power between the sexes, and distinguishes among four major types of relationships: (1) owner-property (absolute power of husband), (2) head-compliment, (3) senior-junior partner, and (4) equal partner (fully balanced). Despite his emphasis on power relations, Scanzoni clearly links the presumed trend toward egalitarian marriages to changes in other family roles, particularly increased sharing of the breadwinner role by husband and wife. Further elaborations of this model point to additional fundamental differences between "traditional" and "modern" marriages: in the goal orientations or "guiding philosophies" spouses pursue, as well as in their negotiation styles (Scanzoni, 1978; Scanzoni and Szinovacz, 1980). The marriage based on traditional prescribed sex-role preferences[3] allows spouses to assume and enact familial roles without open discussion or overt negotiations. In contrast, the flexibility and role interchangeability typical for marriages based on norms of sharing, equality, and sex-role transcendence (Pyke, 1980; Rebecca et al., 1976) do not permit such "salient arrangements." The "modern" couple is, therefore, forced to negotiate openly responsibilities and duties. In addition, while women were traditionally expected to pursue family rather than personal interests, and men's authority and provider role entitled them to primary consideration, the guiding philosophy for the modern marriage is one of joint maximum profit, i.e., both partners' interests are equally important and decision-making assures the wellbeing of all family members.

A somewhat different model is proposed by Dixon (1976). She holds that equality between the sexes requires full abolition of the sexual division of labor. Since traditional marriages are character-ized by a rigid division of labor with the female assuming roles in the domestic realm (sexual relations, reproduction, socialization and homemaking) and the male in the public sphere (politics, education, economic production), full equality can only be achieved if the structural linkages among roles within these two domains decline and roles are no longer ascribed by sex.

The assumption of a linear trend toward companionship, sym-metry, or equal partnership implied in these models has been ques-tioned by Hunt and Hunt (1977, 1982) who envision crystallization of different life styles rather than a general trend toward more role sharing and equality. Three major variations in life styles are dis-tinguished: (1) traditionalists who resist change, (2) prioritizers who arrange their life around distinct priorities (either careers or fami-lies), and (3) integrators, i.e., spouses who work together and at-tempt to integrate family and work roles. Each of these variants is expected to develop independently of the others, leading to in-creased polarization of familial life styles, accompanied by little change in social and economic institutions.

Apart from Hunt's model, these formulations are in basic agree-ment on the direction and content of current and future changes in family roles. Major defining characteristics of the two polar family types which I prefer to call sex-role segregated and sex-role tran-scendent[4] are summarized in Table 1. They should be understood as ideal types in the Weberian sense. Sex-role segregated families fol-low rigid, normatively prescribed sex roles which assign the pro-vider role and authority to the husband/father and the homemaker and childcare roles to the wife/mother. The marital relationship tends to be task-oriented, and women's interests are considered sec-ondary to those of men. Inherently associated with this division of roles and authority is a sexual double standard (Reiss, 1960) and an extension of role segregation to the couple's social networks (Bott, 1957). In contrast, roles and responsibilities in sex-role transcendent marriages are flexible, resulting from negotiation between the part-ners rather than from ascription by sex. Spouses are expected to share all familial responsibilities and to have equal authority and sexual rights. The enactment of familial roles is flexible, based on spouses' personal interests and negotiation outcomes. Power exer-tion processes and outcomes vary from family to family, are not structurally predetermined, and are not contingent on husband's use of force as "ultimate resource" (Gillespie, 1971; Goode, 1970).[5]

TABLE 1: DESCRIPTION OF SEX-ROLE SEGREGATED AND SEX-ROLE
TRANSCENDENT MODELS OF FAMILY ROLES

Domain:	Sex-role segregated	Sex-role transcendent
Sex-role norms	rigid, prescribed, ascribed	flexible, open to negotiation
Division of labor	segregated (husband - provider, wife - homemaker, childcare)	shared responsibilities, negotiated allocation of tasks
Purpose of marriage	emphasis on tasks and duties	emphasis on affection and personal fulfillment
Authority	husband is head of the family	authority is shared
Guiding philosophies	husband's interests are primary, wife's interests are subordinate	all family members' interests are vital, emphasis on joint maximum profit
Sexual relations	double-standard and sex-role prescribed behaviors	single standard, flexible behaviors
Social relations	segregated, close-knit social networks	joint, loose-knit social networks or personal choice

An emphasis on affection, bargaining for joint maximum profit, and shared or individually chosen social relations also constitute elements of the sex-role transcendent model.

In order to assess whether and to what extent families are indeed moving toward the sex-role transcendent model, it is necessary to establish some evaluation criteria for family role changes. Following Bernard (1976) and Dixon (1976), behavioral and normative changes are distinguished and acceptance of the sex-role transcendent model is assumed to have occurred if it is normatively accepted and behaviorally enacted by a majority. Since the sex-role transcendent model postulates role flexibility rather than total role sharing at the behavioral level, the majority criterion remains necessarily somewhat arbitrary. One may expect, however, that role choices which are truly free (i.e., unaffected by norms, socialization experiences, or structural opportunities) would result in a roughly normal distribution of individual attitudes and behaviors. Thus, change toward the sex-role transcendent model would be reflected in increases toward non-traditional role choices.

Given space limitations and serious restrictions in the availability of empirical evidence for some of the dimensions outlined in Table 1, I shall concentrate on three major domains, namely, the division of labor, authority and power, and sexual relations. The specific indicators used here for the assessment of changes toward and acceptance of the sex-role transcendent model as well as the outcomes of the evaluations are summarized in Table 2. The outlined criteria refer exclusively to familial roles. Not assessed are societal, structural, and personality changes which may prevent families from the enactment of sex-role transcendent role choices.

TABLE 2: CRITERIA FOR ASSESSMENT OF CHANGING FAMILY ROLES

Domain	Norms	Change occurred[1]	Implementation by majority[1]
1. Division of labor			
Economic	acceptance of wives' and mothers' labor force participation	yes	yes
	acceptance of shared responsibility for provider role	low	no
Housework	acceptance of mutual and flexible participation in housework	yes	yes
	acceptance of shared responsibility for housework	low	no
Childcare	acceptance of mutual and flexible participation in childcare	yes	yes
	acceptance of shared responsibility for childcare	low	no
Total work	acceptance of equality in spouses' work load	yes	yes
2. Authority	acceptance of shared participation in all family decisions	yes	yes
	acceptance of shared authority	low	no
	acceptance of use of similar power tactics	?[3]	?
	rejection of use of physical force[2]	?	(yes)
3. Sexual relations	acceptance of same sexual standards for both sexes	yes	partially
	acceptance of right to equal sexual gratification	yes	yes
	acceptance of shared participation in sexual decisions	yes	no

[1] Change refers to evidence regarding increased acceptance/enactment of norms/behaviors characteristic of the sex-role transcendent model, implementation refers to the acceptance/enactment of such norms/behaviors by the majority (over 50%).

[2] Application of the majority rule is probably inappropriate here, but the majority of respondents reject use of physical force in marital relations (see text).

[3] ?indicates lack of clear empirical evidence.

TABLE 2 — CONTINUED

Behaviors	Change occurred	Implementation by majority
wives' and mothers' labor force participation	yes	yes
equal contribution of spouses to family income	some	no
mutual and flexible participation in housework	low	no
equal time spent with housework	low	no
mutual and flexible participation in childcare	some	no
equal time spent with childcare	low	no
equal workload of spouses	low	no
shared participation in all family decisions	low	no
not applicable		
use of similar power tactics by both partners	?	no
use of physical force	?	(yes)
equal participation in sexual activities	yes	partially
equal sexual gratification	yes	partially
shared participation in sexual decisions	some	no

CHANGING FAMILY ROLES:
AN ASSESSMENT OF THE PROVIDER ROLE AND ATTITUDES TOWARD WOMEN'S LABOR FORCE PARTICIPATION

There can be little doubt that sex-role norms in general and those regarding women's employment in particular have undergone drastic changes during the last decades, as seen in national survey data. For instance, Cherlin and Walters (1981) report significant increases between the 1960s and late 1970s in the proportion of white men and women who approved of women's working even if their husbands are able to support them. By the late 1970s, a majority of women respondents felt that working mothers could have as warm a relationship with their children as non-working mothers and endorsed equal pay and job opportunities for women (Mason et al., 1976; Thornton and Freedman, 1979; Thornton et al., 1983). In addition, a majority of women rejected assumptions that women would be happier staying at home and caring for their families or that it is more important for women to help their husbands' careers rather than to have one themselves (Thornton et al., 1983). However, over one half of the respondents still believed that it is better if the man earns the main living and the woman takes care of the home and family, a clear rejection of role reversal between the sexes (Mason et al., 1976; Thornton et al., 1983). Similar trends appear in smaller sample investigations (Scanzoni, 1978; Houser and Beckman, 1980) and in other recent national surveys (Spitze and Huber, 1980; Roper, 1980) as well as in comparisons of adolescent and student samples over time (Bayer, 1975; Parelius, 1975; Weeks et al., 1983, King et al., 1978; Herzog et al., 1983), and in generational comparisons of mothers' and daughters' preferences (Rollins and White, 1982; Harris, 1980; Wingrove et al., 1982; Roper and Labeff, 1977; Thornton et al., 1983).

Even though changes in attitudes toward women's labor force participation appear widespread (Mason et al., 1976), they are more pronounced among the young, the highly educated, and among employed women (Scanzoni, 1975, 1978; Cherlin and Walters, 1981; Thornton et al., 1983; Morgan and Walker, 1983; Mason et al., 1976; Houser and Beckman, 1980; Huber and Spitze, 1981). Women tend toward more liberal attitudes than men (Albrecht et al., 1979; Geerken and Gove, 1983; Cherlin and Walters, 1981; Osmond and Martin, 1975; Martin et al., 1980; Stockard, 1980; Tomeh, 1980; Thornton et al., 1983; Herzog et al., 1983).

Some of these studies also demonstrate that the acceptance of women's employment outside the home may be contingent upon familial circumstances, especially family life-cycle stage. For example, it remains a widespread belief that preschool children may suffer if their mothers are employed (Mason et al., 1976). And where survey questions differentiated between part-time and full-time employment, approval rates are highest for part-time employment (Herzog et al., 1983).

Overall, this evidence suggests that approval of wives' employment outside the home has increased substantially within the last two decades, and that the labor force participation of wives, particularly of mothers with schoolchildren, has become an accepted option.

Full-time employment of mothers with preschool children, however, has not achieved the status of a majority opinion.

Responsibility for Economic Support

Are changes in attitudes toward women's labor force participation indicative of a widespread acceptance of shared responsibility for the provider role? While lack of available data renders it difficult to ascertain change in this regard, studies carried out since the mid 1970s leave little doubt that provision for the economic support of families is still thought to be primarily the husband's responsibility. Various surveys, including studies of highly educated or young subjects, reveal that over two-thirds of the respondents disapprove of equal responsibility for the provider role (Caplow et al., 1982; Franz and Mell, 1981; Pleck, 1983; Albrecht et al., 1979; Herzog et al., 1983). And even employed wives do not believe that they fully share economic responsibilities with their husbands (Scanzoni, 1978). Indeed, fulfillment of the provider role continues to be seen as the husband's primary contribution to the family (Yankelovich, 1974; Cazenave, 1979; Pleck, 1983; Lein, 1979; Bernard, 1981; Rubin, 1983), and role reversal between spouses is almost universally rejected (Harris, 1971; Slocum and Nye, 1976; Albrecht et al., 1979).

Thus while work outside the home has become an acceptable option for women and may even be considered as a right (Scanzoni, 1978), it is still not viewed as women's obligation. Women's labor force participation remains optional and voluntary, even though often economically necessary.

Women's Labor Force Participation
and Contributions to the Family Income

The dramatic increase in labor force participation among wives and mothers has been described elsewhere in this volume. According to 1982 data, the dual-earner couple now constitutes the modal pattern both among families without children under 18 years and among families with schoolchildren (U.S. Bureau of the Census, 1983).

The participation of mothers with small children in the work force represents a major departure from the traditional division of labor between spouses, as women now are moving toward a life-long combination of work and family roles (see also Lopata and Norr, 1980). These trends, however, do not imply that spouses are truly sharing the provider role. Not only do many wives and mothers remain homemakers at least through some stages of the family life cycle, but employed wives tend to devote less time to their economic roles than do their husbands: in 1982, 14.6% of employed women, but only 11.9% of men worked one half year or less, and 33.7% of the women, but only 15.2% of the men held part-time jobs (U.S. Bureau of the Census, 1983).

That husbands still carry the major burden of economic support is also reflected in spouses' relative contributions to the family income. From 1965 through 1982, wives' median incomes have remained at about 30% of married males' incomes (U.S. Bureau of the Census, 1967, 1971, 1978, 1982, 1983).[6] Even full-time employed year-round working wives in 1978 contributed only 37% of the family income (Hayghe, 1982). This does not mean, however, that wives' labor force participation is of little consequence, as dual-earner families have higher median incomes than one-earner families and are less likely to fall below the poverty level (Hayghe, 1982, Moen, 1982).

The current situation is probably best characterized by assigning wives a helping role in the economic support of their families. As of the early 1980s, there is little evidence for the acceptance or enactment of a truly shared co-provider pattern.

THE HOMEMAKER AND CHILDCARE ROLES: ATTITUDES AND RESPONSIBILITIES

Existing evidence on attitude changes regarding the homemaker and childcare roles is quite ambivalent, due both to methodological discrepancies among studies (see Hesselbart, in press) as well as to insufficient differentiation between attitudes toward role-sharing and attitudes toward the sharing of responsibility.[7]

Large-scale national surveys indicate increased acceptance of men's participation in household and childcare tasks (Mason et al., 1976; Thornton et al., 1983; Scanzoni, 1978). Data obtained from college students and young adults confirm this trend (Tomeh, 1978; Weeks et al., 1981; Herzog et al., 1983; Keith and Brubaker, 1977; Roper and Labeff, 1977). In direct contrast to these results is evidence based mostly on samples of couples regarding spouses' relative responsibility for household and childcare tasks which shows consistently that wives maintain major responsibility for these roles (Slocum and Nye, 1976; Caplow et al., 1982; Albrecht et al., 1979; Geerken and Gove, 1983; Kamerman, 1980; Herzog et al., 1983; Gross and Arvey, 1977; Gecas, 1976; Stafford et al., 1977).

That husbands' participation in these tasks remains to some extent optional, can also be seen in the rejection of role-reversal (Oakley, 1974; Herzog et al., 1983), especially the involvement of men in heavily stereotyped female tasks such as changing diapers (Oakley, 1974). Negative reactions of male peer groups to high husband involvement in family roles further support the persistence of a sexual division of responsibility for the homemaker and childcare roles (Lein, 1979; see also Stein's chapter in this volume).

The Division of Household and Childcare Tasks

Were families indeed changing toward more sharing of the household role, we could expect a reduction in role segregation of household tasks with spouses spending about the same amount of time with the performance of these activities.

Available evidence suggests that this is not the case. Female household tasks such as cooking, cleaning, or laundry are still predominantly carried out by wives, and male tasks such as repairs and car maintenance are performed by the husbands. Various studies conducted between 1955 and 1979 in fact yield quite similar results and show surprisingly little change in the proportion of nontraditional responses (Gross and Arvey, 1977; Condron and Bode, 1982; Ericksen et al., 1979; Thrall, 1978; Duncan et al., 1973; Caplow et al., 1982; Albrecht et al., 1979; Slocum and Nye, 1976; Gecas, 1976; Scanzoni, 1978; Hesselbart, 1975, 1978; Wheeler and Arvey, 1977; Roper, 1980; Berheide et al., 1976; Atkinson and Huston, 1983).

The persistence of the sexual division of household labor is also evident in children's participation in household work. Several studies show marked sex-typing of children's household duties, especially among older children. Girls also spend more time with household tasks than boys (Goldstein and Oldham, 1979; White and Brinkerhoff, 1981a, b; Lynch, 1975; Cogle and Tasker, 1982; Duncan et al., 1973; Thrall, 1978).

Even though childcare activities are certainly not divided equally between spouses, men are more frequently involved in childcare than in diverse "female" household chores (Geerken and Gove, 1983; Scanzoni, 1978; Gecas, 1976; Caplow et al., 1982; Hesselbart, 1975, 1978; Ericksen et al., 1979; Kamerman, 1980; Stafford et al., 1977; Beckett and Smith, 1981). There is also evidence of a recent increase in fathers' participation in childcare (Hesselbart, 1976, 1978). Other survey and observational studies confirm fathers' interest and involvement in childcare, but they also demonstrate a continuing division of labor between parents, such as the lesser participation of fathers than mothers in the physical care of children. Fathers tend to play with their children (although in absolute terms still less than mothers), but they rarely take part in childcare per se (Lamb, 1977; Katsh, 1981; Kotelchuk, 1976; Rendina and Dickerscheid, 1976; Sawin and Parke, 1979; Davey and Paolucci, 1980; Lamb and Lamb, 1976; Haas, 1982; McHale and Huston, 1983; see also reviews of this literature by Parke and Tinsley, 1981, Russell and Radin, 1983, Yogman, 1981, Pleck, 1983). The few studies that do suggest relative high similarity of spouses' involvement in selected parenting activities, are based on observations in special contexts such as public or hospital settings (Parke and O'Leary, 1976; Mackey and Day, 1979).

Time Allocation for Family Work

Not only are husbands less likely than wives to take part in various household and childcare activities, they also spend considerably less time with family work (Szalai, 1972; Robinson, 1977; Geerken and Gove, 1983; Pleck, 1983; Sanik, 1981; Vanek, 1974; Model, 1982; Berk and Berk, 1979; Meissner et al., 1975; Nickols, 1976; Davis, 1982; Szinovacz, 1979; Arndt et al., 1980; Walker and Woods, 1976). Despite technological developments, there seems to have been little change in time use for household work between the 1920s and the 1960s (Walker and Woods, 1976; Robinson, 1971, 1980; Robinson et al., 1972; Vanek, 1974; Morgan et al., 1966, for contradictory evidence see Caplow et al., 1982). More recent investigations show some reduction in women's time use for family work[8] due largely to demographic changes such as wives' employment, number of children, or marital status (Robinson, 1980). Among families with working wives, the husbands' relative share of time spent on family work has increased in comparison with husbands' in families with full-time homemakers as seen in Table 3. However, given differences in the sample populations and the reliance on aggregate rather than *couple* data for the comparisons shown in Table 3, these conclusions must be regarded as preliminary even though at least two studies using comparable data bases over time come to similar conclusions (Sanik, 1981; Davis, 1982).

Overall, these data suggest some moderate increase in husbands' share of family work since the mid 1960s. Nonetheless, wives con-

TABLE 3:   TIME ALLOCATION IN FAMILIES 1965-1977, BY SEX AND WIFE'S EMPLOYMENT STATUS (HOURS PER DAY)

Source:	Data (year)		Husbands wife employed	wife not employed	Wives employed	not employed
Robinson	1965/66	work	6.9	7.5	5.3	--
(1977)		family work	1.1	1.0	4.0	7.6
		total work	8.0	8.5	9.3	7.6
		share of work %	56.6	100.0	43.4	0.0
		share of family work %	21.6	11.6	78.4	88.4
		share of total work %	46.2	52.8	53.8	47.2
Walker &	1967/68	work[a]	6.3	7.8	5.3	0.5[d]
Woods (1976)		family work	1.6	1.6	4.8	8.1
		total work	7.9	9.4	10.1	8.6
		share of work %	54.3	94.0	45.7	6.0
		share of family work %	20.4	16.5	79.6	83.5
		share of total work %	43.9	52.2	56.1	47.8
Geerken &	1974/75	work[b,c]	9.2	9.5	7.3	--
Gove (1983)		family work	1.7	1.5	4.1	7.4
		total work	10.9	11.0	11.4	7.4
		share of work %	55.8	100.0	44.2	0.0
		share of family work %	29.3	16.9	70.7	83.1
		share of total work %	48.9	59.8	51.1	40.2
Pleck	1975/76	work	6.9	7.0	5.0	0.1
(1983)		family work	1.9	1.8	4.0	6.8
		total work	8.8	8.8	9.0	6.9
		share of work %	58.0	98.6	42.0	1.4
		share of family work %	32.2	20.9	67.8	79.1
		share of total work %	49.4	56.1	50.6	43.9
Pleck	1977	work[c]	6.5	6.9	5.6	--
(1983)		family work	3.9	3.3	7.0	--
		total work	10.4	10.2	12.6	--
		share of work %	53.7	--	46.3	--
		share of family work %	35.8	--	64.2	--
		share of total work %	45.2	--	54.8	--

Sources: Data for Robinson (1977) and Pleck (1983) are from Pleck (1983, Table 7); Data for Walker and Woods (1976) are based on Table 3.17; Data from Geerken and Gove (1983) are based on Table 4.2. Computation of the percentages was performed by this author.

[a] Refers to wives employed 30 or more hours/week.

[b] Weekdays only; all other data reflect weekly averages, including Saturdays and Sundays.

[c] Based on time estimates by the respondents; all other data are based on time-budgets.

[d] Includes volunteer work.

tinue to carry the major burden of family work and to spend considerably more time than their husbands in the performance of household and childcare chores.

TIME USE AND WORK LOADS: ISSUES OF EQUALITY

It is evident from the figures presented in Table 3 as well as from other studies (Hall and Schroeder, 1970; Vanek, 1974; Nickols, 1976; Davis, 1982) that work outside the home leads wives to strongly reduce their own time use for family work. While husbands of housewives spend slightly longer hours than husbands of working wives on their jobs, both groups of husbands seem to maintain their time use for family work at a relatively constant level. However, owing to employed wives' reduction of family work time, their husbands' share of family work is clearly higher than that of the husbands of housewives.[10] But we must recognize that this shift in family work time occurs primarily because of time adjustments on the part of the employed wives. Thus, adjustments to the increased time demands on employed wives are not made by the *couple,* but are left nearly exclusively to the wives themselves.

Another way to assess equality in the division of family work is to compare spouses' total workload or "obligatory" time use (Robinson, 1977). Among families with homemakers, men spend somewhat more time on obligatory activities than the wives, whereas the opposite trend holds for families with employed wives (see Table 3). Nevertheless, the overall time use for employed wives and their husbands in the total population is relatively similar. While spouses' time use may appear relatively balanced, these general figures are misleading because they fail to control for those conditions which have been shown to impact on women's family commitments, namely, the presence and age of children in the family (Hunt and Kiker, 1981; Ericksen et al., 1979; Waldron and Routh, 1981; Huber and Spitze, 1980). One study (Robinson et al., 1977), for instance, shows that employed wives without childcare obligations spend about 1.5 hours more time on obligatory activities than their husbands. This difference increases to 3.5 hours per day for families with three or more children, including at least one preschool child. Similar findings are reported for Canada and Austria (Meissner et al., 1975; Szinovacz, 1979). Pleck's (1983) analysis of the 1975 time use study demonstrates that both employed wives and housewives with preschool children spend over 1.5 hours more time with family work than do women without children in the home, whereas husbands' family work is only marginally affected by family life-cycle status (an increase of less than 8 minutes per day). This inflexibility in husbands' time use for family work is also confirmed by detailed analyses of families' time schedules; especially during the morning hours, husbands are nearly exclusively concerned with getting ready for work while employed wives engage in their own preparation for the work day as well as in various family work activities (Berk and Berk, 1979; Hill and Stafford, 1980).

If equality is judged by mutual adjustment of spouses to each other's time demands rather than by overall obligatory time use, current family work arrangements clearly favor housewives and husbands of employed wives. If mothers today transcend the sex-role segregated model by maintaining employment even when their children are still young, they do so at considerable risk of overload and related stress (see also Robinson et al., 1977; Meissner et al., 1975; Szinovacz, 1979; Schafer and Keith, 1981; Pleck, 1983).

MARITAL POWER RELATIONS

The sex-role segregated model of marital relations implies a dualistic authority structure, with husbands dominating economic and other public issues as well as selected family matters whereas women reign over the domains of housework and childcare. In addition, the husband is the ultimate authority with veto rights over all family issues (Goode, 1970). This right is legitimized by other group members and can be challenged by them, but when "formally institutionalized" (Buckley, 1967, p. 195) such authority becomes socially reinforced and cannot be arbitrarily withdrawn (Szinovacz, in press). To paraphrase Scanzoni (1979a, p. 306), transition to the sex-role transcendent model would indeed "signal the end of authority," but not of power. Implementation of this model would, therefore, imply increased rejection of husbands' veto right over family issues, a decrease in sex-role stereotyped decision-making, and elimination of physical force as a means of ensuring authority.

Authority

Several decades ago, Blood and Wolfe (1960) postulated the end of authority as a significant element in modern marriages, but later research has documented the continued effects of sex-role norms on marital decision-making patterns (Rodman, 1972; Burr et al., 1977; Richmond, 1976; Szinovacz, 1978). Research on spouses' norms and attitudes suggests some questioning of husbands' right to make final decisions, but no full rejection of his authority position. For instance, Thornton et al. (1983) report that while wives' agreement with the statement, "The husband should make important family decisions," declined from 67% in 1962 to 29% in 1980, their adolescent children (interviewed in 1980) were more likely than the mothers to agree with that statement.

Other studies reveal a similar trend toward increased acceptance of spouses' equal participation in important marital decisions along with considerable ambivalence as to husband's authority position in the family, (Weeks et al., 1981; Geerken and Gove, 1983; Scanzoni, 1978). Almost 90% of the wives interviewed by Scanzoni in 1975 favored equal sharing of marital decisions, yet only 49% felt that girls should be permitted as much independence as boys, and a mere 16% disagreed with the statement that the husband should be head of the family (up from 7% in 1971). Since both the Scanzoni (1978) and Thornton et al. (1983) studies are based on female respondents, the trend toward approval of egalitarian decision-making is probably overestimated.

These data therefore suggest continued support for the husband's family authority, although he is expected to consider the needs and wishes of other family members.

Decision-Making and Influence Tactics

Is this trend toward increased acceptance of shared participation paralleled in spouses' actual decision-making patterns? As seen in Table 4, little appears to have changed over the past two decades. Hesselbart (1978) further reports that respondents' implementation of shared decision-making lagged behind their normative preferences. Subjects often felt that decisions should be shared, but did not always realize this preference in their behaviors. Nye (1976) also found that conflicts over selected family domains are only rarely resolved equally in favor of both spouses: husbands dominate in conflicts over socialization, husband's occupation, and recreational issues, whereas wives have more say in conflicts over their own work and housekeeping. It is also clear from this investigation that wives' ability to resolve conflicts in their favor is lower than might be expected in terms of normative preferences and responsibility for the enactment of these roles.

TABLE 4: PARTICIPATION IN FAMILY DECISIONS, 1955 – 1975 (PERCENT REPORTING JOINT PARTICIPATION)

Reference:	Year of study:	Sample:	Car	Life insurance	House	Decision area: Husband's job	Wife's work	Money for food	Doctor	Vacation
Blood and Wolfe (1960)	1955	wives	25	41	58	3	18	32	45	68
Centers et al. (1971)	1964	husbands wives	21 27	28 33	54 64	4 5	24 22	33 32	56 56	71 69
Kandel and Lesser (1972)	1969	wives	31	51	61	8	37	36	52	75
Duncan et al. (1973)	1971	wives	26	36	63	4	24	34	-	-
Hesselbart (1976)	1975	men and women	-	-	-	15	38	35	-	-

Overall, these studies fail to confirm a trend toward shared deci-sion-making. Spouses may pay lip service to egalitarian ideals, but they continue to implement sex-role segregated or husband domi-nant decision-making and conflict resolution patterns.

Bernard (1982, p. 134) observes that changes in marital power relations over time may affect *influence styles* more than decision making or other control patterns. As several researchers have shown, traditional marriages are characterized not only by acceptance of husband dominance and sex-segregation, but also by sex differenti-ated power or influence strategies. Lack of authority as well as tangible, concrete resources, leads women to exert power through indirect, covert techniques (Johnson, 1976; Falbo, 1977; Falbo and Peplau, 1980; Peplau, 1979). This "Lady Macbeth Syndrome" (Bernard, 1982, p. 134) should become less pronounced if women's power position in marriages had indeed improved.

Since there is little published research on marital power *process-es,* it is quite difficult to test Bernard's prediction. One unpublished study (Hoffman, 1982) that examines influence tactics among three cohorts of men and women, found many similarities in the influence strategies used by both sexes, although women in all cohorts were more likely than men to rely on indirect/emotional tactics in intimate relationships (e.g., crying, silent treatment). Other research on power strategies of young adults confirms women's continued use of indirect influence tactics (Falbo and Peplau, 1980).

Physical Force

The final indicator used to assess changes in family power rela-tions is the use of physical force. Current research on family vio-lence provides ample evidence that use of physical force does not constitute a rare feature of today's marriages (Straus et al., 1980). Nor is physical coercion universally condemned: more than one in four respondents in a nationally representative sample approved to some extent of slapping the partner (Dibble and Straus, 1980).

That the use of violence in marriages is linked to the wife's in-ferior status is shown in studies of battered women who remain in abusive relationships, and in data demonstrating a strong correlation between wife's marital dependency and abuse by their husbands. Husbands can take advantage of high wife dependency, but they also ensure their dominance position in families where the wife is less dependent through the use of violence (Dobash and Dobash, 1979;

Marsden, 1978; Allen and Straus, 1980; Yllo and Straus, 1982; Kalmuss and Straus, 1982; Tellis-Nayak and Donoghue, 1982; Brown, 1980; Goode, 1971; Gelles, 1980).

Thus, presently available research evidence lends little support to the notion that marriages are becoming egalitarian. If changes in marital power relations have occurred, they are more subtle than current measurement techniques are able to register. This result is hardly surprising if husbands' authority and power in the marriage flow from their position as family provider (Scanzoni and Scanzoni, 1976). Despite wives' increasing labor force participation rates, the husband's position as major family provider has not been truly challenged.

SEXUAL RELATIONS

The most significant characteristic of the sex-role segregated model in regard to sexual behaviors is the maintenance of a double standard, i.e., men and women are granted different sexual rights, assume different sexual responsibilities, and diverge in the sexual scripts they follow. Although the last decades have often been described as a period of "sexual revolution," debate continues over the fate of the double standard. DeLamater (1981, p. 255), relying primarily on evidence concerning gender similarities in the frequency of permissive sexual attitudes and behaviors, declares that the double standard has "essentially disappeared." Reiss (1981), on the other hand, applying a criterion of male dominance and referring to a wider variety of sexual behaviors, finds that the double standard persists.

Premarital Sexual Attitudes and Behaviors

There can be little doubt that premarital sexual standards and behaviors changed a great deal since the mid 1950s. By the beginning of the 1980s, a majority of males and females both approved of premarital sexual relations for both sexes and engaged in premarital intercourse (Clayton and Brokemeier, 1980; Hopkins, 1977; DeLamater, 1981; Glenn and Weaver, 1979; Singh, 1980; Robinson and Jedlicka, 1982; Bell and Coughey, 1980). Furthermore, sex differences in these attitudes and behaviors have steadily narrowed.

Nevertheless, some sex differences in premarital sexual relations can still be noted. Not only are women today somewhat less likely than men to approve of and engage in premarital sexual relations, they also have fewer dating partners and are more likely than men to respond to premarital sex with feelings of guilt and remorse (Singh, 1980; Robinson and Jedlicka, 1982; Abernathy et al., 1979; Christensen and Johnson, 1978; Staples, 1978).

Thus, while there is evidence of change in the premarital sexual attitudes and behaviors of both sexes, these shifts seem to involve divergent standards. Men are moving toward a standard of permissiveness with *or* without affection, whereas women are changing from a standard of abstinence to one of permissiveness with affection (Reiss, 1980, 1981).

Marital and Extramarital Sexuality

Such changes are not restricted to premarital relations. Research shows a rise in the frequency and variety of sexual activities among married couples, along with evidence that wives are now more likely to be sexually gratified than they were a few decades ago (Kinsey et al., 1948, 1953; Tavris and Sadd, 1977; Hunt, 1974; Westoff, 1974; Gagnon, 1977).

It is questionable, however, whether these trends, including the higher reported rates of female orgasm, are truly indicative of a decisive move toward sexual equality. Women are still less often gratified, while the achievement of mutual orgasm has become a performance norm for *both* sexes. It does not only involve expectations that men ought to sexually satisfy their women, but it also implies that women ought to be able to fulfill this expectation. Given men's success and goal orientation toward sex (Gross, 1978), female orgasm then easily becomes another service for the male sexual partner: *"her orgasm is for him, not for her.* It is his need to validate his manhood that is of primary concern—his need, not hers"* (Rubin, 1976, p. 152, emphasis in original). Standards and behaviors in the area of extramarital relations reinforce the pattern of males' sexual possession of women (Safilios-Rothschild, 1977; Reiss, 1981).

Even though traditional standards concerning extramarital sex have become somewhat relaxed, the majority still disapprove of such behaviors (Glenn and Weaver, 1981; Reiss et al., 1980), particularly for women. For instance, Laner and Housker (1980) report that women's infidelity is more likely to be viewed as a cause for divorce than that of men.

The ideology of men's sexual possession of women is evident in the differential sentencing of rapists, depending on the victim's marital status. Rape of married women tends to result in harsher punishments than rape of the non-married (Jones and Aronson, 1973; Harrell and Sagan, 1974), leading Safilios-Rothschild (1977, p. 29) to conclude "that rape is a more serious crime when a man's 'possession' is molested, despite the fact that women in both cases are similarily injured."

Sexual Decision-Making

Investigations of sexuality both within and outside of marriage have centered on the quantitative aspects of sexual relations (Gross, 1978; Miller and Fowlkes, 1980) rather than on the process of sexual decision-making (Frank and Scanzoni, 1982). The few available studies suggest that men and women exert different types of control over sexual issues. Men, concomitant with their presumably stronger interest in the sexual aspects of intimate relations, play the role of initiator and feel uncomfortable if women take the first step in a sexual encounter (Paplau et al., 1977; Carlson, 1976; Allgeier, 1981; Gross, 1978; Knox and Wilson, 1981). Women, on the other hand, exert "negative control" and seem somewhat successful in resisting male advances (Peplau et al., 1977; Carlson, 1976). This sexual restraint on the part of women, of course, can be viewed as a remnant of the double standard, and, paired with stereotypes of the glamour girl and seductress, is quite characteristic of the inherent ambivalence in women's sexual role (Phelps, 1979; Janeway, 1980).

The observed sex differences in sexual control clearly correspond to the sex-role segregated view of sexuality according to which men actively pursue sexual gratifications, whereas women are expected to please men and exert restraint in their sexual endeavors (Gross, 1978; Miller and Fowlkes, 1980). It is not clear, however, whether women are indeed able persistently to resist male sexual pressures. For example, D'Augelli and D'Augelli (1977) found that in cases of disagreements on sexuality, males dominate in the setting of sexual standards. Recent concern over cases of marital rape leaves little doubt that husbands not infrequently force their sexual wishes on wives (Russell, 1982; Gelles, 1977; Frieze, 1983).

Reiss (1981) also asserts continuing dominance of the male in sexual relations. This, he argues, is obvious from the cultural focus "on intercourse as the major outlet for sexuality" (p. 276) as well as from the fact that sexual relations are "stage-directed" by the male:

> It is the male who is supposed to be the initiator, and at least on first coitus, it is he who decides what positions will be utilized and what sequence of sexual events will occur. Once again, then, the act is set up when the male is ready and to his specifications. (p. 276)

Overall, this literature suggests an increase in permissiveness and greater similarity in sexual standards especially as far as premarital relations are concerned. However, some discrepancies in sexual standards for the sexes remain, and applications of a double standard are quite prominent in sexual decision-making and control patterns.

FACTS AND THEORIES: AN EVALUATION

Overall assessments of change in family roles during the last decades are presented in Table 3. We note considerable attitudinal change, but little movement toward sex-role transcendence in regard to the assignment of family responsibilities and familial role enactment. It is also clear that the rates of observed change diverge for the various role domains (see also Mason et al., 1976).

Are these general trends consistent with current explanations of sex-role differentiation? Among the sociological theories proposed to explain sex-role segregation in general and the sexual division of labor in particular, the functional, exchange, and socialization perspectives are perhaps most widely referred to. In the following section, each of these theories is evaluated in the light of empirical facts and theoretical criticism.

Functionalism and the New Home Economics

Functionalists view sex-role segregation as a necessary outcome of distinct and incompatible leadership roles, and they attribute the sexual allocation of instrumental and expressive roles to biological factors (Parsons and Bales, 1955). The "New Home Economics" (Berk, 1980; Becker, 1981) takes a similar perspective, but emphasizes the economic utility of role differentiation.

Both approaches have undergone heavy criticism and lack consistent empirical support (Slater, 1961; Farkas, 1976; Berk, 1980). More importantly, they neglect linkages between role allocation and power relations in the family and society at large. The "New Home Economics," as Berk (1970, p. 128) remarks, "essentially defines the problem of exploitation away." Owing to their emphasis on legitimate power, functionalists tend to confuse complementarity and reciprocity and, therefore, ignore power inequalities which are characteristic of complementary, but non-reciprocal role relationships (Parsons and Shils, 1951; Claessens, 1970; Gouldner, 1960; Dreitzel, 1972; Haug, 1972). Especially Habermas (1970) has pointed out that complementary role expectations do not guarantee reciprocal need gratification or equal chances of self-representation in interactions. To the extent that norms and role expectations emerge from interactions (role-making rather than role-taking), and familial realities are constructed through negotiations among family members, they are subject to continuous change (Turner, 1962; Berger and Kellner, 1964). It cannot be assumed, as Parsons does, that negotiations of family roles are necessarily oriented toward the achievement of mutual and equal need gratification. Rather, they are likely to reflect power differentials among family members and are, therefore, likely to favor the more powerful partner (Joas, 1973). Additionally, authority can be used to change institutionalized norms and/or to expand one's realm of legitimate influence (Claessens, 1970; Joas, 1973).

EXCHANGE THEORY

Exchange theorists regard family power relations as a function of spouses' relative contributions to the marriage and the value of such contributions. It is argued that under sex-role segregated conditions women exchange domestic services, sex, childcare—and one may also add deference (Blau, 1964)—in return for their economic support and protection by the husband (Scanzoni, 1970). It is further proposed that once women gain more access to economic and other socially valued resources, their power position vis-à-vis the husband will improve (Blood and Wolfe, 1960).

Obviously, partners in intimate relations are always involved in some exchanges of rewards and gratifications, but this exchange need not be equal or fair. The equality of relationships is contingent on spouses' relative dependence on each other's gratifications as well as on the alternatives available to each partner (Emerson, 1976). It has long been suggested that husbands' economic contributions are more important and more effective power bases than wives', leading to fundamental inequalities in the marital relationship (Engels, 1884; Scanzoni and Scanzoni, 1976; Lipman-Blumen, 1976; Safilios-Rothschild, 1970; Johnson, 1976). Whether women's work outside the home constitutes a necessary or sufficient condition for equality remains debatable. Cross-cultural investigations have failed to provide consistent evidence as to the relationship between women's subsistence contributions and their familial and social status (Crano and Aronoff, 1978; Whyte, 1978; Johnson and Hendrix, 1982; Sanday, 1981). Current studies relating wife's labor force participation to her involvement in marital decision-making tend to support the theory to some extent (Bahr, 1974; Hoffman, 1977; Ericksen et al., 1979; Clark et al., 1978; Rank, 1982; Model, 1982; Condron and Bode, 1982), but even this evidence is not always consistent and subject to major methodological shortcomings (Berheide et al., 1976; Safilios-Rothschild, 1970, 1976; McDonald, 1980).

Resource and some family exchange theorists also tend to commit the crucial error of equating women's labor force participation with economic and general personal independence. The marginal economic situation of divorced women and widows (Cherlin, 1981; Szinovacz, 1982) leaves little doubt that many women continue to depend on men for an adequate living standard, even if they are gainfully employed. As long as sociostructural conditions limit women's access to economic opportunities and other socially valued resources and as long as the exchange value assigned to specific resources reflects male dominance at the societal level (Berger et al., 1972), exchange theory tends to legitimize existing power differentials between the sexes (Szinovacz, 1984).

It has also been argued that women's economic dependency on men is counteracted by men's emotional dependency on women (Pleck, 1983; Sattel, 1983; Rubin, 1983). However, present demographic realities (i.e., the sex ratio), unequal economic opportunities, and women's primary role in parenting (Heer and Grossbard-Shechtman, 1981; Guttentag and Secord, 1983; Udry, 1981; Jedlicka, 1978; Pleck, 1980; Vanek, 1980b; Rossi, 1977) render men's marriage alternatives and thus their options for the fulfillment of emotional needs far superior to women's. In other words, men may be dependent on *women* for the fulfillment of emotional (and perhaps also sexual) needs, but not necessarily on their *wives,* whereas wives indeed depend on the *husband* for economic support, social status, and other gratifications.[12]

If men depend on their wives, it is primarily in regard to social fatherhood and personal attachment to the partner (Waller, 1937; Hochschild, 1983). The increasing cases of contested custody suggest, however, that fathers are beginning to extend their rights in this area; and women with children are especially dependent on the husband to ensure their economic well-being. Furthermore, the "motherhood mandate" (Russo, 1976; Petchasky, 1980) and women's, but not men's, stigmatization for illegitimacy render women probably as dependent on men for socially legitimate motherhood as men are on women for social fatherhood. Finally, given the time limits placed on women's reproductive capabilities, they will often be unable to pursue motherhood in subsequent intimate relationships: fathers without custody can remarry younger women and become parents again, but middle-aged women do not have this option. In this sense as well, women are more dependent than men on the continuation of existing family relationships and thus on their husbands.

Socialization Theory

Socialization theorists view learned sex-role norms and role modeling as fundamental forces in maintaining the sexual division of labor. Even though there is considerable empirical support for an effect of sex-role orientations on familial role enactment (Beckman and Houser, 1979; Model, 1982; Cooney et al., 1982; Condron and Bode, 1982; Perrucci et al., 1978; Wheeler and Arvey, 1981; Cordell et al., 1980; Rodman, 1972), we must also recognize that such attitudes usually explain but a small proportion of the variance in role allocation patterns. Indeed, the image of drastic changes in sex-role attitudes within the last decades seems largely overdrawn. Attitudes and norms at the heart of the sex-role segregated model, namely, the assignment of responsibility for family roles by sex, have changed very little. As long as children are exposed to sex-role segregated parental models and are assigned different tasks on the basis of their sex, fundamental attitudinal movement toward the sex-role transcendent model will likely be quite slow. Sex-role change which goes beyond mere lip-service carries the potential of heightened intrapersonal as well as intrafamilial conflict and role strain (Bowen and Orthner, 1983; Keith and Schafer, 1980; Indvik and Fitzpatrick, 1982; Rossi, 1975; Whyte, 1978). Given persistent normative and institutional support for sex-role segregated responsibilities and the internalization of such norms, it is not surprising that both men and women feel reluctant to give up sex ascribed functions even if change is encouraged by social policies (e.g., Sweden) or might follow from sex-role transcendent behavioral choices as in the case of dual-career couples (Haas, 1980, 1981, 1982; Yogev, 1981; Lein, 1979; Rubin, 1983).

CONCLUSION: AUTONOMY VS EQUALITY

The pronounced discrepancies between sex-role attitudes and the assignment of familial responsibilities and tasks raise serious questions about the validity and viability of the projected movement toward sex-role transcendence and equality between the sexes. The attitudinal and behavioral changes in family life styles currently experienced with respect to women's employment, sexually open relations, and divorce, are not necessarily indicative of sex-role change and enhanced equality between the sexes. Rather, they are consistent with societal norms which emphasize individuality, autonomy, personal fulfillment, and achievement (Lasch, 1977). These orientations directly contradict fundamental familial value bases such as communality, togetherness, mutual interests, and ascription. As Degler (1980, p. 471) insists, ''the great values for which the family stands are at odds not only with those of the women's movement, but also with those of today's world.'' More importantly, movement toward individualism and autonomy is *not* identical with movement toward equality. As long as gender equality is not realized, individualistic values can be used by the more powerful (men) to free themselves from traditional responsibilities (economic support, sexual fidelity, emotional commitment) at the cost and against the will of the more dependent partner (women). Such shedding of responsibilities is now legitimized and rendered less costly by individualistic social norms and reduced social controls.

Interpretations which treat women's employment primarily as a sign of changing sex-roles, ignore that many women work out of economic necessity and/or economic insecurity in the face of high unemployment and divorce rates. And even if women find work outside the home personally fulfilling, it has not enabled them to introduce an equal division of responsibilities into their marriages, leading to an accumulation of their work load.

Similarly, the increasing acceptance of emotionally and sexually open relationships seems more representative of autonomous than equalitarian standards. Even if women are granted equal sexual rights, sexual scripts continue to follow a male model (Rossi, 1977) and serve male interests. And even in Europe where sexual standards are more permissive than in the United States, women are less likely than men to engage in extramarital intercourse and tend to perceive sexually open relationships more negatively than men (Buunk, 1980, 1981).

Women's reproductive role and, perhaps, the biosocial bases of the mother-child bond (Rossi, 1977) not only jeopardize their competitive potential in the labor market (at least within rigid organizational and industrial standards), but also make women more dependent than men on the maintenance of stable and relatively secure intimate relationships. If this need is reinforced by societal norms, it is the autonomy-seeking husband who is viewed as deviant and called upon to fulfill his duties (Nazarri, 1980). Under societal norms of individualism and autonomy, on the other hand, women's needs for economic support and emotional commitment are no longer protected. Such demands may then be seen as signs of lacking skills and undue possessiveness. As such they are likely to result in guilt feelings on the part of those women who accept the new individualistic standards, while rejection of such standards can be interpreted as evidence of basic stereotypic sex differences, stereotypes which tend to perpetuate sexual stratification at the societal level.

It has also been argued that the rising divorce rate results at least in part from women's pursuit of personal interests and enhanced sex-role equality (Scanzoni, 1979b). While it is by no means clear that it is the women who initiate and decide on the divorce, there can be little doubt that economic and overload problems following divorce are much more severe for women than for men (Price-Bonham et al., 1983).

Much of the current debate on women's roles has stressed the repressive qualities of family responsibilities and relationships. Women are increasingly encouraged to pursue autonomous and self-fulfilling goals in similar ways as men. This normative mandate supposedly leads to a betterment in women's social position and enhances interpersonal relationships between the sexes. In contrast, it is argued here, that under sociostructural conditions of inequality and lacking social and personal support systems which effectively reduce women's family responsibilities, such calls for autonomy may contribute to rather than diminish exploitation in intimate relationships.

Achievement of sex-role transcendence requires fundamental and simultaneous changes both in societal/institutional structures and in individual orientations (Miller and Garrison, 1982; Pleck, 1976, 1977, 1983). In the traditional family, the husband's provider functions lock him into sex-role segregated family and work patterns as much as do women's economic dependency and their responsibilities for housework and childcare (Glazer, 1976; Dalla Costa, 1972; Pleck, 1977, 1980, 1981). Women's increased participation in the labor force has lightened men's economic burden somewhat, but not to the extent of shared responsibility. The new social norms stress autonomy and self-fulfillment for both sexes. However, men's greater resources and their societal dominance position enable them more than women to define relationship rules and obligations and to use (or abuse) emerging societal norms of autonomy for their own interests rather than to the mutual advantage of all family members. Such onesided application of autonomy standards is probably enhanced by women's increasing demands for equality and the resulting conflicts and power struggles in intimate relationships.

To achieve sex-role transcendence and true equality between the sexes, increased pressure must be exerted on social institutions and organizations to adapt to family needs, and men will have to be convinced (and prepared through socialization) that they can, indeed, profit from such changes. Since women, in a position of greater dependency and less power than men, are seen as victims of exploitation (Mainardi, 1977; Polatchnik, 1973-74; Pleck, 1979), proponents of sex-role change have emphasized women's needs and called for the enlargement of women's options. However, as Marx noted more than a century ago, exploitative human relationships alienate both the victims and their oppressors (Marx, 1966, originally 1844). Unless men envision and are offered advantages from their involvement in equalitarian relationships, they are likely to resist sex-role change (Goode, 1982) and resort to traditional standards and/or individualistic alternatives. The major issue in the achievement of equalitarian relations is not the pursuit of autonomy and personal self-fulfillment, but spouses' willingness and ability to negotiate and implement mutually satisfactory arrangements. For the movement toward sex-role transcendence to succeed, it must profit and enhance the life quality of both men and women.

NOTES

1. For more extensive reivews of this literature see Aldous (1979), Aldous et al. (1979), Scanzoni (1979a), Hochschild (1973), Scanzoni and Fox (1980), Lipman-Blumen and Tickamyer (1975), McDonald (1980), Miller and Garrison (1982), Hesselbart (in press), Szinovacz (1984), Hoffman (1977, 1983).

2. But see also Durkheim's (1921) concept of the "famille conjugale."

3. The sex-role concept used here corresponds with that proposed by Hochschild (1973) and Lipman-Blumen and Tickamyer (1975).

4. This terminology appears to present the core of the conceptual distinction applied in this paper. Other terms such as equality vs patriarchy or modern vs traditional either refer to subdomains (e.g., power relations) or are problematic in terms of their implications (e.g., from a sex-role perspective, some primitive societies are more "modern" than current U.S. society).

5. It is noteworthy that ultimate resource theory raises questions about the proposed close link between husband's breadwinner role and power (rather than authority) in the family.

6. Of course, women's relative income is importantly affected by unequal occupational opportunities and unequal pay, but these are characteristic features of sex-role segregated societal structures. For reviews of women's economic opportunities see Marsh (1982), Oppenheimer (1977), Rosenfeld (1980), Philliber and Hiller (1979).

7. This difference is probably best expressed in terms of voluntary/optional and obligatory involvement in family roles.

8. "Family work" refers to housework plus childcare (Pleck, 1983).

9. For a summary of the debate on this issue see Pleck (1983).

10. Davis' (1982) analysis is of particular interest since the comparisons refer to the same families and to family units rather than unrelated respondents. However, this survey relies on time estimates rather than time diaries. This procedure may affect the validity of results. For instance, in contrast to much other research, Davis finds relatively pronounced differences in family work between husbands of employed wives and housewives.

11. See Pleck (1983) for a more extensive review of this literature.

12. Women's emotional abilities and expressiveness (Notarius and Johnson, 1982; Balswick and Averett, 1977) may have some effect on marital power relations, but they are not likely to fully offset husbands' economic superiority. Also, the causal direction of this relationship is not clear. It has been suggested that emotional abilities and empathy may be a function of powerlessness (Hewitt, 1976; Sattel, 1983), and that women, because of their dependence on men, take a more practical approach to intimate relations and engage in more "feeling work" than men (Hochschild, 1983; Hill et al., 1976). But even if this led women to have higher emotional resources than men, these resources are relationship-specific and, therefore, in the long run probably less effective than the tangible resources possessed and used by men (Johnson, 1976; Raven and Kruglanski, 1970).

REFERENCES

Abernathy, T. J., Robinson, I. E., Balswick, J. O., & King, K. A comparison of the sexual attitudes and behaviors of rural, suburban, and urban adolescents. *Adolescence,* 1979, *14,* 289-295.

Albrecht, S. L., Bahr, H. M., & Chadwick, B. A. Changing family and sex roles: An assessment of age differences. *Journal of Marriage and the Family*, 1979, *41*, 41-50.

Aldous, J. Family interaction patterns. In A. Inkeles, J. Coleman and N. Smelser (Eds.), *Annual review of sociology.* Palo Alto: Annual Reviews, 1979.

Aldous, J., Osmond, M. W., & Hicks, M. W. Men's work and men's families. In W. R. Burr, R. Hill, F. I. Nye, & I. L. Reiss (Eds.), *Contemporary theories about the family, Vol. 1.* New York: Free Press, 1979.

Allen, C. & Straus, M. Resources, power and husband-wife violence. In M. Straus & G. Hotaling (Eds.) *The social causes of husband-wife violence.* Minneapolis: University of Minnesota Press, 1980.

Allgeier, E. R. The influence of androgynous identification on heterosexual relations. *Sex Roles*, 1981, *7*, 321-330.

Arndt, J., Grammo, S., & Hawes, D. K. Allocation of time to leisure activities. *Journal of Cross-cultural Psychology*, 1980, *11*, 498-511.

Atkinson, J. & Huston, T.L. Changes in division of household labor in the first year of marriage. Paper presented at the Meeting of NCFR, St. Paul, 1983.

Bahr, S. J. Effects on power and division of labor in the family. In L. W. Hoffman & F. I. Nye (Eds.), *Working mothers.* San Francisco: Jossey-Bass, 1974.

Balswick, J. & Averett, C. P. Differences in expressiveness: Gender, interpersonal orientation, and perceived parental expressiveness as contributing factors. *Journal of Marriage and the Family*, 1977, *39*, 121-127.

Bayer, A. E. Sexist students in American colleges: A descriptive note. *Journal of Marriage and the Family*, 1975, *37*, 391-400.

Becker, G. S. *A treatise on the family.* Cambridge: Harvard University Press, 1981.

Beckett, J. O. & Smith, A. D. Work and family roles: Egalitarian marriage in black and white families. *Social Service Review*, 1981, 314-326.

Beckman, L. J. & Houser, B. B. The more you have, the more you do: The relationship between wife's employment, sex-role attitudes, and household behavior. *Psychology of Women Quarterly*, 1979, *4*, 160-174.

Bell, R. R. & Coughey, K. Premarital sexual experience among college females, 1958, 1968, and 1978. *Family Relations*, 1980, *29*, 353-357.

Berger, J., Zelditch, M., Anderson, B., & Cohen, B. P. Structural aspects of distributive justice: A status-value formulation. In J. Berger, M. Zelditch, & B. Anderson (Eds.), *Sociological Theories in Progress.* New York: Houghton Mifflin, 1972.

Berger, P. L. & Kellner, H. Marriage and the construction of reality. *Diogenes*, 1964, *46*, 1-23.

Berheide, C. W., Berk, S. F., & Berk, R. A. Household work in the suburbs. *Pacific Sociological Review*, 1976, *19*, 491-517.

Berk, R. A. The new home economics: An agenda for sociological research. In S. F. Berk, (Ed.), *Women and household labor.* Beverly Hills: Sage, 1980.

Berk, R. A. & Berk, S. F. *Labor and leisure at home.* Beverly Hills: Sage, 1979.

Bernard, J. Change and stability in sex-role norms and behavior. *Journal of Social Issues*, 1976, *32*, 207-233.

Bernard, J. The good provider role: Its rise and fall. *American Psychologist*, 1981, *36*, 1-12.

Bernard, J. *The future of marriage.* 2nd Edition. New Haven: Yale University Press, 1982.

Blau, P. M. *Exchange and power in social life.* New York: Wiley, 1964.

Blood, R. O. & Wolfe, D. M. *Husbands and wives.* New York: Free Press, 1960.

Bott, E. *Family and social network.* New York: Free Press, 1957.

Bowen, G. L. & Orthner, D. K. Sex-role congruency and marital quality. *Journal of Marriage and the Family*, 1983, *45*, 223-230.

Brown, B. Wife-employment, marital quality, and husband-wife violence. In M. Straus & G. Hotaling (Eds.), *The social causes of husband-wife violence.* Minneapolis: University of Minnesota Press, 1980.

Buckley, W. *Sociology and modern systems theory.* Englewood Cliffs: Prentice Hall, 1967.

Burgess, E. W. *On community, family, and delinquency.* Chicago: University of Chicago Press, 1973.

Burr, W. R., Ahern, L., & Knowles, E. M. An empirical test of Rodman's theory of resources in cultural context. *Journal of Marriage and the Family,* 1977, *39,* 505-514.

Buunk, B. Extramarital sex in the Netherlands. *Alternative Lifestyles,* 1980, *3,* 11-39.

Buunk, B. Jealousy in sexually open marriages. *Alternative Lifestyles,* 1981, *4,* 357-372.

Caplow, T., Bahr, H. M., Chadwick, B. A., Hill, R., & Williamson, M. H. *Middletown families: Fifty years of change and continuity.* Minneapolis: University of Minnesota Press, 1982.

Carlson, J. The sexual role. In F. I. Nye (Ed.), *Role structure and analysis of the family.* Beverly Hills: Sage, 1976.

Cazenave, N. A. Middle-income black fathers: An analysis of the provider role. *Family Coordinator,* 1979, *28,* 583-593.

Centers, R., Raven, B. H., & Rodrigues, A. Conjugal power structure: A reexamination. *American Sociological Review,* 1971, *36,* 264-278.

Cherlin, A. *Marriage, divorce, and remarriage.* Cambridge: Harvard University Press, 1981.

Cherlin, A. & Walters, P. B. Trends in United States men's and women's sex-role attitudes: 1972 to 1978. *American Sociological Review,* 1981, *46,* 453-460.

Christensen, H. T. & Johnson, L. B. Premarital coitus and the Southern black: A comparative view. *Journal of Marriage and the Family,* 1978, *40,* 721-732.

Claessens, D. *Rolle und Macht.* Muenchen, 1970.

Clark, R. A., Nye, F. I. & Gecas, V. Husbands' work involvement and marital role performance. *Journal of Marriage and the Family,* 1978, *40,* 9-21.

Clayton, R. R. & Bokemeier, J. L. Premarital sex in the seventies. *Journal of Marriage and the Family,* 1980, *42,* 759-775.

Cogle, F. L. & Tasker, G. E. Children and housework. *Family Relations,* 1982, *31,* 359-399.

Condron, J. G. & Bode, J. G. Rashomon, working wives, and family division of labor: Middletown, 1980. *Journal of Marriage and the Family,* 1982, *44,* 421-426.

Cooney, R. S., Rogler, L. H., Hurrell, R., & Ortiz, V. Decision-making in intergenerational Puerto Rican families. *Journal of Marriage and the Family,* 1982, *44,* 621-631.

Cordell, A. S., Parke, R. D., & Sawin, D. B. Fathers' view on fatherhood with special reference to infancy. *Family Relations,* 1980, *29,* 331-338.

Crano, W. D. & Aronoff, J. A cross-cultural study of expressive and instrumental complementarity in the family. *American Sociological Reivew,* 1978, *43,* 463-471.

DallaCosta, M. Women and the subversion of community. *Radical America,* 1972, *6,* 67-102.

D'Augelli, J. F. & D'Augelli, A. R. Moral reasoning and premarital sexual behavior. Toward reasoning about relationships. *Journal of Social Issues,* 1977, *33,* 46-66.

Davey, A. J. & Paolucci, B. Family interaction: A study of shared time and activities. *Family Relations,* 1980, *29,* 43-49.

Davis, M. R. *Families in a working world: The impact of organizations on domestic life.* New York: Praeger, 1982.

Degler, C. N. *At odds.* New York: Oxford University Press, 1980.

DeLamater, J. The social control of sexuality. In R. H. Turner & J. F. Short (Eds.), *Annual Review of Sociology.* Palo Alto: Annual Reviews, 1981.

Dibble, U. & Straus, M. Some social structural determinants of inconsistency between attitudes and behavior: The case of family violence. *Journal of Marriage and the Family,* 1980, *42,* 71-80.

Dixon, R. B. Measuring equality between the sexes. *Journal of Social Issues,* 1976, *32,* 19-32.

Dobash, R. E. & Dobash, R. *Violence against wives.* New York: Free Press, 1979.

Dreitzel, H. P. *Die gesellschaftlichen Leiden und das Leiden an der Gesellschaft.* Stuttgart, 1972.

Duncan, O. D., Schuman, H., & Duncan, B. *Social change in a metropolitan community.* New York: Russell Sage, 1973.

Durkheim, E. La famille conjugale. *Revue Philosophique,* 1921, *91,* 1-14.

Emerson, R. M. Social exchange theory. In A. Inkeles, J. Coleman, & N. Smelser (Eds.), *Annual Review of Sociology.* Palo Alto: Annual Reviews, 1976.

Engels, F. *Der Ursprung der Familie, des Privateigentums und des Staats.* Zuerich: Schweizerische Volksbuchhandlung, 1884.

Ericksen, J. A., Yancey, W. L. & Ericksen, E. P. The division of family roles. *Journal of Marriage and the Family,* 1979, *41,* 301-313.

Falbo, T. Relationships between sex, sex role, and social influence. *Psychology of Women Quarterly,* 1977, *2,* 62-72.

Falbo, T. & Peplau, L. A. Power strategies in intimate relationships. *Journal of Personality and Social Psychology,* 1980, *38,* 618-628.

Farkas, G. Education, wage rate, and the division of labor between husband and wife. *Journal of Marriage and the Family,* 1976, *38,* 473-483.

Frank, D. I. & Scanzoni, J. Sexual decision-making: Its development and dynamics. In G. L. Fox (Ed.), *The childbearing decision.* Beverly Hills: Sage, 1982.

Franz, W. K. & Mell, M. B. Perception of parental roles in preschool children. *Home Economics Research Journal,* 1981, *10,* 2-9.

Freeman, J. The women's liberation movement: Its origins, organizations, activities, and ideas. In J. Freeman (Ed.), *Women: A Feminist Perspective.* Palo Alto: Mayfield, 1979.

Frieze, I. H. Investigating the causes and consequences of marital rape. *Signs,* 1983, *8,* 532-553.

Gagnon, J. *Human sexualities.* Glenview: Scott, Foresman and Co., 1977.

Gecas, V. The socialization and child care roles. In F. I. Nye (Ed.), *Role structure and analysis of the family.* Beverly Hills: Sage, 1976.

Geerken, M. & Gove, W. R. *At home and at work.* Beverly Hills: Sage, 1983.

Gelles, R. Power, sex, and violence: The case of marital rape. *Family Coordinator,* 1977, *26,* 339-347.

Gelles, R. Violence in the family: A review of the seventies. *Journal of Marriage and the Family,* 1980, *42,* 873-885.

Gillespie, D. L. Who has the power? The marital struggle. *Journal of Marriage and the Family,* 1971, *33,* 445-458.

Glazer, N. Housework. *Signs,* 1976, *1,* 905-922.

Glenn, N. D. & Weaver, C. N. Attitudes toward premarital, extramarital, and homosexual relations in the U.S. in the 1970's. *Journal of Sex Research,* 1979, *15,* 108-118.

Goldstein, B. & Oldham, J. *Children and Work: A Study of Socialization.* New York: Transaction Books, 1979.

Goode, W. J. *World Revolution and Family Patterns.* New York: Free Press, 1970.

Goode, W. J. Force and violence in the family. *Journal of Marriage and the Family,* 1971, *33,* 625-636.

Goode, W. J. Why men resist. In B. Thorne and M. Yalom (Eds.), *Rethinking the Family,* New York: Longman, 1982.

Gouldner, A. W. The norm of reciprocity: A preliminary statement. *American Sociological Review,* 1960, *25,* 161-178.

Gross, A. E. The male role and heterosexual behavior. *Journal of Social Issues,* 1978, *34,* 87-107.

Gross, R. H. & Arvey, R. D. Marital satisfaction, job satisfaction, and task distribution in the homemaker job. *Journal of Vocational Behavior,* 1977, *11,* 1-13.

Guttentag, M. & Secord, P. F. *Too many women? The sex ratio question.* Beverly Hills: Sage, 1983.

Haas, L. Role-sharing couples: A study of egalitarian marriages. *Family Relations,* 1980, *29,* 289-296.

Haas, L. Domestic role sharing in Sweden. *Journal of Marriage and the Family,* 1981, *43,* 957-967.

Haas, L. Parental sharing of childcare tasks in Sweden. *Journal of Family Issues,* 1982, *3,* 389-412.

Habermas, J. *Arbeit, Erkenntnis, Fortschritt.* Amsterdam, 1970.

Hall, F. T. & Schroeder, M. P. Time spent on household tasks. *Journal of Home Economics,* 1970, *62,* 23-29.

Harrell, W. A. & Sagan, J. *Sex differences in the perception of rape and the sentencing of rapists.* Paper presented at the Meeting of the American Sociological Society, Montreal, 1974.

Harris, L. & Associates. *The Harris Survey Yearbook of Public Opinion 1970.* New York: Louis Harris, 1971.

Harris, R. J. An examination of the effects of ethnicity, socioeconomic status and generation on familism and sex-role orientations. *Journal of Comparative Family Studies,* 1980, *11,* 173-193.

Hartmann, H. Capitalism, patriarchy, and job segregation by sex. *Signs,* 1976, *1,* 137-169.

Hartman, H. The family as the locus of gender, class, and political struggle: The example of housework. *Signs,* 1981, *6,* 366-394.

Haug, F. *Kritik der Rollentheorie.* Frankfurt, 1972.

Hayghe, H. Dual-earner families: Their economic and demographic characteristics. In J. Aldous (Ed.), *Two Paychecks.* Beverly Hills: Sage, 1982.

Heer, D. M. & Grossbard-Shechtman, A. The impact of the female marriage squeeze and the contraceptive revolution on sex roles and the Women's Liberation Movement in the United States, 1960 to 1975. *Journal of Marriage and the Family,* 1981, *43,* 49-65.

Herzog, A. R., Bachman, J. G., & Johnston, L. D. Paid work, child care, and housework: A national survey of high school seniors' preferences for sharing responsibilities between husband and wife. *Sex Roles,* 1983, *9,* 109-135.

Hesselbart, S. L. *Does charity begin at home? Attitudes toward women, household tasks, and household decision-making.* Paper presented at the Meetings of the American Sociological Association, New York, 1976.

Hesselbart, S. L. *Project TAL 1978.* Unpublished research report, Florida State University, 1978.

Hesselbart, S. L. Changes in gender roles and changes in family life. Chapter to appear in M. B. Sussman & S. Steinmetz (Eds.), *Handbook of Marriage and the Family,* in press.

Hewitt, J. P. *Self and Society.* Boston: Allyn and Bacon, 1976.

Hill, C. R. & Stafford, F. P. Parental care of children: Time diary estimates of quantity, predictability and variety. *Journal of Human Resources,* 1980, *15,* 219-239.

Hill, C. T., Rubin, Z. & Peplau, L. A. Breakups before marriage: The end of 103 affairs. *Journal of Social Issues,* 1976, *32,* 147-168.

Hochschild, A. R. A review of sex role research. *American Journal of Sociology,* 1973, *78,* 1011-1029.

Hochschild, A. R. Attending to, codifying and managing feelings: Sex differences in love. In L. Richardson & V. Taylor (Eds.), *Feminist Frontiers.* Reading: Addison-Wesley, 1983.

Hoffman, L. W. Changes in family roles, socialization, and sex differences. *American Psychologist,* 1977, *32,* 644-657.

Hoffman, L. W. Increased fathering: Effects on the mother. In M. E. Lamb & A. Sagi (Eds.), *Fatherhood and Family Policy.* Hillsdale: Erlbaum, 1983.

Hoffman, S. B. *The interpersonal influence strategies of adult cohorts.* Unpublished PhD Dissertation, Pennsylvania State University, 1982.

Hopkins, J. R. Sexual behavior in adolescence. *Journal of Social Issues,* 1977, *33,* 67-85.

Houser, B. B. & Beckman, L. J. Background characteristics and women's dual-role attitudes. *Sex Roles,* 1980, *6,* 355-366.

Huber, J. & Spitze, G. Wives' employment, household behaviors, and sex role attitudes. *Social Forces,* 1981, *60,* 150-169.

Hunt, J. G. & Hunt, L. L. Dilemmas and contradictions of status: The case of the dual-career family. *Social Problems,* 1977, *24,* 407-416.

Hunt, J. G. & Hunt, L. L. Dual-career families: Vanguard of the future or residue of the past? In J. Aldous (Ed.), *Two Paychecks*. Beverly Hills: Sage, 1982.

Hunt, J. C. & Kiker, B. F. The effect of fertility on the time use of working wives. *Journal of Consumer Research*, 1981, *7*, 380-387.

Hunt, M. *Sexual Behavior in the 1970's*. New York: Dell, 1974.

Iglehart, A. P. *Married Women and Work*. Lexington: Heath, 1979.

Indvik, J. & Fitzpatrick, M. A. If you could read my mind, love: Understanding and misunderstanding in the marital dyad. *Family Relations, 31*, 43-51.

Janeway, E. Who is Sylvia? On the loss of sexual paradigms. *Signs*, 1980, *5*, 573-589.

Jedlicka, D. Sex inequality, aging, and innovation in preferential mate selection. *Family Coordinator*, 1978, *27*, 137-140.

Joas, H. *Die gegenwaertige Lage der soziologischen Rollentheorie*. Frankfurt, 1973.

Johnson, G. D. & Hendrix, L. A cross-cultural test of Collins' theory of sexual stratification. *Journal of Marriage and the Family*, 1982, *44*, 675-684.

Johnson, P. Women and power: Toward a theory of effectiveness. *Journal of Social Issues*, 1976, *32*, 99-110.

Jones, C. & Aronson, E. Attribution of fault to a rape victim as a factor of respectability of the victim. *Journal of Personality and Social Psychology*, 1973, *26*, 415-419.

Kalmuss, D. S. & Straus, M. Wife's marital dependency and wife abuse. *Journal of Marriage and the Family*, 1982, *44*, 277-286.

Kamerman, S. B. *Parenting in an Unresponsive Society*. New York: Free Press, 1980.

Kandel, D. B. & Lesser, G. S. Marital decision-making in American and Danish urban families: A research note. *Journal of Marriage and the Family*, 1972, *34*, 134-138.

Katsh, B. S. Fathers and infants. Reported caregiving and interaction. *Journal of Family Issues*, 1981, *2*, 275-296.

Keith, P. M. & Brubaker, T. H. Sex-role specific expectations associated with specific household tasks: Perceived age and employment differences. *Psychological Reports*, 1977, *41*, 15-18.

Keith, P. M. & Schafer, R. B. Role strain and depression in two-job families. *Family Relations*, 1980, *29*, 483-488.

King, K., Abernathy, T. J., & Chapman, A. H. Do adolescents believe the employment of wives is a threat to marital relationships? *Family Coordinator*, 1978, *27*, 231-235.

Kinsey, A. C., Pomeroy, W. B., & Martin, C. E. *Sexual Behavior in the Human Male*. Philadelphia: Saunders, 1948.

Kinsey, A. C., Pomeroy, W. B., Martin, C. E., & Gebhard, P. H. *Sexual Behavior in the Human Female*. Philadelphia: Saunders, 1953.

Knox, D. & Wilson, K. Dating behaviors of university students. *Family Relations*, 1981, *30*, 255-258.

Kotelchuk, M. The infant's relationship to the father: Experimental evidence. In M. E. Lamb (Ed.), *The Role of the Father in Child Development*. New York: Wiley, 1976.

Lamb, M. E. Father-infant and mother-infant interaction in the first year of life. *Child Development*, 1977, *48*, 167-181.

Lamb, M. E. & Lamb, J. E. The nature and importance of the father-infant relationship. *Family Coordinator*, 1976, *25*, 379-385.

Laner, M. R. & Housker, S. L. Sexual permissiveness in younger and older adults. *Journal of Family Issues*, 1980, *1*, 103-124.

Lasch, C. *Haven in a heartless world*. New York: Basic Books, 1977.

Lein, L. Male participation in home life: Impact of social supports and breadwinner responsibilities on the allocation of tasks. *Family Coordinator*, 1979, *28*, 489-495.

Lipman-Blumen, J. Toward a homosocial theory of sex roles: An explanation of the sex segregation of social institutions. *Signs*, 1976, *1*, 15-31.

Lipman-Blumen, J. & Tickamyer, A. R. Sex roles in transition: A ten-year perspective. In *Annual Review of Sociology*. Palo Alto: Annual Reviews, 1975.

Lopata, H. Z. & Norr, K. F. Changing commitments of American women to work and family roles. *Social Security Bulletin*, 1980, *43*, 3-13.

Lynch, M. Sex role stereotypes: Household work of children. *Human Ecology Forum*, 1975, *5*, 1-5.

Mackey, W. C. & Day, R. D. Some indicators of fathering behaviors in the United States: A cross-cultural examination of adult male-child interaction. *Journal of Marriage and the Family*, 1979, *41*, 287-298.

Mainardi, P. The politics of housework. In R. Morgan (Ed.), *Sisterhood is Powerful.* New York: Vintage, 1971.

Marsden, D. Social perspectives on family violence. In J. P. Martin (Ed.), *Violence and the Family.* New York: Wiley, 1978.

Marsh, L. C. Hours worked by husbands and wives. In J. Aldous (Ed.), *Two Paychecks.* Beverly Hills: Sage, 1982.

Martin, P. Y., Osmond, M. W., Hesselbart, S. L., & Wood, M. The significance of gender as a social and demographic correlate of sex role attitudes. *Sociological Focus*, 1980, *13*, 383-396.

Marx, K. *Pariser Manuskripte 1844.* Texte zur Methode und Praxis, Reinbek: Rowohlt, 1966.

Mason, K. O., Czajka, J. L., & Arber, S. Change in U.S. women's sex-role attitudes, 1964-1974. *American Sociological Review*, 1976, *41*, 573-596.

McDonald, G. W. Family power: The assessment of a decade of theory and research, 1970-1979. *Journal of Marriage and the Family*, 1980, *42*, 841-854.

McHale, S. M. & Huston, T. L. *The assumption of parental roles.* Unpublished manuscript, Pennsylvania State University, 1983.

Meissner, M., Humpheys, E. W., Meis, S. M., & Scheu, W. J. No exit for wives: Sexual division of labour and the cumulation of household demands. *Canadian Review of Sociology and Anthropology*, 1975, *12*, 424-439.

Miller, J. & Garrison, H. H. Sex roles: The division of labor at home and in the workplace. In R. H. Turner & J. F. Short (Eds.), *Annual Review of Sociology.* Palo Alto: Annual Reviews, 1982.

Miller, P. Y. & Fowlkes, M. R. Social and behavioral constructions of female sexuality. *Signs*, 1980, *5*, 783-800.

Model, S. Housework by husbands. In J. Aldous (Ed.), *Two paychecks.* Beverly Hills: Sage, 1982.

Moen, P. The two-provider family. In M. E. Lamb (Ed.), *Nontraditional families: Parenting and child development.* Hillsdale: Erlbaum, 1982.

Morgan, C. S. & Walker, A. J. Predicting sex-role attitudes. *Social Psychology Quarterly*, 1983, *46*, 148-151.

Morgan, J., Sirageldin, I. & Baerwaldt, N. *Productive Americans.* Ann Arbor: ISR, 1966.

Nazzari, M. The significance of present-day changes in the institution of marriage. *The Review of Radical Political Economics*, 1980, *12*, 63-75.

Nickols, S. Y. *Work and housework: Family role in productive activity.* Paper presented at the Meetings of the National Council on Family Relations, New York, 1976.

Norton, A. J. Family life-cycle: 1980. *Journal of Marriage and the Family*, 1983, *45*, 267-275.

Notarius, C. I. & Johnson, J. S. Emotional expression in husbands and wives. *Journal of Marriage and the Family*, 1982, *44*, 483-489.

Nye, F. I. Family roles in comparative perspective. In F. I. Nye (Ed.), *Role Structure and Analysis of the Family.* Beverly Hills: Sage, 1976.

Oakley, A. *The Sociology of Housework.* New York: Pantheon, 1974.

Oppenheimer, V. K. The sociology of women's economic role in the family. *American Sociological Review*, 1977, *42*, 387-405.

Osmond, M. W. & Martin, P. Y. Sex and sexism: A comparison of male and female sex-role attitudes. *Journal of Marriage and the Family*, 1975, *37*, 744-758.

Parelius, A. P. Emerging sex-role attitudes, expectations, and strains among college women. *Journal of Marriage and the Family*, 1975, *37*, 146-154.

Parke, R. D. & O'Leary, S. E. Father-mother-infant interaction in the newborn period: Some findings, some observations, and some unresolved issues. In K. Riegel & J. Meachman (Eds.), *The Developing Individual in a Changing World, Vol. 2.* The Hague: Mouton, 1976.

Parke, R. D. & Tinsley, B. R. The father's role in infancy: Determinants of involvement in caregiving and play. In M. E. Lamb (Ed.), *The Role of the Father in Child Development, Second edition.* New York: Wiley, 1981.

Parsons, T. & Bales, R. F. *Family, Socialization, and Interaction Process.* New York: Free Press, 1955.

Parsons, T. & Shils, E. A. (Eds.) *Toward a General Theory of Action.* New York: Harper, 1951.

Peplau, L. A. Power in dating relationships. In J. Freeman (Ed.), *Women: A Feminist Perspective.* Palo Alto: Mayfield, 1979.

Peplau, L. A., Rubin, Z., & Hill, C. T. Sexual intimacy in dating relationships. *Journal of Social Issues,* 1977, *33,* 86-109.

Perrucci, C. C., Potter, H. R., & Rhoads, D. L. Determinants of family role performance. *Psychology of Women Quarterly,* 1978, *3,* 53-66.

Petchesky, R. P. Reproductive freedom: Beyond a woman's right to choose. *Signs,* 1980, *5,* 661-685.

Phelps, L. Female sexual alienation. In J. Freeman (Ed.), *Rethinking the Family.* New York: Longman, 1979.

Philliber, W. W. & Hiller, D. V. A research note: Occupational attainment and perceptions of status among working wives. *Journal of Marriage and the Family,* 1979, *41,* 59-62.

Pleck, J. H. The male sex-role: Definitions, problems, and sources of change. *Journal of Social Issues,* 1976, *32,* 155-164.

Pleck, J. H. The work-family role system. *Social Problems,* 1977, *24,* 417-427.

Pleck, J. H. Men's family work: Three perspectives and some new data. *Family Coordinator,* 1979, *28,* 481-488.

Pleck, J. H. Men's power with women, other men, and society: A men's movement analysis. In E. H. Pleck & J. H. Pleck (Eds.), *The American Man.* Englewood Cliffs, NJ: Prentice Hall, 1980.

Pleck, J. H. *The Myth of Masculinity.* Cambridge: MIT Press, 1981.

Pleck, J. H. Husband's paid work and family roles: Current research issues. In H. Z. Lopata & J. H. Pleck (Eds.), *Research on the Interwave of Social Roles, Vol. 3.* Greenwich: JAI Press, 1983.

Polatchnik, M. Why men don't rear children: A power analysis. *Berkeley Journal of Sociology,* 1973, *18,* 45-86.

Price-Bonham, S., Wright, D. W., & Pittman, J. F. Divorce: A frequent "alternative" in the 1970's. In E. D. Macklin and R. H. Rubin (Eds.), *Contemporary Families and Alternative Lifestyles.* Beverly Hills: Sage, 1983.

Pyke, S. W. Androgyny: A dead end or a promise. In C. Stark-Adamec (Ed.), *Sex roles: Origins, Influences, and Implications for Women.* Montreal: Eden Press, 1980.

Rank, M. R. Determinants of conjugal influence in wife's employment decision-making. *Journal of Marriage and the Family,* 1982, *44,* 591-604.

Raven, B. H. & Kruglanski, A. W. Conflict and power. In P. Swingle (Ed.), *The Structure of Conflict.* New York: Academic Press, 1970.

Rebecca, M., Hefner, R., & Oleshansky, B. A model of sex-role transcendence. *Journal of Social Issues,* 1976, *32,* 197-206.

Reiss, I. L. *Premarital Sexual Standards in America.* New York: Free Press, 1960.

Reiss, I. L. *Family Systems in America, Third edition.* New York: Holt, Rinehart and Winston, 1980.

Reiss, I. L. Some observations on ideology and sexuality in America. *Journal of Marriage and the Family,* 1981, *43,* 271-283.

Reiss, I. L., Anderson, R. E., & Sponaugle, G. C. A multivariate model of the determinants of extramarital sexual permissiveness. *Journal of Marriage and the Family*, 1980, *42*, 395-411.

Rendina, I. & Dickerscheid, J. D. Father involvement with first-born infants. *Family Coordinator*, 1976, *25*, 373-378.

Richardson, L. & Taylor, V. *Feminist Frontiers*. Reading: Addison-Wesley, 1983.

Richmond, M. L. Beyond resource theory: Another look at factors enabling women to affect family interaction. *Journal of Marriage and the Family*, 1976, *38*, 257-266.

Robinson, I. E. & Jedlicka, D. Change in sexual attitudes and behaviors of college students from 1965-1980: A research note. *Journal of Marriage and the Family*, 1982, *44*, 237-240.

Robinson, J. P. Historical changes in how people spend their time. In A. Michel (Ed.), *Family Issues of Employed Women in Europe and America*. Leiden: Brill, 1971.

Robinson, J. P., Converse, P., & Szalai, A. Everyday life in twelve countries. In A. Szalai (Ed.), *The Use of Time*. The Hague: Mouton, 1972.

Robinson, J. P. *How Americans Use Time: A Social-Psychological Analysis*. New York: Praeger, 1977.

Robinson, J. P. Housework technology and household work. In S. F. Berk (Ed.), *Women and Household Labor*. Beverly Hills: Sage, 1980.

Robinson, J. P., Yerby, J., Fieweger, M., & Somerick, N. Sex-role differences in time use. *Sex Roles*, 1977, *3*, 443-458.

Rodman, H. Marital power and the theory of resources in cultural context. *Journal of Comparative Family Studies*, 1972, *3*, 50-67.

Rollins, J. & White, P. N. The relationships between mothers' and daughters' sex-role attitudes and self-concepts in three types of family environment. *Sex Roles*, 1982, *8*, 1141-1155.

Roper, B. S. & Labeff, E. Sex roles and feminism revisited: An intergenerational attitude comparison. *Journal of Marriage and the Family*, 1977, *39*, 113-119.

Roper, Inc. *The 1980 Virginia Slims American Women's Opinion Poll. A Survey of Contemporary Attitudes*, Roper Inc., 1980.

Rosenfeld, R. A. Race and sex differences in career dynamics. *American Sociological Review*, 1980, *45*, 583-609.

Rossi, A. S. Sex equality: The beginnings of ideology. In K. W. Kammeyer (Ed.), *Confronting the Issues: Sex roles, Marriage, and the Family*. Boston: Allyn and Bacon, 1975.

Rossi, A. S. A biosocial perspective on parenting. *Daedalus*, 1977, *106*, 1-31.

Rubin, L. B. *Worlds of Pain*. New York: Basic Books, 1977.

Rubin, L. B. *Intimate Strangers. Men and Women Together*. New York: Harper and Row, 1983.

Russell, D. E. H. *Rape in Marriage*. New York: Macmillan, 1982.

Russel, G. & Radin, N. Increased parental participation: The fathers' perspective. In M. E. Lamb & A. Sagi (Eds.), *Fatherhood and Family Policy*. Hillsdale: Erlbaum, 1983.

Russo, N. F. The motherhood mandate. *Journal of Social Issues*, 1976, *32*, 143-153.

Safilios-Rothschild, C. The study of family power structure: A review 1960-1969. *Journal of Marriage and the Family*, 1970, *32*, 539-552.

Safilios-Rothschild, C. A macro- and micro-examination of family power and love: An exchange model. *Journal of Marriage and the Family*, 1976, *38*, 355-362.

Safilios-Rothschild, C. *Love, Sex, and Sex Roles*. Englewood Cliffs, NJ: Prentice Hall, 1977.

Sanday, P. R. *Female Power and Male Dominance*. Cambridge: Cambridge University Press, 1981.

Sanik, M. M. Division of household work: A decade comparison—1967-1977. *Home Economics Research Journal*, 1981, *10*, 175-180.

Sattel, J. W. Men, inexpressiveness, and power. In L. Richardson & V. Taylor (Eds.), *Feminist Frontiers*. Reading: Addison-Wesley, 1983.

Sawin, D. B. & Parke, R. D. Fathers' affectionate stimulation and care-giving behaviors with newborn infants. *Family Coordinator*, 1979, *28*, 509-513.

Scanzoni, J. *Opportunity and the Family.* New York: Free Press, 1970.

Scanzoni, J. *Sex Roles, Life Styles, and Childbearing.* New York: Free Press, 1975.

Scanzoni, J. *Sex roles, women's work, and marital conflict.* Lexington: Lexington Books, 1978.

Scanzoni, J. Social processes and power in families. In W. R. Burr, R. Hill, F. I. Nye, & I. L. Reiss (Eds.), *Contemporary Theories About the Family, Vol. 1.* New York: Free Press, 1979. (a)

Scanzoni, J. A historical perspective on husband-wife bargaining, power, and marital dissolution. In G. Levinger & O. C. Moles (Eds.), *Divorce and Separation.* New York: Basic Books, 1979. (b)

Scanzoni, J. Contemporary marriage types. *Journal of Family Issues,* 1980, *1,* 125-140.

Scanzoni, J. & Fox, G. L. Sex roles, family and society: The seventies and beyond. *Journal of Marriage and the Family,* 1980, *42,* 743-756.

Scanzoni, J. & Szinovacz, M. *Family decision-making. A developmental sex-role model.* Beverly Hills: Sage, 1980.

Scanzoni, L. & Scanzoni, J. *Men, Women, and Change.* New York: McGraw-Hill, 1976.

Schafer, R. B. & Keith, P. M. Equity in marital roles across the family life cycle. *Journal of Marriage and the Family,* 1981, *43,* 359-367.

Singh, B. K. Trends in attitudes toward premarital sexual relations. *Journal of Marriage and the Family,* 1980, *42,* 387-393.

Slater, P. Parental role differentiation. *American Journal of Sociology,* 1961, *67,* 296-311.

Slocum, W. L. & Nye, F. I. Provider and housekeeper roles. In F. I. Nye (Ed.), *Role Structure and Analysis of the Family.* Beverly Hills: Sage, 1976.

Spitze, G. & Huber, J. Changing attitudes toward women's nonfamily roles, 1938 to 1978. *Sociology of Work and Occupations,* 1980, *7,* 327-335.

Stafford, R., Backman, E. & DiBona, P. The division of labor among cohabiting and married couples. *Journal of Marriage and the Family,* 1977, *39,* 43-57.

Staples, R. Race, liberalism-conservativism and premarital sexual permissiveness: A bi-racial comparison. *Journal of Marriage and the Family,* 1978, *40,* 733-742.

Stockard, J. Developing attitudes toward the role of women. A comparison of females and males. *Youth and Society,* 1980, *12,* 61-82.

Straus, M., Gelles, R. & Steinmetz, S. *Behind Closed Doors.* New York: Anchor, 1980.

Szalai, A. (Ed.) *The Use of Time.* The Hague: Mouton, 1972.

Szinovacz, M. Another look at normative resource theory: Contributions from Austrian data—A research note. *Journal of Marriage and the Family,* 1978, *40,* 413-421.

Szinovacz, M. *The situation of women in Austria: Economic and family issues.* Vienna: Ministry of Social Affairs, 1979.

Szinovacz, M. (Ed.) *Women's Retirement: Policy Issues of Current Research.* Beverly Hills: Sage, 1982.

Szinovacz, M. Family power relations and processes. In M. B. Sussman & S. Steinmetz (Eds.), *Handbook of Marriage and the Family,* in press.

Tavris, C. & Sadd, S. *The Redbook Report on Human Sexuality.* New York: Delacorte, 1977.

Tellis-Nayak, V. & Donoghue, G. O. Conjugal egalitarianism and violence across cultures. *Journal of Comparative Family Studies,* 1982, *13,* 277-290.

Thorne, B. Feminist rethinking of the family: An overview. In B. Thorne & M. Yalom (Eds.), *Rethinking the Family. Some Feminist Questions.* New York: Longman, 1982.

Thornton, A. & Freedman, D. Changes in the sex role attitudes of women, 1962-1977: Evidence from a panel study. *American Sociological Review,* 1979, *44,* 831-842.

Thornton, A., Alwin, D. F., & Camburn, D. Causes and consequences of sex-role attitude change. *American Sociological Review,* 1983, *48,* 211-227.

Thrall, C. A. Who does what: Role stereotypy, children's work, and continuity between generations in the household division of labor. *Human Relations,* 1978, *31,* 249-265.

Tomeh, A. K. Sex-role orientation: An analysis of structural and attitudinal predictors. *Journal of Marriage and the Family,* 1978, *40,* 341-354.

Turner, R. H. Role-taking: Process versus conformity. In A. Rose (Ed.), *Human Behavior and Social Processes.* Boston: Houghton Mifflin, 1962.

Udry, J. R. Marital alternatives and marital disruption. *Journal of Marriage and the Family,* 1981, *43,* 889-897.

U.S. Bureau of the Census. Current population reports, Series P-60, No. 51. *Income in 1965 of Families and Persons in the United States.* Washington, D.C.: U.S. Government Printing Office, 1967.

U.S. Bureau of the Census. Current population reports, Series P-60, No. 80. *Income in 1970 of Families and Persons in the United States.* Washington, D.C.: U.S. Government Printing Office, 1971.

U.S. Bureau of the Census. Current population reports, Series P-60, No. 113. *Money Income and Poverty Status in 1975 of Families and Persons in the United States and the West Region, by Divisions and States.* Washington, D.C.: U.S. Government Printing Office, 1978.

U.S. Bureau of the Census. Current population reports, Series P-20, No. 366. *Household and Family Characteristics: March 1980.* Washington, D.C.: U.S. Government Printing Office, 1981.

U.S. Bureau of the Census. Current population reports, Series P-60, No. 132. *Money Income of Households, Families, and Persons in the United States, 1980.* Washington, D.C.: U.S. Government Printing Office, 1982.

U.S. Bureau of the Census. Current population reports, Series P-60, No. 140. *Money Income and Poverty Status of Families and Persons in the United States, 1982.* Washington, D.C.: U.S. Government Printing Office, 1983.

Vanek, J. Time spent on housework. *Scientific American,* 1974, *231,* 116-120.

Vanek, J. Work, leisure and family roles: Family households in the United States, 1920-1955. *Journal of Family History,* 1980a, *5.*

Vanek, J. Household work, wage work, and sexual equality. In S. F. Berk (Ed.), *Women and Household Labor.* Beverly Hills: Sage, 1980b.

Waldron, H. & Routh, D. K. The effect of the first child on the marital relationship. *Journal of Marriage and the Family,* 1981, *43,* 785-788.

Walker, K. E. & Woods, M. E. *Time Use: A Measure of Household Production of Family Goods and Services.* Washington, D.C.: American Home Economics Association, 1976.

Waller, W. The rating and dating complex. *American Sociological Review,* 1937, *2,* 727-734.

Weeks, M. O., Crosby, J. F. & Tackett, J. Changing marriage role expectations: A comparison of college women in 1961 and 1978. *International Journal of the Sociology of the Family,* 1981, *11,* 115-126.

Westoff, C. F. Coital frequency and contraception. *Family Planning Perspectives,* 1974, *6,* 136-141.

Wheeler, C. L. & Arvey, R. D. Division of household labor in the family. *Home Economics Research Journal,* 1981, *10,* 10-20.

White, L. K. & Brinkerhoff, D. B. The sexual division of labor: Evidence from childhood. *Social Forces,* 1981a, *60,* 170-181.

White, L. K. & Brinkerhoff, D. B. Children's work in the family: Its significance and meaning. *Journal of Marriage and the Family,* 1981b, *43,* 789-798.

Whyte, M. K. *The Status of Women in Preindustrial Societies.* Princeton: Princeton University Press, 1978.

Wilkie, J. R. The trend toward delayed parenthood. *Journal of Marriage and the Family,* 1981, *43,* 583-591.

Wingrove, C. R. & Slevin, K. F. Age differences and generational gaps. College women and their mothers' attitudes toward female roles in society. *Youth and Society,* 1982, *13,* 289-301.

Yankelovich, D. The meaning of work. In J. Rosow (Ed.), *The Worker and the Job.* Englewood Cliffs: Prentice Hall, 1974.

Yllo, K. & Straus, M. *Patriarchy and violence against wives: The impact of structural and normative factors.* Paper presented at the Theory Construction and Methodology Workshop, Washington, D.C., 1982.

Yogev, S. Do professional women have egalitarian marital relationships? *Journal of Marriage and the Family,* 1981, *43,* 865-871.

Yogman, M. W. Development of the father-infant relationship. In H. Fitzgerald, B. Lester, & M. W. Yogman (Eds.), *Theory and Research in Behavioral Pediatrics, Vol. 1.* New York: Plenum.

Young, M. & Willmott, P. *The Symmetrical Family.* Harmondsworth: Penguin, 1973.

Chapter 11

Missing Links:
Notes on an Impossible Mission

Marilyn Johnson
Beth B. Hess

The question is intriguing: has the Women's Movement affected childrearing practices in the family? The answer is elusive: the research literature to date does not provide sufficient information for even a tentative conclusion. An extensive search of social science sources yielding over 400 items, reveals more about the need for a reasoned agenda of research on socialization and sex/gender roles than about the substantive questions posed. Thus, while these brief notes cannot shed much light on the original topic, we offer some observations as lessons for future researchers.

NATURE OF THE LITERATURE

The bulk of research on childrearing and feminism is published by women in journals of relatively low prestige. Since one can hardly argue that the subject is low in social significance or intellectual challenge, we suspect that the disproportionately small number of male authors reflects a low academic ranking (male defined) of family/sex role studies and, more fundamentally, a general societal tendency for men to distance themselves from family concerns. Whatever the causes, the absence of males from the family is literally reproduced in the literature.

Despite where the information is published or who does the re-

Marilyn Johnson is an antiquarian in Metuchen, NJ. Beth B. Hess is Professor of Sociology at the County College of Morris, Randolph, NJ.

203

search, one might expect an extensive literature addressing the influence of the Women's Movement on childrearing. Alas, such is not the case. Among the 400 studies reviewed, such influence is more often assumed than examined empirically. Very few studies focus directly on the issue of whether and how the sex-role ideology of parent affects the way in which they raise their children and/or their children's subsequent characteristics, behavior, and values. The few studies that have this focus are quite limited in generalizability because of sample size, sample composition, or conceptually inappropriate research strategies. A few studies examine changes over time in childrearing norms and practices, attributing these to the changing status of women and family structures. However plausible these interpretations, little evidence is presented that the women's movement has been responsible for measurable family change, in part because the very question posed forces us to confront what may be insurmountable difficulties in connecting macro-level to micro-level, ideology to behavior, and cause to effect.

In a more positive vein, however, increasing attention is being paid to topics that would probably not have evoked interest or even reached the level of social fact had there not been a resurgence of feminism: e.g., single-parent families, the involvement of fathers in child care, dual-career families, effects of mother's employment, and influence of mother's occupation on children's achievement— all of which are discussed in this issue of *Marriage and Family Review*. In addition, the particular problems of gay fathers and lesbian mothers are receiving serious consideration (Miller, 1979; Mucklow and Phelan, 1979; Kirkpatrick et al., 1981). Nonetheless, in setting the agenda for family researchers in the 1980s, Felix Berardo (1981) places sex-role studies at the top of his list, most particularly those that focus on (1) spousal decision-making and sex-role preferences, (2) the links between micro- and macro-level processes, (3) the effects of children on parental relationships, and (4) the impact of feminism on the black family.

Whether such an ambitious agenda can be realized in the coming decade remains problematic at this writing, given the state of the art: the low valuation of "women's studies" in the academic reward structure, the low priority accorded such studies by most funding agencies, the neglect of appropriate research training in the typical graduate program, and the frequent failure to create and apply clear conceptualizations that would enlarge the theoretical scope of research findings.

SPECIFICATION OF THE RESEARCH QUESTION

Research is needed that will document sequences of change in family structure and childrearing, relate these to the sex-role ideology of parents, and discover what differences might ensue for children of either sex. Yet a meaningful agenda for future research can be developed only if we first come to grips with tantalizing questions of what it is we really want to know and of whether what we want to know is reasonably knowable through social science research. No doubt an additional source of our disappointment with the research literature is the fact that our initial question—has the women's movement affected childrearing practices in the family?—is framed improperly. The question both lacks specificity and unjustifiably implies asymmetry of causation.

Problems of Causal Attribution

How can the impact of a social movement be assessed? One can document family change—childrearing practices in this instance—but it is very difficult to pinpoint the women's movement was a causal agent. In fact, both the trend toward relatively egalitarian treatment of sons and daughters and the trend toward increased family involvement of men were well documented before the flowering of the new feminism. Sociologists who were in graduate school in the late 1950s and early 1960s were introduced to a family literature which, while heavily influenced by Parsonian functionalism, nonetheless contained clues of important changes already underway—e.g., Urie Bronfenbrenner (1958) on the increasing spread of middle-class egalitarian norms of childrearing to other social classes; and Morris Zelditch, Jr. (1955) on the relative flexibility of instrumental and expressive task allocation in the contemporary American family. In a seminal critique of the Parsonian model, Slater (1961) perceived a trend in modern society toward an egalitarian "de-differentiated" pattern of childrearing and argued that such a pattern is more functional for the socialization of children, especially of boys.

One recent study (Shepard, 1980) of college students (who would have been born in the late 1950s) found that daughters and sons reported very similar treatment from their fathers and mothers; that is, on a majority of the items being measured, mothers and fathers were perceived as responding similarly. Possibly, such trends were responses to other changes taking place in the society that also set the stage for the rebirth of feminism: namely, women's rising levels of educational attainment and labor force participation. Attitude changes from 1962-on are, however, amply documented (Thornton et al., 1983), and are clearly in the direction of increasing egalitarian conceptions of women's roles, among a sample of young people and their mothers. While the children (age 18) were less traditional their mothers, the latter had also changed over the 18 years of the study. Work experience and education, as well as youth were associated with egalitarian attitudes.

It is important to keep in mind that the family is not merely a dependent variable in social analysis, reacting to events in the world outside; it is also possible that changes in relationships between spouses and among parents and children have effects on other institutions. A similar circularity pervades the discussion of the impact of ideology vs structural variables. Certainly, children today are being raised in a family environment radically different from that in which their parents grew up. The list of such changes is formidable: working mothers, older parents, fewer siblings, larger percentages of college-educated parents, more living members of the extended family, more single parents and step parents, pre-school education and day care, and less "official" gender differentiation.

To what extent are these trends *reflecting* a rise in feminist activity and to what extent were they *pre-existing,* serving to energize the women's movement? The issue requires careful historical analysis. Even if one were to find that sex-role ideology makes a difference in childrearing practices, such a finding cannot delineate the full impact of the women's movement. Numerous indirect effects would remain unmeasured. Large numbers of American men and women who do not consider themselves ideological feminists cannot have escaped fully the subtle and pervasive influence of the movement. For example, many women today are active in fields that might not have been open to them only two decades ago. Furthermore, the variable of "mother's occupation," not merely her labor force participation, is increasingly recognized as a potentially important explanatory variable in socialization research.

Definition of the consequences. The difficulty of assessing fully the explanatory power of the Women's Movement—more precisely, the set of independent variables for which "Women's Movement" is linguistic shorthand—is compounded by the difficulty of defining just *which* aspects of childrearing should be examined as potential consequences. That is, future research would benefit from more conscious deliberation about what are the dependent variables of interest. The potential outcomes of childhood socialization are infinite. What researchers select for study is limited not only by the state of art of their theories and methods, but also, as several other authors in this volume have pointed out, by implicit and often unexamined value positions. These value positions were only barely hidden under the banner of "objective science" in the early research on children of divorced parents or of working mothers. A far more subtle form of bias may still be seen in the use of dependent variables such as achievement and nurturance in attempts to find out whether girls are becoming more like boys, and vice versa, although on balance there is more research interest in female emulation of male patterns.

Contextual Variables

Evaluation of childrearing consequences must also take into account the larger structural and normative context of variant or changing family forms and behaviors. We might speculate, for example, that the child whose mother is gainfully employed will suffer less today, when most mothers work outside the home, than in the past when a wife's employment was socially disapproved. Employment in the work force implied neglect of maternal obligations and a failure of the husband as provider, when most mothers were available to their children at lunchtime and immediately after school, and when most children of employed mothers were *expected* to display signs of poor social, emotional, and intellectual development.

As a contextual variable, the climate of social opinion will have an independent effect on children in different family situations: single parent, dual worker, step parent, gay father or lesbian mother. In addition, the level of societal approval or tolerance of variant family practices is likely to affect the extent to which extrafamilial institutions develop supportive arrangements e.g., flexitime, paternity leave, in-school cafeterias. Societal approval or tolerance depends in part on how many similar families are recognized.

The parental pair. In most family research, parents are treated either as unrelated individuals or as undifferentiated pairs. Too little attention has been paid to the differential effects of particular dyadic combinations. Attitudes of fathers toward the mothers' role, for example, may be crucial. Fathers who care for their children willingly create a different family dynamic from that which characterizes families in which the father's involvement is coerced. Effects on daughters of maternal encouragement of independence are likely to differ widely depending on whether the father's attitudes reinforce or undermine the mother's efforts. Clearly, various mother/father combinations are deserving of far more systematic research effort than currently expended.

Ideology/attitudes vs behavior/roles. As a final caveat in specifying questions for future research, we warn against the too frequent confusion of orientation and behavior in the published literature. Many studies, for example, have used mother's work role (homemaker vs paid employee) as a proxy for "traditional/nontraditional" orientations. We are likely to learn far more about feminism and family socialization if, instead, we regard the connection between parental sex-role ideology and parental statuses and behaviors as a matter for empirical observation. While there appears to be a correlation between feminist ideology and employment status—although the causal connection may be either way—the association is not so close as to warrant treatment of the two as interchangeable indicators. Indeed, we want to know more about the effects on children of *incongruence* between parental ideology and behavior.

METHODOLOGICAL ISSUES

Running through almost all of these comments is a larger critique which is basically methodological—that what appears in the research literature is constrained by the techniques employed and/or by a failure to adopt the appropriate level of analysis.

As an example of the first type of problem—the limits of measurement—the development of standardized sex-role scales and inventories, while necessary for comparability among diverse studies, also inhibits further exploration of other aspects of behavior and development likely to be influenced by the changing status of women. Since much of the published literature on sex role socialization has been produced by psychologists, the use of standardized instruments is widespread, as is the use of extremely small and nonrepresentative samples. The social science laboratory is, of course, an artificial environment manipulated by "experts" with a particular agenda. The same charge of Procrusteanism can be leveled at those who shape the data to fit sophisticated statistical models (see Baumrind, 1980 for a full discussion of this point).

The most flagrant violations of sound methodology, however, are of the second type: failures to analyse at the system level under study. While the authors claim that their research case is the dyad (parent-child) or the family system as a whole, their findings are all too often derived from aggregate data. For example, in one recent large-scale study, a statewide random sample of over 2000 households, where data were collected from wife-husband dyads, the researchers present tables that split pairs by aggregating all wife and all husband responses—including one table in which the dependent variable was spousal agreement on household division of labor! (Albrecht, Bahr, and Chadwick, 1979).

Indeed, the key independent variable in studies of socialization may not be mothers' or fathers' roles, attitudes, or behaviors but whether and how these are combined within a given dyad. That is, we need to measure a characteristic of the parental unit such as agreement or disagreement on sex-role orientation, and expectations of sons or daughters. Spouses do affect one another, and parents exert a joint effect on their offspring—and children can influence parents (see Lerner and Spanier, 1978). There is some hint in the literature, for example, that fathers, regardless of their sex-role ideology, are more likely to participate in parenting when their wives have a nontraditional orientation (Russell, 1978; Baruch and Barnett, 1981; see also Stein, this issue). But we do not know if the outcomes for these parents are similar to those for parents who share a nontraditional ideology. Although both types of dyad may display a similar allocation of household tasks, the internal dynamics could be very different, generating strain and resentment in one set of parents, while easing tension in the other. Such differences in atmosphere are likely to affect the child's perceptions. Yet too many researchers remain locked into an opposite-sex/same-sex paradigm of parental influence without examining the family constellation. Having carefully selected intact families, they fail to use their data fully.

Lastly, the cross sectional nature of the vast majority of studies makes generalizations about change somewhat tenuous. Even where similar subjects are used at different time periods—e.g. university sociology students and their parents in 1934 and 1974 (Roper and Labeff, 1976)—the two populations may not be comparable.

SOME TENTATIVE ANSWERS

Despite all these caveats, there are some substantive gleanings to be culled from the existing research literature.

1. There is little doubt that the secular trend in attitudes of American men and women is toward greater egalitarianism (Thornton et al., 1983, for data from an 18-year panel study; and Ferree and Hess, 1984, Chapter 4 for a review of survey data). As other authors in this issue have pointed out, however, these attitudes have not been reflected in the division of household labor.

2. This trend toward egalitarianism appears to exemplify the Weberian process of ideological preceding behavioral change. That is, despite dramatic shifts in sex-role attitudes, women have actually made little progress toward equality within the family, the economy, or the polity—especially the latter two spheres. Conversely, behavioral changes often occur regardless of ideological disposition, ultimately leading to attitude modifications.

3. In addition, the evidence for major changes in sex-role patterns of socialization is very weak, at least through the mid-1970s (Beuf, 1974; Bush et al., 1977-78; Sidorowicz and Lunney, 1980; Leuptow, 1980; Birnbaum et al., 1980). Children appear to arrive very early and firmly at relatively traditional and stereotypical views of appropriate gender behavior, although children of working mothers seem to be more flexible than children of nonworking mothers (Jones and McBride, 1980). Girls continue to display lower levels of aspiration than their male counterparts (Brook et al., 1979). In addition, girls' occupational expectations remain constrained by domestic role considerations, while boys continue to see these as discrete spheres of activity (Aneshensel and Rosen, 1980; but data are from 1974).

4. The preference for male offspring remains strong, particularly with respect to first-born and only children (Norman, 1974; Fidell et al., 1979). However, since the preferred family size today is two children, most adults also express a desire for a daughter as the second-born.

5. Boys appear to be psychologically more vulnerable than girls to changes in family structure and functioning. A number of studies report that marital break-up adversely affects sons (Hetherington et al., 1978), but so does parental lack of agreement (Block et al., 1981), alternative daycare (Moskowitz et al., 1977), and, at least for working class boys, maternal employment in general (Gold and

Andres, 1978; Baker, 1981). It should, however, be noted that some of these oft-quoted findings are based upon small nonrepresentative samples (e.g., 110 nursery school children for Gold and Andres, and 83 largely middle-class self-selected parental dyads involved in a longitudinal study for Block et al.).

Conversely, female offspring seem to be less affected by lack of parental agreement and more resilient to changes in family structure. In one study (Mullins, 1980, based on 1972 data), the likelihood of a daughter having feminist attitudes was independently related to her perception of maternal unhappiness in the housekeeping role and father's dissatisfaction with his job. In general, a mother's attitudes and expectations were more powerful predictors of a daughter's sex-role attitudes than was the mother's behavior (Meyer, 1980; Smith and Self, 1980; Rollins and White, 1982). The direct effect of maternal employment *per se* appears strong in some studies (e.g., Stevens and Boyd, 1980) and non-existent in others (Meyer, 1980, with a working class sample; Rosenthal and Hansen, 1981). Much depends what variables are being measured—daughters' attitudes, occupational plans, self-concept, feelings about parents, or family-size expectations.

6. The effect of fathers' sex-role attitudes and/or behaviors is not much clearer. There is some indication that extreme closeness to father encourages traditional sex typing in daughters (Orlofsky, 1979; McBroom, 1981). At the same time, a father's independent participation in child care was found to reduce his daughter's stereotyping (Baruch and Barnett, 1981).

7. Much of the work on parental influence, especially that of the father, is designed to test hypotheses regarding models of socialization; namely, do children reach an appropriate sex-role identity through modeling, social learning, or other cognitive strategies? Thus far, this issue remains unresolved, confounded by changes in parental attitudes and behaviors, as well as by changes at the societal level. In addition, several recent studies challenge the assumption of parental dominance in sex-role socialization (Shepard, 1980; Seegmiller, 1980; Barry, 1980). Rather, peers, older siblings, school experiences, and the generalized expectations of the culture impress their mark regardless or in addition to parental pressure (Philliber, 1980).

8. Clearly, future research must take into account the sex-role attitudes of both parents and how these may differentially affect girls and boys. In this respect, the work of Barnett (1981) might well

serve as a guide; with a heavily upper-middle class sample of white mothers and fathers, she found that parental sex-role orientation did not affect the socialization of male offspring with regard to independence training or achievement pressure. For daughters, however, parents with nontraditional sex-role orientations initiated independence training at earlier ages than parents with traditional attitudes. Further, the mother's own sense of competence was positively related to independence demands on daughters, while fathers who saw women as competent placed high value on achievement for their daughters.

Similar analyses on other subpopulations might help us answer the question of whether or not parental sex-role attitudes have specific effects on offspring, even though this research may not be able to tell us if such attitudes represent an historical change, much less one related to the women's movement. It would be most instructive, for example, to know the consequences for black children of the apparently more egalitarian marriages of their parents compared to white couples (Beckett and Smith, 1981)—would these children display less stereotypical attitudes and behaviors?

Indeed, the really important question might be: will the involvement of fathers in child care stop the cycle whereby gender-related insufficiencies are reproduced through exclusive rearing by mothers? According to the powerful analyses of Dinnerstein (1977) and Chodorow (1978), both boys and girls are psychologically crippled in a family structure that makes women fully responsible for childrearing; boys fail to develop communal capacities (friendliness, cooperation, empathy, and self-control), and girls inhibit assertiveness, autonomy, and strong feelings of self-worth. If fathers were to share childrearing tasks, would children then be enabled to develop fully both their instrumental and expressive potentials?

We simply do not yet know. But this is clearly *the* agenda item for the 1980s. To quote Diana Baumrind (1980):

> In particular, socialization researchers will want to examine the effects on child development of the most radical and possibly beneficial change in the social structure to emerge from the turbulence of the 1960s, namely greater sexual symmetry in child care. The women's movement has liberated the mother from the home and has allowed the father to enter the home as a primary caretaker to share more equally in the day-to-day of

children intentionally conceived by both. The phenomenon of fathers nurturing their young is now sufficiently prevalent to permit systematic investigation of its effects on the development of character. (p. 642)

REFERENCES

Albrecht, S.L., Bahr, H.M., & Chadwick, B.A. Changing family and sex roles: An assessment of age differences. *Journal of Marriage and the Family,* 1979, *41,* 41-50.

Aneshensel, C.S., & Rosen, B.C. Domestic roles and sex differences in occupational expectations. *Journal of Marriage and the Family,* 1980, *42,* 121-130.

Baker, M.H. Mother's occupation and children's attainments. *Pacific Sociological Review,* 1981, *24,* 237-254.

Barnett, R.C. Parental sex-role attitudes and child-rearing values. *Sex Roles,* 1981, *7,* 837-846.

Barry, R.J. Stereotyping of sex role in preschoolers in relation to age, family structure, and parental sexism. *Sex Roles,* 1980, *6,* 795-806.

Baruch, G.K., & Barnett, R.C. Fathers' participation in the care of their preschool children. *Sex Roles,* 1981, *7,* 1043-1055.

Baumrind, D. New directions in socialization research. *American Psychologist,* 1980, *35,* 639-652.

Beckett, J.O., & Smith, A.D. Work and family roles: Egalitarian marriage in white and black families. *Social Service Review,* 1981, 315-326.

Berardo, F.M. Family research and theory: Emergent topics in the 1970s and the prospects for the 1980s. *Journal of Marriage and the Family,* 1981, *43,* 251-254.

Beuf, A. Doctor, lawyer, household drudge. *Journal of Communication,* 1974, *24,* 142-145.

Birnbaum, D.W., Nosanchuk, T.A., & Croll, W.L. Children's stereotypes about sex differences in emotionality. *Sex Roles,* 1980, *6,* 435-443.

Block, J.H., Block, J., & Morrison, A. Effects of childrearing orientations and gender-related personality correlates in children. *Child Development,* 1981, *52,* 965-974.

Bronfenbrenner, U. Socialization and social class through time and space. In E.E. Maccoby, T.M. Newcomb, & E.H. Hartley (Eds.), *Readings in social psychology.* New York: Holt, 1958.

Brook, J.S., Whiteman, M., Lukoff, I.F., & Gordon, A.S. Maternal and adolescent expectations and aspirations as related to sex, ethnicity, and socioeconomic status. *The Journal of Genetic Psychology,* 1979, *135,* 209-216.

Bush, D.E., Simmons, R.G., Hutchinson, B., & Blyth, D.A. Adolescent perceptions of sex-roles in 1968 and 1975. *Public Opinion Quarterly,* 1977-78, *41,* 459-473.

Chodorow, N. *The reproduction of mothering: Psychoanalysis and the sociology of gender.* Berkeley: University of California Press, 1978.

Dinnerstein, D. *The mermaid and the minotaur: Sexual arrangements and human malaise.* New York: Harper and Row, 1977.

Ferree, M.M., & Hess, B.B. *Controversy and Coalition: The new feminist movement.* Boston: Twayne, in press.

Fidell, L., Hoffman, D., & Kieth-Spiegel, P. Some social implications of sex-choice technology. *Psychology of Women Quarterly,* 1979, *4,* 32-42.

Gold, D., & Andres, D. Relations between maternal employment and development of nursery school children. *Canadian Journal of Behavioural Science,* 1978, *10,* 116-129.

Jones, L.M., & McBride, J.L. Sex-role stereotyping in children as a function of maternal employment. *The Journal of Social Psychology,* 1980, *111,* 219-223.

Kirkpatrick, M., Smith, C., & Roy, R. Lesbian mothers and their children: A comparative survey. *American Journal of Orthopsychiatry,* 1981, *51,* 545-551.

Lerner, R.M., & Spanier, G.B. *Child influences on marital and family interaction: A life-span perspective.* New York: Academic, 1978.

Lueptow, L.B. Social structure, social change and parental influence in adolescent sex-role socialization: 1964-1975. *Journal of Marriage and the Family,* 1980, *42,* 93-103.

McBroom, W.H. Parental relationships, socioeconomic status, and sex-role expectations. *Sex Roles,* 1981, *7,* 1027-1033.

Meyer, B. The development of girls' sex-role attitudes. *Child Development,* 1980, *51,* 508-514.

Miller, B. Gay fathers and their children. *The Family Coordinator,* 1979, *28,* 544-553.

Mucklow, B.M., & Phelan, G.K. Lesbian and traditional mothers' responses to adult response to child behavior and self-concept. *Psychological Reports,* 1979, *44,* 880-882.

Mullins, E.I. Perceived parental role satisfaction and daughter's sex role attitudes and aspirations. *Sociological Focus,* 1980, *13,* 397-411.

Norman, R.D. Sex differences in preferences for sex of children: A replication after 20 years. *Journal of Psychology,* 1974, *88,* 229-239.

Orlofsky, J.L. Parental antecedents of sex-role orientation in college men and women. *Sex Roles,* 1979, *5,* 495-512.

Philliber, S.G. Socialization for childbearing. *Journal of Social Issues,* 1980, *36,* 30-44.

Rollins, J., & White, P.N. The relationship between mothers' and daughters' sex-role attitudes and self-concepts in three types of family environment. *Sex Roles,* 1982, *8,* 1141-1155.

Roper, B.S., & Labeff, E. Sex roles and feminism revisited: An intergenerational attitude comparison. *Journal of Marriage and the Family,* 1976, *39,* 13-19.

Rosenthal, D., & Hansen, J. The impact of maternal employment on childrens' perceptions of parents and personal development. *Sex Roles,* 1981, *7,* 593-598.

Russell, G. The father role and its relation to masculinity, femininity, and androgyny. *Child Development,* 1978, *49,* 1174-1181.

Seegmiller, B.R. Sex-role differentiation in preschoolers: Effects of maternal employment. *The Journal of Psychology,* 1980, *104,* 185-189.

Shepard, W. Mothers and fathers, sons and daughters: Perceptions of young adults. *Sex Roles,* 1980, *6,* 421-433.

Sidorowicz, L.S., & Lunney, G.S. Baby X revisited. *Sex Roles,* 1980, *6,* 67-73.

Slater, P.E. Parental role differentiation. *American Journal of Sociology,* 1961, *67,* 296-311.

Smith, M.D., & Self, G.D. The Congruence between mothers' and daughters' sex-role attitudes: A research note. *Journal of Marriage and the Family,* 1980, *42,* 105-109.

Stevens, G., & Boyd, M. The importance of mother: Labor force participation and intergenerational mobility of women. *Social Forces,* 1980, *59,* 186-199.

Thornton, A., Alwin, D.F., & Camburn, D. Causes and consequences of sex-role attitude and attitude change. *American Sociological Review,* 1983, *48,* 211-227.

Zelditch, M., Jr. Role differentiation in the nuclear family: A comparative study. In T. Parsons & R.F. Bales (Eds.), *Family, socialization and interaction processes.* Glencoe, IL: Free Press, 1955.

Chapter 12

Family Roles
and the Impact of Feminism
on Women's Mental Health
Across the Life Course

Elizabeth W. Markson

"Who are you?" said the caterpillar.

"I-I hardly know, Sir, just at Present," Alice replied rather shyly, "at least I know who I *was* when I got up this morning, but I think I must have been changed several times since then" (Lewis Carroll, *Through the Looking Glass, Alice's Adventures in Wonderland*).

Gender roles are assigned at birth to both males and females. These roles are not exterior to the self but rather create it and become internalized. The self is thus not an abstract concept or a biological given but a constantly shifting social product. Like Alice, whose experiences in Wonderland produced many self-changes within a short time, we are actively engaged in learning appropriate role behavior by interpreting the reactions of others, selecting behavioral cues, and responding accordingly. It is through interaction with others and self-reflection that we develop a sense of selfhood and learn masculine or feminine roles.

Yet definitions of gender roles have begun to change markedly within the last two decades, during which time at least some people have changed two or three times. It thus seems reasonable to ask: has the recent women's movement begun to produce a new type of woman? Many years ago, Karl Mannheim posed the question: why did the Middle Ages and Renaissance produce different kinds of

Elizabeth W. Markson is Director for Social Research, Boston University Gerontological Center and Associate Research Professor, Department of Sociology, Boston University.

215

people? He noted that answers to this question required study of changes of the human mind within a historical context, in close connection with changes in the social structure, as well as at generational factors. Yet most social changes defy a simple account of their effects on any particular group because of their varied and sometimes contradictory consequences. Adaptation to social change at the individual level is filtered through one's own age cohort experience, stage in the life course, and one's other social roles (Elder, 1982). The impact of the recent feminist movement upon women in general and upon their mental health and self esteem in particular is no exception. To answer the question posed earlier would require a view not only of historical events, but also of the relative importance of age cohort variations and stage in the life-course—a perspective not easily gained as we ourselves experience a particular slice of history. In this paper, some recent social-structural changes specifically affecting women and their family roles are examined and speculations about their relationship to mental health and sense of well-being offered.

Socially constructed, gender roles are historically and culturally defined. Until recently, women's roles in the United States included the following core elements:

1. concentration on marriage, home, and children as their legitimate work sphere;
2. reliance on a male provider for sustenance and status;
3. emphasis on nurturance and compassion;
4. notion of fulfillment through others' accomplishments rather than through one's own active mastery;
5. emphasis on personal beauty and sexual attractiveness;
6. ban on direct expressions of aggression, assertiveness, power, and sexual initiative (Keller, 1974).

Although the actual roles of many American women have varied from this model due to the effects of race, socio-economic status, and other factors (see for example, Ladner, 1971; Ehrenreich and English, 1979), much of the social science literature has defined women within this almost purely "domestic" frame. In psychology, for example, the social context of behavior has generally been ignored in descriptions of what is "natural" or "healthy" behavior for women and theories without evidence have been widely accepted (Weisstein, 1971). It is only within the last decade or so that women's roles beyond the maternal, familial, and nurturant spheres have been viewed as "healthy" by either the general public or mental health professionals, as an unprecedented expansion of knowledge and literature analyzing the female experience has been published (Carmen, Russo, and Miller, 1981).

Yet gender roles remain a powerful influence on life chances and mental and physical well-being. Age cohort is also a powerful factor, interacting with gender to filter the affects of social change and events. This paper is concerned with the interactions of age cohort, gender, and recent historical changes brought about by the new feminist movement as they relate to physical and mental well being.

RECENT HISTORICAL CHANGES AFFECTING WOMEN

In the early 1960s, the mention of feminism or a feminist movement was anathema to most Americans. Nonetheless, a series of events, some of which are reviewed briefly here, heightened awareness of women as a class (see Ferree and Hess, in press, for an extended analysis). For example, the short-lived Commission on the Status of Women (1961-63) of President Kennedy documented many inequalities faced by women. The 1963 report of this Commission was issued in the same year that Betty Friedan called attention to "the problem that has no name"—the discontent of the baby-boom housewife, surrounded by appliances and inundated by homemaking, childcare, waxy buildup on the kitchen floor, and the low self-esteem associated with minority group status. By 1966 Friedan had founded the National Organization for Women (NOW) to address women's second class status. Other organizations, both formal and informal, rapidly evolved as well.

Many younger women were attracted to the new feminism as a consequence of their experiences in other social movements of the 1960s. As Robin Morgan observed:

> Thinking we were involved in the struggle to build a new society, it was a. . .depressing realization that we were doing the same roles in the (civil rights) movement as out of it—typing. . . making coffee. . .being accessories to the men. (Morgan, 1970)

Not only were women increasingly aware of their minority status, but dramatic social structural and public policy changes have taken place in the two decades or so since the Commission on the Status of Women was formed. Some of these changes were accidental, as in Title VII of the Civil Rights Act of 1964, to which "sex" was added with the intent of ridiculing and defeating the bill. Others, like Title IX of the Education Amendments of 1972, were deliberate. Selected key policy and legislative changes since 1963 are shown in Table 1.

Not all age cohorts, of course, were affected equally by these and other changes. For example, the passage of Title IX was important primarily to younger age cohorts as well as to middle aged women employed by schools, colleges, or universities receiving Federal funds. Abortion law changes had dramatic implications for women in their reproductive years but less meaning for those in older age cohorts. The major piece of legislation that would have affected females in all age cohorts—the Equal Rights Amendment—failed, as we all know, to achieve ratification. Moreover, resistance from political and religious conservatives (see Brown, this issue) and actions by the Reagan administration have effectively reduced and even rescinded many legislative and judicial gains made thus far.

Nor has this legislation been free from problems. For example, Title IX, now under attack from the Right, has also been criticised by its proponents because of the weakness of its sports provisions for females and because of difficulties in enforcement. And despite the Equal Pay Act's provision of "equal pay for equal work," working the same job as a man does not guarantee women equal wages even when she has the same training and experience. The thornier issue of equal pay for comparable worth (i.e., similar credentials, experience, and job responsibilities) has only recently been addressed. Nonetheless women's civil rights have expanded greatly since the early 1960s. In less than a generation, the size of the paid female labor force has more than doubled, primarily due to employment of women aged 20 to 44 and of married women with preschool and school age children (see Moore, Spain, and Bianchi, this issue). In spite of the clustering in "female," low paying jobs that remains, coupled with inadequate resources for day care, risks of sexual harassment, and often greater workload as both wage earner and houseworker, women today have more freedom to seek education and a paid occupation, to delay marriage, and to have fewer children than did their sisters of twenty years ago. What impact, if any, have these role modifications had upon the mental well-being of adult women?

TABLE 1

SELECTED LEGISLATIVE AND JUDICIAL CHANGES SINCE 1960 AFFECTING THE STATUS OF AMERICAN WOMEN

CHANGE	COVERAGE	AGE COHORTS MOST AFFECTED
Equal Pay Act of 1963 (P.L. 88-38)	Prohibits differential rates of pay for men and women who "do equal work on jobs." Until 1972, the Equal Pay Act covered only certain types of employees. In 1972, coverage was extended to executive, administrative, and professional employees as well as outside sales workers.	Young women (20-39)
Title VII of the Civil Rights Act of 1964 (P.O. 88-352)	Provides that: "It shall be unlawful employment practice for any employer to fail or refuse to hire or to discharge or otherwise discriminate against any individual with respect to his (sic) compensation, terms, conditions, or privileges of employment because of such individual's race, color, religion, sex, or national origin." Prior to 1972, Title VII covered only private employers with 25 or more employees and labor unions with 25 or more members. Amended in 1972 to extend to state and local government agencies and public and private educational institutions. Amended in 1973 to cover employers of 15 or more people and labor unions with 15 or more members. Still excluded: religious educational institutions and associations, elected officials, and other categories.	Young women (20-39) and midlife women (40-65)
Title IX of the Education Amendments of 1972	Prohibits schools, colleges, and universities from discriminating on the basis of sex in any education program or activity receiving Federal financial assistance. This act, however, contains many exceptions, including separate teams for men and women students in contact sports, exemptions from the requirement that male and female applicants to undergraduate institutions have the same admission criteria applied, and provisions for equal athletic budgets.	Children, young women (20-39), and midlife women employees of educational institutions
Roe vs. Wade	U.S. Supreme Court struck down state laws prohibiting or restricting abortion during the first three months of pregnancy.	Young women (20-39)
Equal Credit Opportunity Act of 1975	Provides that a woman may get credit in her own name except in community property states; creditors may not ask questions about spouse, birth control, or make inferences thereon.	All adult women
Equal Rights Amendment of 1972	Passed by Congress after being introduced each session since 1923, the ERA provided: "Equality of rights under the law shall not be denied or abridged by the United States or by any state on account of sex." It failed to be ratified within the requisite time frame.	All females through the life course

MENTAL HEALTH, SELF-ESTEEM, AND MORALE

Traditional psychotherapeutic assumptions about mentally healthy women have employed essentially a "woman as wimp" model and a double standard of mental health. As Freud commented, thus setting the tone for subsequent formulations:

> I cannot escape the notion (though I hesitate to give it expression) that for woman the level of what is ethically normal is different from what it is in man. We must not allow ourselves to be deflected from such conclusions by the denials of the feminists who are anxious to force us to regard the two sexes as completely equal in position and worth. (Freud, 1956, cited in Foxley, 1979, p. 21)

Indeed, although trend data are very limited, women continue to substantially outnumber men in most mental health facilities. They are overrepresented as patients in private mental hospitals, community mental centers, general hospital inpatient units, and outpatient psychiatric facilities. Only in state and county mental hospitals and public general hospitals is this situation reversed (Felipe, Russo, and Sobel, 1981). Whether this is due to women's greater likelihood of admitting unpleasant feelings and sensations, or to the stereotypical and diffuse expectations inherent in the feminine role, or to the greater probability that women will be diagnosed as mentally ill by significant others and by physicians has been hotly debated in the literature for over a decade (see, for example, Chesler, 1972; Phillips and Segal, 1969; Gove and Tudor, 1973).

For disorders that are incongruent with societal stereotypes of the feminine role, such as alcoholism, females have much lower utilization rates than males, and estimates of prevalence indicate that women alcoholics are untreated or misdiagnosed more often than men (Felipe, Russo, and Sobel, 1981). Yet female alcoholism has been proposed as revolving around gender role and the emotional problems generated by difficulties in adapting to that role (Gomberg, 1974). The relationship between depression and alcoholism among women is strong; indeed, women "self-medicate" their depression with alcohol as well as with prescribed tranquillizers, hypnotics, antidepressants, and over-the-counter solutions to what Seidenberg (1973) has called the "trauma of eventlessness" that characterizes the traditional feminine role in the twentieth century.

It is no accident that the British call gin "mother's ruin." Nor is it an accident that women who are alcoholics are regarded as "worse" than their male counterparts; they are violating norms for good (i.e., feminine) behavior. Men who get drunk to dim the hard edges of everyday life and to express hostility and anger are, after all, fitting into masculine role stereotypes, albeit unpleasant ones. The alcoholic woman, like the crowing hen, is viewed as fit neither for God nor men.

It is thus perhaps not surprising that one of the most consistent findings on mental health is that depression has been and remains closely associated with being female. Recent estimates indicate that 20 to 30 percent of all American women experience depressive episodes, often of moderate severity, at some point during their lives (Klerman and Weissman, 1980). These higher rates of depression among females are not sufficiently explained by biological, genetic, or hormonal differences between the sexes (Weissman and Klerman, 1980). Rather, social and individual circumstances generally accepted as normal may lead to heightened despair among women.

Within the past two decades many of the traditional psychotherapeutic assumptions about women have been challenged, keeping pace with and sometimes going beyond social-structural changes affecting the status of women (Rice and Rice, 1973; Nickerson, 1978; Stone, 1980). Inequities and conflict in marriage, family, reproduction, childrearing, divorce, education, work, and aging that make women particularly vulnerable to mental illness have been increasingly documented (see, for example, Subpanel on the Mental Health of Women of the President's Commission on Mental Health, 1978). Given increased attention and structural change, how have women fared? What age cohorts have been most affected by changes in the status of women? And how may developmental changes associated with the aging process be differentiated from age cohort effects?

DEVELOPMENTAL CHANGES AND COHORT CHANGES

The last question, that of developmental changes versus age cohort effects, raises another thorny issue: can developmental change be considered apart from cohort effects? Much of what we know about normal development in adulthood is based on cross-sectional data and may measure period effects and/or cohort differences rather than consistently patterned longitudinal developmental change.

Moreover, models of normal development such as those of Erikson and others have been based on the male experience, stressing chronological age which may not be as central a variable for women, whose lives are less characterized by continuous, uninterrupted series of events (Barnett and Baruch, 1978).

What we do know is that at all ages, women appear to have lower self-esteem and poorer self-concepts than do men (Gurin, Veroff, and Feld, 1960; Turner, 1979). Again, these findings may simply reflect historical influence, inasmuch as self-concepts and self-esteem are based upon cultural definitions of femininity and masculinity throughout the life course. As Turner (1979) has pointed out, "Since so few studies have been longitudinal or cross-sequential in design, we must continue to speculate about cause-effect relationships, and even whether these age-related 'shifts' occur at all" (p. 476).

Whether due to developmental change, cohort effects, or social-structural changes, older women do seem to be different from younger ones; they are more self assertive, autonomous, and active, perhaps due to release from role responsibilities of parenting (Gutmann, 1977; Neugarten, 1968). Contrary to popular opinion, the empty nest years are not inevitably associated with low self-esteem, feelings of worthlessness, and depression (Neugarten et al., 1968; Campbell, 1976; McKinley and Jeffries, 1974). Consistently, a number of studies indicate that depression is most common among women with young children (Campbell et al., 1976; Guttentag, Salasin, and Belle, 1980; Lowenthal, 1975; Radloff, 1975). Again, however, there may be an interaction of age cohort, developmental changes, and social options. For example, one longitudinal study of elderly men and women reported that the late-life adaptation of highly feminine, other-oriented women was dependent upon their marital status and nearness to children (Maas and Kuypers, 1974). Like the Mrs. Portnoys described by Pauline Bart (1970) these women had no investments or involvement outside their family and were particularly at risk when their traditional roles were terminated. The evidence thus suggests that development, sense of self-esteem, and mental health across the life course are influenced by availability and access to social roles. As greater access to a variety of roles is made available, women's development through adulthood and their mental health at any point in time may be positively influenced.

Most of the major epidemiological population studies on mental health were done over two decades ago and are virtually useless for estimating the extent of change among either women or men. That societal change affects self-esteem is given some support by limited data collected by Goodman (1980) on lesbian women she treated before and after the gay liberation movement in 1969. While by no means a representative sample of all women, all lesbians, or even of lesbian psychotherapy patients, her two cross-sectional samples indicate greater self-esteem among the post-liberation group. Whether the greater level of self-esteem among post-liberation patients is also an age cohort effect whereby younger women were more likely to benefit from changes in societal norms is unclear from this study, although the post-liberation sample had a larger proportion of 20 to 30 year old and fewer midlife (40 to 50 year old) women.

YOUNG WOMEN—18 TO 40 YEARS OLD

Young women have been generally more affected by the feminist movement than any other age group, whether or not they support feminist goals. Because they were born and grew up at a different time than did their mothers, even the same event may have had different meanings. For example, the impact of *Roe vs. Wade* upon the lives of young women today has been vastly different than upon their mothers; the 22-year-old middle-class female today may find it almost impossible to imagine a time when legal abortion was not an alternative to an unwanted pregnancy. Age cohort is thus a salient point for identity and for mental health. Yet class differences bisect age cohort differences. Paradoxically, for example, recent data suggest that young, poor women, especially low income mothers, have shown the greatest rise in the rate of both treated and untreated depression (Carter and Scott, 1976; Guttentag, Salasin, and Belle, 1980; Weissman and Klerman, 1977). At present, women head nearly one in three households compared to one in seven in 1950, and almost two-thirds of female-headed family heads are caring for children under 18 (Spain and Bianchi, 1983). Women are almost twice as likely as men to have incomes below the poverty level; 26 percent of white poor and 57 percent of black poor live in families headed by women (Hess, 1983). It is young, poor women who head single-parent families, and young married women who work at dead-end jobs who are most likely to be depressed (Carmen, Russo, and Miller, 1981). A disproportionate number of such women are black and Hispanic. The social and economic powerlessness traditionally associated with the feminine role remains a key factor in the development of psychological distress. Moreover, it is precisely those most powerless to cope with the repeated frustrations associated with blocked employment opportunities, inadequate housing, lack of protection against abuse, violence, and crime, and lack of child care alternatives who are most vulnerable (Greywolf, Reese, and Belle, 1980). Clearly, not all young women have benefited equally from the feminist movement!

MIDLIFE WOMEN—40 TO 65 YEARS OLD

Socio-cultural changes impinge most directly upon the behavior of the young, and the now-midlife woman is no exception. Middle-aged women are undergoing developmental change in a changing society and may be fascinated or repelled by the changes in traditional gender roles. That roughly the same age cohort produced both Betty Friedan and Phyllis Schlafly highlights the contradictory responses to feminism within one generation. Although "midlife crisis" is part of the American vocabulary, compared to men, midlife women have received relatively little research attention. When studied, they have most often been defined according to their familial and reproductive roles. Few studies have examined the importance of paid employment on the self-esteem or mental health of midlife women (Baruch and Barnett, 1978; Markson and Gognalons-Nicolet, 1982; Targ, 1980). Nor is it clear what impact midlife career transitions and the increasingly common phenomenon of career reentry have upon women's mental health.

Perhaps the most interesting data on the possible impact of the feminist movement upon midlife female mental health are those of Srole and Fischer (1980). Following up a sample of 1,294 randomly selected Manhattan residents initially interviewed in 1954, Srole and Fischer were able to locate and obtain interviews with 695 people (approximately 81 percent of the accessible target sample) again in 1974. On the basis of their initial survey, Srole and his associates concluded that mental illness increases with age and that rates of psychiatric impairment increase by decade of birth (Srole et al., 1962). Although the 1974 sample showed somewhat lower rates of overall impairment (11.9 vs. 14 percent), the same tendency for greater pathology associated with the aging process was noted. However, when age at time of interview was taken into account so that those 50 to 59 in 1954 were compared to those 50 to 59 in 1974, the data indicate that mental health does *not* decline with age *per se* but rather is related to birth cohort. Thus those who were 40 to 49 or 50 to 59 in 1954 were "sicker" than their 1974 counterparts.

This finding was most dramatic among women; women who were in midlife in 1954 were significantly more impaired than their 1974 counterparts. Men, on the other hand, demonstrated no significant cohort differences in midlife mental health. It is tempting to relate these findings to changes in employment status among women; for example, the number of years an average woman could expect to spend in the labor force nearly doubled between 1962 and 1974. And although women were (and remain today) concentrated in the traditionally female occupational fields of secretarial, nursing, and elementary school teacher, greater societal support for such employment among midlife women occurred during the two decades elapsing between the initial and follow-up Manhattan studies. While the majority of studies of the impact of employment on the mental health and self-esteem of women have ignored differences in age cohort, life stage, and familial roles, and socio-economic status (Warr and Parry, 1982), at least one study suggested that women—particularly midlife women—with paid employment were significantly less likely to commit suicide: a finding especially pronounced among married and widowed women compared with unmarried and divorced women (Cumming, Lazer, and Chishold, 1975). Perhaps even a little bit of freedom from reproductive, parental, and familial roles may go a long way to enhancing the mental health of midlife women—whether or not these women would call themselves feminists!

OLD AGE WOMEN—65 YEARS OLD AND OVER

Least likely to be actively involved in the women's movement and most untouched by it are the now-old women. Socialized in eras when the feminine graces were considered desirable albeit not accessible to those of lower socioeconomic or minority group status, relatively few women over the age of 65 are attracted to feminism or to radical causes—perhaps one reason the ranks of the Grey Panthers remain small. Yet the now-old woman is the most disadvantaged of all.

Throughout the life course, mental health and sense of self-esteem are related to socio-economic well-being and to availability and accessibility of support networks. Old age puts women at particular risk because of their relatively low incomes and greater likelihood of being widowed. Women at age 65 and over account for half of the women living below the poverty level, and widows over the age of 75 comprise most of the elderly poor. For many today, their greater poverty in old age is a crystallization of a lifelong pattern of limited options: low income, truncated education, and minimal work choices. Nor has the now-old woman benefited much from judicial and legislative changes affecting women in general. The major problem afflicting women in old age—poverty—remains untouched by recent policy decisions.

Financial insecurity and inadequate retirement income contribute significantly to impaired feelings of physical and psychological well-being (Research and Forecasts, 1981). Despite extensive discussion and concern about both the funding and coverage of the Social Security Act, for example, most older women still are eligible only for minimal Social Security benefits and find it more advantageous to take half their husband's benefits than to apply for their own entitlements. In 1981, for example, the monthly full Social Security benefit was about $370 for women and $480 for men, but only 31 percent of women received full benefits in comparison to 44 percent of the male recipients. Relatively few women—about 12 percent of those in paid employment—are covered by private pension schemes, with benefits that average $1,471 per year less than that of men (Markson, 1983, p. 73). Six of every ten women 65 and over depend on Social Security as their only source of income; men, however, rarely rely on Social Security as their sole income in retirement.

As a result, many now-old women are faced with three unattractive choices, none of which enhances mental health and may even promote depression: eking out a meager existence; relinquishing their independence by moving into the home of a child or other relative; or entering an institution. In general, the majority of now-old women value their autonomy so that forfeiting one's own home to live with adult child or grandchild may produce lower morale and impaired mental health (Grams and Fengler, 1980; Hughes and Gove, 1981).

It is only recently that depression has been recognized as a common problem of old people. Patients who would have heretofore been diagnosed as suffering from one of the so-called senile dementias are now properly seen as clinically depressed. Distinguishing depression from dementia remains a difficult problem, because of the retardation, poverty of thought, poor concentration, and inattention that characterize both illnesses. Moreover, the risk of false diagnosis increases with age of the patient. In this context it is interesting to note that, although old men are much more likely to commit suicide than old women, it is women who are more likely to be diagnosed as suffering from a senile dementia. This in part reflects their greater life expectancy inasmuch as the condition appears most often in the eighth decade of life. But there is at least some suggestion in the literature that the dementias of old age may be an end result of depression—the final stage of ego depletion (Cath, 1976). The extent to which the disadvantaged position of the very old woman contributes to mental illness in later life remains an area for investigation.

DISCUSSION

How then has the mental health and self-esteem of successive cohorts of women been affected by the changes associated with the feminist movement? The data are fragmentary and primarily anecdotal. Srole and his associates were confined to a follow-up of the original 1954 sample; accordingly no data are available on the psychological well being of women born since 1939. Nor has sufficient time elapsed for other longitudinal studies to be completed. Yet young women (those now 20 to 39) are precisely the age cohorts whose socialization and opportunities have been most altered by feminism. Women are now marrying almost two years later than in 1950, and the proportion of women 20 to 24 who had never married rose from about one-third to one-half. Families are smaller; the birth rate declined from 24.1 per 1,000 in 1950 to 15.7 in 1981. During the 1960s and 1970s, labor force participation rates for married women with children under the age of six increased dramatically—from 12 percent in 1950 to 50 percent in 1982. Worklife expectancy for women has increased faster than life expectancy, so that by 1977 a 20-year-old woman could expect to spend 45 percent of her life in the labor market as compared to 27 percent in 1950.

Educational attainment—a close correlate of mental health and psychological well being—has increased as well. Traditionally, women have been less likely than men to attend or to graduate from college, but 1981 college enrollment among 18- to 19-year-old women surpassed that of men. Younger women also earn more than older women; women of all ages earned 59.6 cents for every dollar earned by men in 1980, but those over age 45 earned only 55 cents. Moreover, although the unemployment rate for women typically has been higher than the rate for men, the gap has narrowed during recent recessions, as joblessness rises most sharply in the cyclical goods-producing industries in which most women work.

But, plus ça change? The 1980s thus far have not been good years for females in general and the woman worker in particular. Recent occupational gains made in non-traditional and male-dominated occupations has slowed perceptibly. Women can find little solace in the fact that their unemployment rates have been somewhat lower than those for men, for if discouraged workers are counted as unemployed, the unemployment rate of women in 1982 exceeded that of men (11.2 vs. 10.7). As among all workers, unemployment rates are higher for black and Hispanic women; in 1982, for example, the rate for black females was about twice that for white females.

Even women employed in relatively recession-proof industries have remained concentrated in low-paid, dead-end jobs. The plight of the female single parent is especially acute; although three out of five women maintaining families were in the labor force in 1982, on the average they had completed fewer years of school than wives and were concentrated in lower skilled, lower paying jobs. Female family heads typically lack sources of income other than employment, yet they are also about twice as likely as married women living with spouse to be unemployed. If one accepts the premise that "stress and powerlessness are the deadly combination" most often associated with depression among women (Guttentag and Salasin, 1976), the prognosis for psychological well-being among low income, minority, and female headed families is negative within the near future. The consequences of these hard times on women as they progress through the life course may be far reaching.

Even relatively advantaged young women have made only modest strides. Women still tend to major in "feminine," low-paying fields and may lack readily transferable skills in an increasingly technological economy. In part, this could reflect the fact that traditional gender role stereotypes continue to predominate and govern female behavior (Der Karabetian and Smith, 1977; Gilbert, Detusch, and Strahan, 1978). There is some evidence that degree of feminist orientation influences individual perception of appropriate masculine or feminine behavior (Mexydlo and Betz, 1980). Young women in particular receive pressures from feminists to behave in one way, and from nonfeminists to behave in another. As one young woman noted:

> One of the biggest worries I hear from older feminists (the author is 22) is that younger ones are reluctant or unable to act or speak out on issues. Part of this reluctance is the lack of a springboard, the lack of a clear idea of what kind of a new woman to be. . . . We could be any kind of woman we wanted to be. Instead, it was a classic case of sensory overload. With too many options, we panicked and retreated into old roles or new apathy. (*Young Feminists Speak for Themselves,* 1983, p. 43)

Nor are relationships with men authentically egalitarian.

> What's new for my generation is that there's a whole new breed of men who know what women like to hear. They've really got it down. . . . But they really haven't looked inside themselves. . . it only goes so far. (ibid, p. 90)

That younger age cohorts are confused about gender role expectations is not surprising. Behavioral and attitudinal changes, especially those linked to so basic a part of socialization as gender role, occur gradually and at unequal rates, influenced by one's position in the opportunity structure as well as by age cohort. Moreover, the formal opposition to the gains of the feminist movement that have been increasingly voiced since 1980 have done little to promote the rights of women as a class, although it has crystallized the "gender gap." Recently proposed legislation designed to reverse the gains made by the feminist movement (the Family Protection Act and the numerous bills introduced to prohibit abortion are two examples) have, however, been defeated, and there is some doubt that there is sufficient popular support for their reintroduction in Congress within the near future.

Has a new type of woman developed as a result of the feminist movement? The answer would seem to be both yes and no. Life for younger women, while by no means a bed of roses, is no longer as much of a procrustean bed as for their mothers. If increased options for choice are associated with psychological well-being, one would anticipate that at least the relatively economically advantaged younger age cohorts of women will have greater self-esteem and experience lower levels of psychic impairment than their mothers or grandmothers throughout the life course. For members of socioeconomically disadvantaged groups, however, the feminist movement has as yet not beneficially impinged upon their lives.

REFERENCES

Barnett, R.C. and Baruch, J.K. Women in the middle years: A critique of research and theory. *Psychology of Women Quarterly,* 1978, 3:2, 187-197.

Bart, P. Portnoy's mother's complaint. *Trans-Action,* 1970, 8, 69-74.

Campbell, A. Subjective measures of well-being. *American Psychologist,* 1976, 31, 117-124.

Campbell, A., Converse, P.E., and Rodgers, W.L. *The Quality of American Life.* New York: Russell Sage, 1976.

Carmen, E.H., Russo, N.F., and Miller, J.B. Inequality and women's mental health: an overview. *American Journal of Psychiatry,* 1981, 138: 10, 1319-1330.

Carter, L.A. and Scott, A.F. (Eds.). *Women and Men: Changing Roles, Relationships, and Perceptions.* New York: Aspen Institute, 1976.

Cath, S. Psychoanalytic Perspectives on Aging—An Historical Survey. In D.P. Kent, R. Kastenbaum, and Sylvia Sherwood (Eds.), *Research Planning and Action for the Elderly.* New York: Behavioral Publications, 1976.

Chesler, P. *Women and Madness.* New York: Doubleday, 1972.

Cumming, E., Lazer, C., and Chisholm, L. Suicide as an index of role strain among employed and not employed married women in British Columbia. *Canadian Review of Sociology and Anthropology,* 1975, 12, 462-470.

Der-Karabetian, A. and Smith, A.J. Sex-role stereotyping in the United States: Is it changing? *Sex Roles,* 1977, 3, 193-198.

Ehrenreich, D. and English, B. *For Her Own Good.* New York: Anchor, 1979.

Elder, G. Historical Experiences in the Later Years. In T.K. Hareven and K.J. Adams (Eds.). *Aging and Life Course Transitions.* New York: Guilford, 1982.

Ferree, M.M. and Hess, B.B. *Controversy and Coalition: The New Feminist Movement.* Boston: Twayne, in press.

Foxley, C.H. *Nonsexist Counseling: Helping Women and Men Redefine their Roles.* Dubuque, Iowa: Kendall-Hunt, 1979.

Gilbert, L., Deutsch, C., and Strahan, R. Feminine and masculine dimensions of the typical, desirable, and ideal woman and man. *Sex Roles,* 1978, 4, 767-778.

Gomberg, E.S. Women and alcoholism. In V. Franks and V. Burtle (Eds.) *Women in Therapy.* New York: Brunner/Mazel, 1975.

Goodman, B. Some mothers are lesbians. In E. Norman and A. Mancuse (Eds.), *Women's Issues and Social Work Practice.* Itasca, IL: Peacock, 1980.

Gove, W.R. and Tudor, J.F. Adult sex roles and mental illness. *American Journal of Sociology,* 1973, 78, 812-835.

Grams, A. and Fengler, A.F. *The older parent in the extended family.* Paper presented at the Gerontological Society of America Annual Meeting. San Diego, November, 1980.

Greywolf, E.S., Reese, M.F., and Belle, D. Stressed mothers syndrome: How to short-circuit the stress depression cycle. *Behavioral Medicine,* 1980, 7:11, 12-18.

Gurin, G., Veroff, J., and Feld, S. *Americans View their Mental Health.* New York: Basic Books, 1960.

Gutmann, D. The cross-cultural perspective: Notes toward a comparative psychology of aging. In J. E. Birren and K.W. Schaie (Eds.), *Handbook of the Psychology of Aging*. New York: Litton, 1977.

Guttentag, M. and Salasin, S. Women, men, and mental health. In L.A. Carter and A.F. Scott (Eds.). *Women and Men: Changing Roles, Relationships, and Perceptions*. New York: Aspen Institute, 1976.

Guttentag, M., Salasin, S., and Belle, D. (Eds.). *The Mental Health of Women*. New York: Academic Press, 1980.

Hess, B.B. New faces of poverty. *American Demographics*, 1983, 5, 5, 26-31.

Hughes, M. and Gove, W.R. Living alone, social integration, and mental health. *American Journal of Sociology*, 1981, 87, 48-74.

Keller, S. The female role: Constants and change. In V. Franks and V. Burtle (Eds.), *Women in Therapy*. New York: Brunner/Mazel, 1974.

Klerman, G.L. and Weissman, M.M. Depressions among women: Their nature and causes. In M. Guttentag, S. Salasin, and D. Belle (Eds.). *The Mental Health of Women*. New York: Academic Press, 1980.

Ladner, J.A. *Tomorrow's Tomorrow: The Black Woman*. New York: Doubleday, 1971.

Lowenthal, M.F., et al. *Four Stages of Life*. San Francisco: Jossey-Bass, 1975.

McKinley, S.M. and Jeffreys, M. The menopausal syndrome. *British Journal of Preventive and Social Medicine*, 1974, 28, 108-115.

Maas, H.S. and Kuypers, J.A. *From Thirty to Seventy*. San Francisco, Jossey-Bass, 1974.

Mannheim, K. *Man and Society in an Age of Reconstruction*. New York: Harcourt Brace Jovanovich, 1940.

Markson, E.W. *Older Women*. Lexington, MA: Lexington Books of D.C. Heath, 1983.

Markson, E.W. and Gognalons-Nicolet, M. *Midlife adaptation among women: Risk and opportunities affecting their future old age*. Paper presented at the International Sociological Association, Mexico City, August, 1983.

Mezyldlo, L.S. and Betz, D.E. Perceptions of ideal sex roles as a function of sex and feminist orientation. *Journal of Counseling Psychology*, 1980, 27, 3, 282-285.

Morgan, R. *Sisterhood is Powerful*. New York: Random House, 1970.

Neugarten, B. *Middle Age and Aging*. Chicago: University of Chicago Press, 1968.

Nickerson, E.T. *How helpful are the helpers? A review of sexist helping practices and competencies needed by helpers of women*. (xerox)

Phillips, D. and Segal, B. Sexual status and psychiatric symptoms. *American Sociological Review*, 1969, 34, 58-72.

Radloff, L.S. Risk factors for depression: What do we learn from them? In M. Guttentag, S. Salasin, and D. Belle (Eds.), *The Mental Health of Women*. New York: Academic Press, 1980.

Research and Forecasts. *Aging in America: Trials and Triumphs*. New York: Rudder & Finn, 1980.

Rice, J.K. and Rice, D.G. Implications of the women's liberation movement for psychotherapy. *American Journal of Psychiatry*, 1973, 130, 191-196.

Russo, N.F. and Sobel, S.B. Sex differences in the utilization of mental health facilities. *Professional Psychology*, 1981, 12, 7-19.

Seidenberg, R. The trauma of eventlessness. In J.B. Miller (Ed.), *Psychoanalysis and Women*. New York: Brunner/Mazel, 1973.

Spain, D. and Bianchi, S.M. How women have changed. *American Demographics*, 1983, 5, 19-25.

Srole, L. (with Fischer, A.K.). The midtown Manhattan longitudinal study vs. the "mental paradise lost" doctrine. *Archives of General Psychiatry*, 1980, 37, 209-221.

Srole, L., et al. *Mental Health in the Metropolis*. New York: McGraw Hill, 1962.

Stone, A.A. Presidential address: conceptual ambiguity and morality in modern psychiatry. *American Journal of Psychiatry*, 1980, 137, 887-891.

Subpanel on the Mental Health of Women, President's Commission on Mental Health, Task Panel Report, Vol. III. Washington, DC: U.S. Government Printing Office, 1978.

Targ, D. Toward a reassessment of women's experience at middle age. *Family Coordinator,* 1980, 28, 377-382.

Turner, B.F. The self-concepts of older women. *Research on Aging,* 1979, 1, 464-480.

Warr, P. and Parry, G. Paid employment and women's psychological well-being. *Psychological Bulletin,* 1982, 91: 3, 498-516.

Weissman, M.M. and Klerman, G.L. Sex differences and the epidemiology of depression. *Archives of General Psychiatry,* 1977, 34, 98-111.

———. Sex differences and the epidemiology of depression. In E. S. Gomberg and V. Franks (Eds.), *Gender and Disordered Behavior.* New York: Brunner/Mazel, 1979.

Weisstein, N. Psychology constructs the female. In V. Gornick and B. Moran (Eds.), *Woman in Sexist Society.* New York: Mentor, 1971.

Young feminist speak for themselves. *Ms,* April, 1983, 43, 90.

Chapter 13

Cinderella: Her Multi-Layered
Puissant Messages Over Millennia

Kris Jeter

Women's roles in the modern world are not simple products of societal complexity with its endemic occupational specialization, high geographic and social mobility, small size family, and more recent worldwide legislation either banning or encouraging gender equity in all life sectors. The current status of women and their roles within the family and other life areas are rooted in historic experience dating to primordial times. Each generation, in the pattern of a genetic clock, receives from the previous one deep seated beliefs and concomitant behaviors. The transmission of perceptions of reality are deeply rooted in the subconscious. Appropriate norms of behavior for family members are prescribed and their form evolves from the values institutionalized deep in the psyche and embedded in cultural traditions.

In this chapter, the Cinderella fairy tale is examined; its ancient and historic representations of family structure and dynamics are deveined. Unabridged are discussions of incestuous feelings and expressions, oedipal relationships, parent and stepparent relationships, the romantic tradition, and sibling rivalry. Basic to the Cinderella tale is the hope that male/female inequalities will be overcome or ameliorated by unrelinquished love while living happily ever after.

In 1892, Marian Roalfe Cox wrote *Cinderella: Three Hundred and Forty-Five Variants;* her voluminous work was republished in

Kris Jeter, PhD, is Principal, Beacon Associates Ltd., Inc. and Adjunct Associate Professor, Department of Individual & Family Studies, University of Delaware.

1967. In this detailed and scholarly work, Cox presented the Cinderella variations from four continents, although primarily Europe, which were written from 1636 to 1892. These variations are cross referenced according to category, chronology, country of origin, and source. Each varient is briefly abstracted according to the inclusion of common incidents and then is abstracted in a more fluent fashion which includes details and quotations.

Cox identified 39 common incidents which may be used to classify the 345 Cinderella variations into five categories. These five categories, the number of their variations, descriptions, and examples follow.

1. Cinderella—All 57 basic variations have the mistreated heroine identified by the hero because of an object. The Brothers Grimm's "Aschenputtel" and Perrault's "Cendrillon" are two examples of the Cinderella category.
2. Catskin—In these 44 variations, the father of Cinderella wishes to marry his daughter and so Cinderella flees him. In the course of this exile, she meets her hero. She assumes a "catskin" to hide her menial existence. The "catskin" is detected by the hero and they marry. The Brothers Grimm's "Allerleirauh" and Perrault's "Peau d'Ane" are examples of the Catskin category.
3. Cap o'Rushes—Each of these 17 variations contain the initial decision found in Shakesphere's 1606 tragedy, *King Lear.* The King tests his three daughters' love for him. In many of these variations the youngest is usually disowned because she likens her love for her father to her love for salt. He divides his kingdom in half for the two eldest daughters and disinherits his youngest. While an outcast, she meets and in time marries the hero. When salt is short in supply, the father admits the need for it and repents. An English tale called "Cap o'Rushes," because the outcast daughter wears rushes as a disguise, is the story on which Cox based the title of this category.
4. Hero-Tales—In these 16 variations, the hero is a male. This hero, however, is not in the traditional mythical heroic cycles more recently discussed by Joseph Campbell. Although Cox does not abstract these variations, the popular "Puss in the Boots" story could be an example of the hero-tales category.
5. Indeterminate—Cox identified 52 variations as indistinctive according to the preceding categories. Basile's "The Three

Fairies'' and the Brothers Grimm's "One-Eye, Two-Eyes, and Three-Eyes" are examples of the indeterminate category.

The Cinderella story basic to all of the above five categories is similar. A mistreated, menial person is assisted by an ally. While in disguise, wearing a magic garment, a prospective mate is met at a special point de reunion. Three times the heroine/hero flees the prospective mate. The menial person is later recognized by the prospective mate because of the unique fit of a ring, shoe, or other object. The marriage tests are passed, resulting in a happy marriage.

For the purposes of this article, two versions of Cinderella will be distinguished: the sanitized French Perrault version of 1697, later adopted by Walt Disney; and the German Brothers Grimm's 1812 version. Perrault is thought to have borrowed from the 1550 Straparola published work. As an adroit writer for the royal court, Perrault created a docile, obedient, and passive Cinderella. The father's only act in this version is to marry Cinderella's stepmother. Cinderella chooses to debase herself by bedding in the hearth. At the command of the heretofore unknown Fairy Godmother, Cinderella goes to the Prince's ball and returns home at the appointed hour. The "happily ever after" ending depicts Cinderella arranging marriages between her stepsisters and Court lords and sharing with them her wedding ceremony to the Prince.

The Grimm Brothers wrote stories in the early 1800s that they heard being told by German mothers to their children. In their version, Cinderella is commanded to sleep in the hearth. She requests from her father a hazel branch and plants it on the burial place of her natural mother. Cinderella asserts herself to her stepmother, requesting to go to the ball. Cinderella's stepmother assigns her unreasonable tasks which she completes with the assistance of animal friends. The hazel tree, a reincarnation of the natural mother, provides Cinderella with elegant garments. At the ball, Cinderella meets the prince. She flees the prince, hiding first in a pigeon house and then in a pear tree—both of which are then destroyed by her father. Cinderella loses her slipper and a search is conducted to find the woman whose foot the slipper fits. First one stepsister and then the second stepsister mutilate their feet to fit in the shoe and be accepted as the bride until the doves pronounce the trickery. On the way to the wedding of Cinderella and the Prince, the stepsisters are forever blinded by the doves.

Freudian trained, Bruno Bettelheim in 1975 has written *The Uses of Enchantment: The Meaning and Importance of Fairy Tales.* Cinderella "tells about the agonies of sibling rivalry, of wishes coming true, of the humble being elevated, of true merit being recognized even when hidden under rags, of virtue rewarded and evil punished—a straightforward story. But under this overt content is concealed a welter of complex and largely unconscious material, which details of the story allude to just enough to set our unconscious associations going" (p. 239).

Of all the fairy tales, Cinderella, one of the most popular, best explores sibling rivalry. The child listening to the simple appearing story can empathize with Cinderella, who is harshly assigned many callous, meritless tasks by her stepmother and stepsisters. The siblings by marriage in the story may be easily transposed to be siblings by birth or retain, especially in the past ages of death and remarriage and in this age of divorce and remarriage, their step relationship. The child may cognitively know that the treatment of all children in the family is fair. However, affectively, the child feels unappreciated, inferior, and stuck in an unbalanced relationship with no hope of emergence with a sense of personal power. The source of sibling rivalry is the child's apprehension that the parents, when comparing children, will evaluate her or him to be the least loveable.

Cinderella, to speak to the primordial preconscious, should be more accurately named Ashrella. The English word, "Cinderella," is an unprecise translation of the French word, "Cendrillon," Cinders are partially burned filth, remains of the fire. Ashes are fine particles of mineral matter, the solid residue remaining from thoroughly burned combustible materials. Ashes have long been assigned spiritual import in many cultures and times. For example, consider the terms, "ashes to ashes" and "Ash Wednesday." Martin Luther used the term, "ash brother," to describe the relationships of Abel to Cain and Esau to Jacob. Phoenix rises to victory from the ashes. Ashes symbolize grief, humiliation, mourning, repentance, and resurrection.

Cinderella's role model was the Vestal Virgin, the honored high class woman consecrated to Vesta, the Roman Goddess of hearth, fire, and of the state. The Vestal Virgin was selected from among her peers between the ages of six to ten. For five years (and in later times for 30 years), the Vestal Virgin would serve Vesta by maintaining the sacred fire perpetually burning on the altar. After this life of immaculacy, purity, and virtue, the Vestal Virgin would marry a man of honored position.

Cinderella lives in a paradoxical world, not unlike that of the child listening to her story. Cinderella wears soiled, tattered clothing, a sign of mourning, while living in the hearth, a symbol of the times when her mother nurtured her in the warm intimacy of the kitchen to the smell of baking bread. The listening child remembers the innocent joy and the devastating guilt of playing in the dirt: the push-pull tension of the parent/child relationship and the loss of the all attentive parent of the newborn to the adolescent and the adult.

Cinderella may be interpreted to be a story of oedipal origins speaking to the child in the oedipal stage between ages three and six. To Freud, the young boy in this oedipal or phallic stage discovers new aspects about his penis and imagines being a sexual adult and marrying his mother. Likewise, the young girl in the corresponding oedipal or electra stage experiences penis envy and then fantasizes about marrying her father and presenting him with a gift of a baby.

In some variations of Cinderella, her mistreatment is due to her entering the oedipal relationship with her father. To avoid marriage to her father, she flees. This version may well speak to the listening child's oedipal wishes and guilt. In other variations, Cinderella is banished because she will not enter the oedipal relationship with her father. This version may hold import to the child wishing that her father would request more love from her. Both versions bring rise to the oedipal feelings tended by both child and parent. Most versions parallel Freud's actual stages of development. The girl child's original love for her mother is replaced between ages three and six by love for her father and intense rivalry with her mother and sisters for this love. With normal puberty, love for the mother is usually reintensified.

The mutilation of some characters by others is not a usual action in fairy tales. The self mutilation performed by the stepsisters in the Brothers Grimm version is a rarity. The cutting off of toes and heels may be the unconscious act of symbolic self-castration or removal of a fantasized penis and demonstration of menstruation to verify femininity. The stepsisters' blood is revealed by the birds and seen by the Prince. In comparison, Cinderella has no emission of blood. A girl who has yet to menstruate is thought to be more virginal than her menstruating stepsisters.

Bettleheim briefly compares the story development of Cinderella to the first six of Erik H. Erikson's eight psychosocial stages of development. This discussion is expanded below. Erikson theorizes that biological maturation and social expectations create choices.

Positive choices made in the earlier stages generally promote positive choices at later stages.

1. Trust vs. Mistrust (birth to one-and-a-half years)—Cinderella is nurtured to trust by her natural mother near the hearth.
2. Autonomy vs. Shame and Doubt (one-and-a-half to three years)—Cinderella becomes autonomous when she accepts her blended family and her new role in this family.
3. Initiative vs. Guilt (three to six years)—Cinderella's process of mourning evolves into a positive form of initiative when she plants a branch and nurtures the tree with her expression of emotions, prayers, and tears. Because of her initial successful development of trust with her natural mother, her image of her birth mother dematerializes and matures into a positive influence with Cinderella.
4. Industry vs. Inferiority (six to eleven years)—Cinderella faces the task of industry by completing debasing, seemingly impossible tasks (picking lentils from ashes, sifting grain, spinning) and learns that these tasks can be inwardly rewarding and that she can distinguish evil from virtue. Cinderella completes these tasks successfully both because and in spite of her step relatives.
5. Identity vs. Role Confusion (adolescence)—Cinderella confronts her true identity of opposite characteristics by arranging for the Prince to see her total self—positive in gifted ball wear with an entourage and negative in tattered rags by the hearth.
6. Intimacy vs. Isolation (young adulthood)—Cinderella chooses intimacy. The symbolic act for the consumation is the Prince's placement of the shoe on Cinderella's foot. This outward act signifies her retention of the unbroken hyman and the Prince's tight fitting of his penis into Cinderella's vagina.

The Cinderella story was originally a nature tale consciously steeped by the ancients in the essence of the creative cycles of the universe, adapting to each culture's interpretation of animal and plant life. As the Cinderella story was told from generation to generation it transversed seasons, ages, and cultures. In later times the verbalized images of Cinderella manifested in other art forms: Rossini's opera, D'Erlanger and Fokine's ballet, Prokofiev's ballet, and Disney's motion picture. Each retelling was infused and infiltrated with the prevailing thought of each era.

Cinderella was transformed from an explicit pornographic tale born in the Eastern tradition to be a formula story for propaganda written to further the Protestant work ethic. The emphasis shifted from ancestor worship, foot fetishes, oedipal relationships with the father desiring incestual favors from his daughter, and the Vestal Virgin to the good life which is earned through hard menial work. The seventeenth and eighteenth century "literature of aspiration" transformed Cinderella into Benjamin Franklin's autobiography, Horatio Alger's stories, and Samuel Richardson's *Pamela*.

The earliest known version of Cinderella printed in the United States is believed to be *Cinderella or The History of the Little Glass Slipper*. In 1800, Mathew Carey, an Irish immigrant, published 1000 copies and one was acquired in 1951 by the Huntington Library. This version reflects the American philosophy of self determinism, democracy, and reward through hard work. It is prefaced with the following:

> Through Cinderella's humble state we show,
> Yet pray, like her, in virtue learn to grow:
> So shall some friend support your honest cause,
> and guide you through the world in spite of foes. (Foreword)

Eric Berne, the founder of Transactional Analysis, in 1972 wrote *What Do You Say After You Say Hello?,* and in his discussion of the influence of a fairy tale on the formation of a script used Cinderella as his primary example. Scripts are preconscious life plans determined in childhood and continually reinforced by parents and society. Often, a person will live out a script that was heard as a child in the form of a fairy tale and gravitate towards persons who will enact supporting character roles and participate in games or devious, self satisfying transactions. Berne analyses the scripts of the primary characters in the Perrault version.

1. Cinderella—The heroine experiences happiness early in life and with her mother's death assumes a tragic role. She accepts the time restrictions imposed by the Fairy Godmother and plays a version of "Hide and Go Seek" known in transactional analysis as "Try and Catch Me" with the Prince. Then after the ball, she wears for her family a knowing "I've Got a Secret" facial expression. After the Prince's rescue, she communicates a "Now She Tells Us" transaction.

2. Father—With the death of his first wife, he forgets his daughter and marries an imposing, frigid woman and takes the Fairy Godmother as a mistress.

3. Stepmother—Through seduction, she arranges a good marriage for herself. After the nuptials she shows her negative intentions.

4. Stepsisters—They imitate their mother and believe in getting theirs first without concern for their new step family. Then, as caught "schlemiels" they apologize and are even rewarded with Lords as husbands.

5. Godmother—She tells Cinderella that her magic will evaporate at midnight, thus, knowing that Cinderella will be out of the house until that time and will be home before the others, allowing her to spend time alone with Cinderella's Father.

6. Prince—In short, the Prince is a wimp. He cannot in two evenings learn information about the woman with whom he dances and cannot even "catch her in a fast race even though she is limping along with only one shoe" (p. 235). He sends another man to identify the woman "of dubious upbringing and questionable family" (p. 235) and then marries Cinderella.

7. The Gentleman—As an employee of the Prince, the Gentleman completes his work assignment in an effective manner expressing integrity in his clear communication patterns. He could have appropriated Cinderella as his own if he were not ethical.

8. The Two Lords—Without appropriate conscious pre-thought and communication, the two Lords marry the stepsisters they meet on their wedding day and lock them into a prescribed life style.

Eric Berne then gives two current examples of Cinderella scripts. One is a tragic story with characteristics acting according to the original script and the second a rewritten script with characters identifying verbal and non-verbal patterns and scripts and living consciously.

Six years after Eric Berne's death in 1970, Dorothy Jongeward and Dru Scott elaborated further on Cinderella in their book, *Women as Winners: Transactional Analysis for Personal Growth.* They describe the Cinderella in a woman's life as the character who waits until she is in the right garments and in the right time and space to be saved by the Godmother and the Prince.

Jongeward and Scott recommend that the woman who has internalized the Cinderella role refrain from procrastinating, finding meaning in the lives of children and spouses rather than internally, and waiting to be saved in the future. Rather, the woman is to become her own Fairy Godmother, embrace her personal strengths, define demonstrable goals, accomplish activities which support these goals, and live in the present. She is to chronologize her life, determining if she often engages in relationships of persecution which she then forgives and forgets. Friendships are to be developed with men who feel comfortable with themselves, enjoy the company of women and are attuned to equitous relationships. A viable, rewarding life is to be imagined and forecast which does not necessitate rescue by a man. The varied facets of her career are to be investigated. Alternative strategies are to be ascertained for attaining goals. And this woman scripted to be Cinderella is to reflect upon, "What do I expect after the ball is over?" (p. 44).

In 1979, Madonna Kolbenschlag wrote *Kiss Sleeping Beauty Good-Bye: Breaking the Spell of Feminine Myths and Models.* "Because myths are no less powerful than nature and because they mirror as well as model our existence, I have introduced six familiar fairy tales as heuristic devices for interpreting the experience of women. These tales are parables of what women have become; and at the same time, prophecies of the spiritual metamorphosis to which they are called" (p. x).

Kolbenschlag analyzes the Cinderella story as a role model for the economic structure of society. She has listed in a hierarchy six motives for work:

1. subsistence, survival
2. human dignity, security
3. "sense of duty"—social approval
4. increased status, "the good life"
5. pleasure, significance—creative fulfillment
6. redemption of the social order, "the future." (p. 79)

Work is thought to have developed historically in each culture to translate into satisfaction all of the above six motives. With slavery and servitude, particular forms of work were denigrated. Autonomous work roles were elevated by devaluing supportive work roles. The industrial revolution in particular separated women from rewarding and satisfying work.

Today, in the United States, most adults do follow in the footsteps of Cinderella and the Prince. The major life decision for men is considered to be the choice of vocation; energy and resources are focused on education and apprenticeship for the designated vocation. After the choice, an appropriate wife is selected to fit into the academic, corporate, political or other particular vocational world. In the Cinderella story, the Prince, already trained and installed in his ministerial position, then searches for a suitable mate.

Meanwhile, Cinderella is engaged in non-goal directed behavior and is cleaning the ring around the hearth which requires less risk in today's environmentally protected society, waiting to be discovered by her Prince Charming. Her energy is not focused on choosing a vocation and attaining appropriate education and apprenticeship. Rather, she works at unrewarding menial tasks living only for her major decision made by not deciding—marriage. After conforming to the restricted size and conforming fit of the shoe, she is deemed proper by the Prince to be his wife. She probably assumes his birth name and lives "happily ever after" supporting his goals. She marries to survive and then survives the marriage.

The statistical woman in the United States works outside the home and works to exist. As Cinderella meeting an imposed midnight deadline, she punches her time card into an underpaid menial job and then punches her time card out to the second unpaid menial job of wife and mother. In fact, she is probably being the supportive wife both at the job and at home.

Like Phoenix, "Cinderella is rising from the ashes" (p. 91). Many first generational American women and Black women are more assertive, less dependent on men mentors and spouses, and have greater enterprise and stamina than other American women. These role models plus raised individual and societal consciousness speak to current generations of women whose children have grown up and younger generations growing up. Once again, women are merging work and family into the cottage industry. Women are working for policy change at work and at home, requesting the status and equity once assigned to all work.

In 1981, professional writer, Colette Dowling, wrote *The Cinderella Complex: Women's Hidden Fear of Independence*. Reflecting on her personal life, she applies psychological theory to women's stories. "It is the thesis of this book that personal, psychological dependency—the deep wish to be taken care of by others—is the chief force holding women down today. I call this 'The Cinderella Complex'—a network of largely repressed attitudes and fears that keeps women in a kind of half-light, retreating from the full use of their minds and creativity. Like Cinderella, women today are still waiting for something external to transform their lives'' (p. 21).

Dowling traces and compares the development of the woman and the man relating it to child rearing practices. Both the boy and girl as infants are passive and dependent upon adults. Parents reply more often to the cries of the girl baby than the boy baby. Thus, between ages two and six, the boy changes from dependence to independence. From birth, the girl is developmentally more cognitive, perceptual, and verbal than the boy. Before entrance into first grade, the girl is fully one year more advanced in these areas than the boy. However, the girl employs these skills to foresee events and to adapt and comply with authority. Throughout childhood, the girl has retained her identity with her mother; little conflict has been experienced between the two. Affective ties are built, valued, and needed. Being guarded more closely than the boy, independence, self confidence, and survival skills are not fostered resulting in ''learned helplessness.'' The girl reacts; the boy acts.

With adolescence, the young woman fulfills desires for social acceptance by not entering competitions and by downgrading abilities, thus becoming even more dependent. Unless there is a crisis, independence is never developed.

An adolescent woman may transfer dependence on parents to dependence on a husband. Or she may complete her education and work, and then, as independence is found to be tiresome, become apprehensive and wish to return to the perceived security of dependency, taking on a husband. With marriage, the man retains his routine and the woman adjusts to the new boundaries, to wifehood, and to motherhood. On the paid job, success is feared by the woman because it would threaten human relationships. The woman does not act, compete, or discuss personal talents.

Furthermore, the woman denies this dependent role. In the act of suppression, energy and time are robbed by indecisiveness and inertia. Procrastination and negligence cause self-chastisement and self-debasement which, in turn, cause purposeless frustration and hostility, leading to more procrastination and negligence.

Dowling suggests that the modern day Cinderella stop waiting for the Fairy Godmother, the Prince, or anyone and witness reality each moment of the day. ''Ultimately, the goal is emotional spontaneity—an inner liveliness that pervades everything. . ., every work project, every social encounter, every love relationship. It comes from the conviction: 'I am the first force in my life.' And it leads to what Karen Horeny calls wholeheartedness—the ability 'to be without pretense, to be emotionally sincere, to be able to put the whole of oneself into one's feelings, one's work, one's beliefs' " (p. 235).

The current status of women and their roles within the family and other life vocations is rooted in historic experience dating to primordial times. The Cinderella story has been traced to African, Mediterranean, Near and Far Eastern cultures before the birth of Christ. As other fairy tales and myths, it has endured with variations because seemingly appropriate roles for family members are prescribed; the form of these roles evolve from the values institutionalized deep in the psyche and embedded in cultural traditions.

What is the conscious parent and story teller to do today? Does the story of Cinderella indeed assist children to deal with incestuous feelings and expressions, oedipal relationships, parent and step parent relationships, and sibling rivalry? And does the story of Cinderella keep women in heavily laden unrewarded work roles and dependent relationships?

Perhaps Cinderella can be told with explanations, injunctions, and modifications? If the Wolf in the "Peter and the Wolf" story is now taken to the zoo and a feather in his nose causes the Wolf to cough out the live duck he had eaten, then Cinderella can attain and control her independence by becoming educated at night school for a goal directed career in which she can continue to advance after contracting for an equitous relationship with the Prince.

Some people may want to tell modern day stories. These, while consistent with the twentieth century literary form, should acknowledge feminine and masculine sensibilities plus affective, cognitive, and psychomotor processes and reconcile everyday consciousness with a philosophical concern for the human race, the mutually shared planet and the solar system. For example, the telling of Madeleine L'Engle's *A Wind in the Door,* empowers all of its hearers. Meg Murray, a young adolescent, is the heroine. In order to save her brother from death due to the illness, "mitochondritis," she, with a group of two children and two angels, a school principal, a Black teacher, a cherubim, and a tree set out to meet three tests. These tests are "naming" or the identification of the true reality; "deepening" or centering and empathy; and "kything" or unconditional love. Are these not the tasks of the twentieth century and future Cinderellas and Princes? The woman's and man's roles can be positively influenced through conscious story telling. Mindfully told fairy tales and myths and selective current stories have a well of historic information and symbolic representations for inculcating awareness of sex roles and conflicts and for modeling means to change.

REFERENCES

Berne, E. *What Do You Say after You Say Hello? The Psychology of Human Destiny.* New York: Grove Press, Inc., 1972.

Bettelheim, B. *The Uses of Enchantment: The Meaning and Importance of Fairy Tales.* New York: Random House, Inc., 1975.

Carey, M. *Cinderella or The History of The Little Glass Slipper.* Photolythic fascimile of 1800 edition. Alhambra, CA: Private Press, C.F. Braun and Company, 1979.

Cox, M. R. *Cinderella: Three Hundred and Forty-Five Variants.* London: The Folk-Lore Society, 1892 and Nendeln/Liechtensteini The Folk-Lore Society, 1967.

Dowling, C. *The Cinderella Complex: Women's Hidden Fear of Independence.* New York: Pocket Books, Simon and Schuster, 1981.

Jongeward, D. and Scott, D. *Women as Winners: Transactional Analysis for Personal Growth.* Reading, MA: Addison-Wesley Publishing Company, 1976.

Kolbenschlag, M. *Kiss Sleeping Beauty Good-Bye.* Doubleday and Company, 1979.

L'Engle, M. *A Wind in The Door.* New York: Dell Publishing, 1973.

Selective Guide
to Current Reference Sources
on Women and the Family

Jonathan Jeffery

This section of *Marriage and Family Review* is devoted to reference sources pertaining to the theme of this issue. The sources listed here will provide additional information on the topic of women and the family. This information is selective, not comprehensive, and the material will generally be current.

The usefulness of the source is often indicated by sample keyword suggestions; however, the reader should consider other possible subject terms and all synonymous words when searching these sources.

Assistance of a librarian may be required to utilize computer data bases or to respond to individual research interests.

Indexing and Abstracting Sources-Publisher, start date, and frequency of publication are noted.

America: History and Life. (Indexes articles on the history of the United States and Canada.) Santa Barbara, Calif., ABC Clio Press, 1964- , quarterly.
See: Marriage, Feminism, Women's liberation movement.
Historical Abstracts. Santa Barbara, Calif., ABC Clio Press, 1955- , quarterly.
Inventory of Marriage and Family Literature. Minneapolis, MN, Family Study Center and the Institute of Life Insurance, 1967- .
See: keywords in title.
Psychological Abstracts. Lancaster, Pa., American Psychological Association, 1927- , monthly.

Jonathan Jeffery is Associate Librarian, Reference Department, Morris Library, University of Delaware.

Public Affairs Information Service. New York, PAIS, 1915- , weekly.
    See: Black women, Employment-Women, Feminism, Women.
Readers Guide to Periodical Literature. New York, Wilson, 1905- , semimonthly.
Sage Family Studies Abstracts. Beverly Hills, Sage Publications, 1979- , published 34 times a year.
Social Sciences Citation Index. Philadelphia, Institute for Scientific Information, 1969- , published 3 times a year.
Social Sciences Index. New York, Wilson, 1974- , quarterly.
    See: Feminism, Family, Husband and wife, Marriage.
Sociological Abstracts. New York, Sociological Abstracts, 1952- , published 6 times a year.
    See: Woman/Women, Feminist/Feminists/Feminism, Institutional(ism).
Women's Studies Abstracts. New York, Rush, 1972- , quarterly.
    See: Feminism, Family Roles, Socialization.

On-Line Bibliographic Data Bases. Examples of search aids to assist searching are given for selected data bases. Consult a librarian for search information.

CATALYST RESOURCES (contains citations to current information on women in the workforce) 1963- .
COMPREHENSIVE DISSERTATION INDEX (definitive subject, title, and author guide to American dissertations) 1861- .
FAMILY RESOURCES (producer-National Council on Family Relations), includes online access to *Inventory of Marriage and Family Literature.*
LC MARC (comprehensive file of worldwide collection of books that can be searched by author, title, subject, and other access points) 1968- .
MAGAZINE INDEX (offers broad coverage of general magazines) 1976- .
NATIONAL NEWSPAPER INDEX (indexing of *Christian Science Monitor, New York Times, Wall Street Journal*) 1979- .

Afterword

Beth B. Hess

When we first set fifteen of our colleagues to the task of analysing the changes in American family systems wrought by two decades of feminism, we needlessly wondered how the essays might fit together to present a coherent picture. As the reader has undoubtedly noticed, one basic theme has informed almost every essay: pervasive changes are taking place in women's lives, largely as a result of increased labor force participation, but comparable changes in the division of family labor and in the roles of men have lagged considerably. The "question of the family" remains stubbornly at the heart of the matter, and until this issue is addressed, there can be no genuine equality between the sexes. The goal of "sex role transcendence" is as elusive as ever.

The forces of resistance are powerful; not only the organized countermovement of the antifeminist right, but also in the presumably value-neutral professional and popular literature. Despite their own experience in dual-earner families, many Americans express a lingering loyalty to "traditional values," which, when buttressed by a psychologically-oriented fear of depriving children of maternal attachment, still stigmatizes the working mother. The past few years have seen the publication of books and articles with such titles as *In Defense of Family* (Kramer, 1983), *The Erosion of Childhood* (Suransky, 1982), and "The Loss of Childhood" (Winn, 1983). Clearly, there is a wide audience that wishes to believe that the problems of contemporary childhood can be safely laid at the feet of "selfish" or self-serving mothers who place their own interests above those of other family members. Yet we also know that it is precisely full-time homemakers with childcare responsibilities who tend to have lowest levels of self-esteem and highest rates of depressive symptoms.

Beth B. Hess is Professor of Sociology, County College of Morris, Randolph, NJ.

In addition, Barbara Ehrenreich (1983) claims that it was not women, but men, who first deserted the modern family in search of personal fulfillment, encouraged by mental health experts to "become their own person," and by the medical profession to protect themselves against heart attacks by reducing interpersonal stressors. Despite the "flight from commitment" of many men, the willingness of others to become more deeply involved in childcare continues to be stymied by the demands of employers, the structuring of work itself, and the subtle pressures of peer expectations of "manliness." The conclusion of most of the authors in this volume is that so long as men do not fully participate in the domestic world, not only will genuine equality be forfeited but children will continue to be socialized to asymmetric gender roles.

Thus it appears that the theme enunciated in the historical perspective that opens this volume—the limited impact of feminism on patterns of family life—runs throughout the other essays. Is it indeed the case that the nature of family interaction—the intimate relationships of adults and their offspring—must always be counterposed to those of the world outside the domestic sphere? The historian Carl Degler (1980), for example, claims that the universalistic norms of individual achievement in the larger society will always be "at odds" with the particularistic norms of intimacy within the family. Other analysts who identify themselves as feminists (e.g., Elshtain, 1982) argue that women must reimmerse themselves in family and community as necessary bases for the struggle against corporate power. Many, such as Friedan (1981) argue that if feminists continue to perceive family life as antithetical to women's full participation in society, this vital symbol of emotional power will become, by default, the exclusive rallying point of the religious and political right.

In language reminiscent of a generation ago, the choices for contemporary women are often phrased in "either/or" terms: that success in one sphere must be at the cost of lowering aspirations in the other. We read frequently today of a "post-feminist" generation of young women angered at not being able "to have it all" as they assumed they had been promised by the new Women's Movement. Their rage is directed at the Movement rather than at the social structural obstacles that continue to allow men but not women to have it all.

Despite all the sound and fury over lost childhoods and empty promises of fulfillment, there are important signs of both continued change *and* the capacity of American families to adapt. A recent national sample survey of attitudes toward work and homemaking (New York Times, 1983) found the following startling differences:

Percentages of women who say that they think the two or three most enjoyable things about being a woman today are:

	1970	1983
Being a mother; raising a family	53	26
Being a homemaker	43	8
Being a wife	22	6
Respect; special treatment	20	12
Careers, jobs, pay	9	26
General rights and freedoms	14	32

If these data have any validity, it would be most unrealistic to expect a sudden resurgence of domesticity among American women, particularly since the attractiveness of work outside the home was greatest for women at younger ages.

The data also suggest that being a wife and/or homemaker are not perceived as very fulfilling roles at this time. Perhaps the realization that one will not have much assistance from one's husband has contributed to this decline in support. But must such attitudinal change translate into the abandonment of marriage or childbearing? Not according to the most recent extensive examination of data by Thornton and Freedman (1983). As most readers of this volume are well aware, nine of ten Americans will marry at least once, and ninety percent of those will have at least one child. Marriage and parenthood remain crucial and central to the life experience. Yet there are many trends that most Americans find disturbing: high divorce rates (although these have leveled off in the past few years), the increase in single parent households below the poverty level (particularly among blacks and Hispanics), and a rise in out-of-wedlock birth, especially to teenagers.

Other trends, while distressing to some, would be considered positive to others: the delay in age at first marriage, for example, should moderate the divorce rate while allowing women to receive the education and work experience that will benefit them in the likelihood of having to support themselves between marriages or during widowhood. A lowered birth rate will bother those who perceive strength in numbers, but please those who favor minimal population growth. The rise in independent households can also be seen as a positive sign of the ability of elderly widows to maintain their separate residences, much to the pleasure of themselves and their adult offspring. And while the thought of large numbers of children growing up in single-parent households evokes public concern, most will spend the greater part of their childhood in two-parent families (the original and the reconstituted).

Within families, as the chapters in this issue amply document, the balance between work and family roles is shifting for both spouses. At the moment, spouses appear to be negotiating in a normative vacuum, but it seems likely that their individual decisions will eventually add up to a pattern of shared responsibility, though perhaps not as extensive as most of our authors might wish. The next decade may be crucial for the achievement of egalitarian relationships in the domestic sphere, which is both the necessary condition and ultimate consequence of equality between the sexes.

REFERENCES

Degler, C.N. *At odds.* New York: Oxford, 1980.
Ehrenreich, B. *The hearts of men: American dreams and the flight from commitment.* Garden City, NY: Anchor Press/Doubleday, 1983.
Elshtain, J.B. Feminism, family, and community. *Dissent,* Fall, 1982.
Friedan, B. *The second stage.* New York: Summit, 1981.
Kramer, R. *In defense of the family: Raising children in America today.* New York: Basic, 1983.
New York Times Poll, Sunday, December 4, 1983: p. 1 ff.
Suransky, V.P. *The erosion of childhood.* Chicago: University of Chicago, 1982.
Thornton, A. and Freedman, D. The changing American family. *Population Bulletin,* 38, October, 1983. Washington, D.C.: Population Reference Bureau.
Winn, M. *The loss of childhood.* New York Times Magazine, May 8, 1983.